Alexandra E. Lindhout

The Routes of African Diaspora Life Writing in Germany and the United States of America: A Comparative Analysis

Alexandra E. Lindhout

The Routes of African Diaspora Life Writing in Germany and the United States of America: A Comparative Analysis

Deutscher Wissenschafts-Verlag (DWV)
Baden-Baden

Cover-Gestaltung: Q, www.q-home.de

Bibliografische Information Der Deutschen Nationalbibliothek
Die Deutsche Nationalbibliothek verzeichnet diese Publikation in der
Deutschen Nationalbibliografie; detaillierte bibliografische Daten sind
im Internet über http://dnb.ddb.de abrufbar.

Bibliographic information published by Die Deutsche Nationalbibliothek
Die Deutsche Nationalbibliothek lists this publication in the Deutsche
Nationalbibliografie; detailed bibliographic data are available in the
Internet at http://dnb.ddb.de.

Information bibliographique de Die Deutsche Nationalbibliothek
Die Deutsche Nationalbibliothek a répertorié cette publication dans la
Deutsche Nationalbibliografie; les données bibliographiques détaillées
peuvent être consultées sur Internet à l'adresse http://dnb.ddb.de.

Die vorliegende Arbeit wurde vom Fachbereich 05 – Philosophie und Philologie – der Johannes Gutenberg-Universität Mainz im Jahr 2010 als Dissertation zur Erlangung des akademischen Grades eines Doktors der Philosophie (Dr. phil.) angenommen.

1. Auflage
Gedruckt auf alterungsbeständigem, chlorfrei gebleichtem Papier

© Copyright 2011 by
Deutscher Wissenschafts-Verlag (DWV)®
Postfach 11 01 35
D–76487 Baden-Baden

www.dwv-net.de
www.UniversityPress.de

Alle Rechte, insbesondere das Recht der Vervielfältigung und Verbreitung sowie der Übersetzung, vorbehalten. Kein Teil des Werkes darf in irgendeiner Form (durch Photokopie, Mikrofilm oder ein anderes Verfahren) ohne schriftliche Genehmigung des Verlages reproduziert oder unter Verwendung elektronischer Systeme verarbeitet, vervielfältigt oder verbreitet werden.

ISBN: 978-3-86888-035-9

Acknowledgements

One can pay back the loan of gold, but one dies forever in debt to those who are kind.

Malayan Proverb

The arduous but overall highly gratifying and enlightening path of writing this dissertation would not have been possible without the support of the many people whom I want to thank.

First, I owe deep gratitude to my mentor and advisor Prof. Dr. Hornung at my home university, the Johannes Gutenberg-Universität Mainz, Germany. Despite the burdens placed on his time, he always supported and inspired me throughout my studies. He made possible a year of research as visiting scholar at Columbia University in New York City, USA.

I would also like to especially thank my second advisor, Prof. Dr. Gernalzick. Her patience and profound knowledge in many fields stimulated my interest and pushed me to always learn and achieve more. In addition, many thanks to my editor L. Frew and to the Graduiertenförderung of the Johannes Gutenberg-Universität Mainz for the fellowship that supported me financially for a full year while I was researching in New York City.

I would like to express my appreciation to my friends, who proofread selected parts and shared their expertise and ideas with me. Special thanks to Martina for keeping me sane and distracted; your friendship is indispensable. In addition, I would like to thank my mother-in-law for her support as well as my American "parents," who are responsible for broadening my horizons and who taught me to cope abroad.

With all my heart I thank my entire family, especially my mother and my father, who throughout my life have never challenged my decisions and who have always believed in me and my abilities. I owe everything to them. I deeply admire what they have achieved in their lives.

Last but definitely not least, my heartfelt thanks and deep love go out to my wonderful husband and to our beautiful son. My husband's refreshing views made me look at my research in different and fruitful perspectives. My son's carefree laugh gave so much joy to me when I needed it most. They have given me their love and the courage to go on. I owe a lot of quality time to them.

For my family

Table of Contents

Chapter One: Preliminary Thoughts — 1

Chapter Two: Theoretical Framework and Theses – Autobiography Theory and Criticism — 6

2.1	Brief History: The Beginnings and the Second Wave	6
2.2	Contemporary Approaches and Key Concepts for this Study	9
2.3	Postcolonial Approaches: Brief Introduction	24
2.4	Postcolonial Identity	25
2.5	African-American Criticism	29

Chapter Three: Roots en Route – African-American Life Writings — 37

3.1	A Brief Contemplation on Slave Narratives and the African-American Tradition of Life Writing	37
3.2	Selection and Significance of Contemporary African-American Life Writings	40
3.2.1	Marita Golden's *Migrations of the Heart: An Autobiography* (1983)	41
3.2.2	Barack Obama's *Dreams from My Father: A Story of Race and Inheritance* (1995/2004)	43
3.2.3	Saidiya Hartman's *Lose Your Mother: A Journey Along the Atlantic Slave Route* (2007)	44
3.3	Political Agency and Activism as Continuity? Analysis of *Migrations*, *Dreams from My Father*, and *Lose Your Mother*	46
3.3.1	Communal and Individual Issues at the Interface with Political Motivation: The Fight Against Silence	47
3.3.2	Writing to Shape Their Lives: The Route to Success via the Fight Against Racism, Sexism, and Exoticism	61

Chapter Four: Roots en Route – African-German Life Writings — 83

4.1	A Brief Contemplation on African-German vis-à-vis African-American Life Writing	83
4.2	Selection and Significance of Contemporary African-German Life Writings	85
4.2.1	Ika Hügel-Marshall's *Daheim unterwegs: Ein deutsches Leben* (1998)	86
4.2.2	Hans Jürgen Massaquoi's *Destined to Witness: Growing Up Black in Nazi Germany* (1999)	87

4.2.3	Thomas Usleber's *Die Farben unter meiner Haut: Autobiographische Aufzeichnungen* (2002)	88
4.3	Political Agency and Activism as the Catalysts for the Formation of an African-German Culture: Analysis of *Daheim unterwegs*, *Destined to Witness*, and *Die Farben unter meiner Haut*	89
4.3.1	Isolation and Initial Political Motivation: The Fight Against Silence	90
4.3.2	Writing Oneself into Being to Overcome Racism, Sexism, and Exoticism	105

Chapter Five: Autobiography as Healing – A Comparative Analysis of the African-American and African-German Life Writings 123

5.1	Individualism versus Community versus Kinship	123
5.1.1	Massaquoi and Obama as Bonding Agents	127
5.1.2	Idolization and Realism in Usleber and Golden	135
5.1.3	Courageous Women: Hügel-Marshall and Hartman	143
5.2	Identity, Catharsis, and Wholeness	150

Chapter Six: Concluding Thoughts 166

Appendix

German Abstract 169

Works Cited and Consulted 171

Chapter One: Preliminary Thoughts

The field of the African diaspora is vast and very diverse. Contemporary African-American culture and literature are still highly influenced by African-American history, dating back to when the first enslaved Africans crossed the Atlantic and were brought to America to serve their white masters under the most cruel and inhuman conditions. From those horrific days up to the struggles against deprivation and racism today, distinct African-American cultural and literary traditions have emerged, enriched by customs stemming from African heritage. I consciously and intently use a hyphen between African and American, not only as adjectives, as most people nowadays do as in "African-American culture" but because I want to stress that both terms are equal partners and that a specific culture has shaped itself. By using a hyphen I want to make a clear statement to underline that the person can be both African *and* American at the same time, and that both heritages are of equal importance while doing away with former notions of slave and master hierarchies.[1] In the following, when talking about African-Germans, I also opt for the hyphen on account of similar reasons of equality.[2]

Due to a special history, an African-American community has come into existence that is unique in its togetherness and determination to fight for equal rights. History and culture of African-Americans take a great part in shaping America on the one hand and the African-American community as well as the African diaspora on the other. African-Americans are larger in number than descendants of Africans in other non-African countries, which has contributed to the formation of a strong African-American community and tradition. This community is responsible for the many achievements reached by African-Americans, such as the Civil Rights Movement. These developments have led to the establishment of scholarly fields investigating African-American culture and tradition. Today, most colleges and universities in the United States of America (USA) dedicate departments or programs to this field of research, such as African-American Studies Departments.

African-Germans are another group of the African diaspora and remain much less acknowledged and studied.[3] In 2005, I investigated the autobiography

---

[1] It is clear, though, that African-Americans usually see themselves as Americans because they have been born and socialized in America and thus their American idenitity takes priority. Nevertheless, many African-Americans still suffer from their slave backgrounds and feel the urge to investigate and search for their African roots. I am aware that not all African-Americans are of slave ancestry as the analysis also show.

[2] If written without a hyphen, *American* or *German* would be the dominant term described by the adjective *African*; and consequently the term *African* becomes the defining aspect of the *American* or *German* person described, thus hinting at his or her slave ancestry or racial issues.

[3] African-German is usually used as an umbrella term for people of either only African descent having gained German citizenship, or individuals of parents who are German and

of Hans J. Massaquoi, *Destined to Witness: Growing Up Black in Nazi Germany*.[4] This and his subsequent memoir, *Hänschen klein, ging allein . . . Mein Weg in die Neue Welt*,[5] inspired me and became the subject of my Master's thesis.[6] As presented in the following, I wanted to learn more about the African diaspora, especially about the similarities and differences between African-American and African-German experiences. Surprisingly, when starting out the research, I did not find much information on African-German issues or on a comparative view of African-German and African-American literature. Thus, apart from the similarities, I started to look at obvious differences apparent at first sight. African-Germans have a different historical background compared to African-Americans, and they are not as numerous within German society as are African-Americans in the USA. African-Germans continue to struggle to be accepted and heard, to be part of German society, and to be recognized as Germans with an African heritage who can enrich German culture. African-Germans have only recently begun to form a community and have started to speak out about their lives and experiences in Germany in the past twenty to thirty years.

It is due time to raise the awareness for the African-German experience and to conduct recondite and meaningful research in this field, that is, in African-German literature and its comparative analysis to African diaspora literature. In the past, there was a lack of academic interest in the lives and histories of the relatively marginal group of African-Germans. Only recently, more and more scholars have discovered this fascinating field of research. American scholars Tina Campt and Michelle Wright, for instance, are among those who have contributed profound surveys. With this research I continue to fill in the gaps in historiography as well as in the academic and popular realms. The literature of this research opens up the "possibility of another history" (Williams and Chrisman 8). I believe the conduct of the analysis at hand to be of great importance not only to the fields of (African-) American studies, (African-) German studies and diaspora studies, but to the development, understanding, and acknowledgement of cultural diversity in Germany and the (African diasporic) world. Yet, how can African-German literature and culture be part of an American studies dissertation? Globalization has not halted at the doorstep of the humanities, and American studies, therefore, has also turned towards transnational and transatlantic contexts. Today we live, as Welsch would call it, in a transcultural world and we cannot simply ignore the increasing complexity

---

African or African-American. There are more terms, like Black German, which also include other groups.

[4] This work is known as *Neger, Neger, Schornsteinfeger* in Germany and was produced as a two-piece film by the ZDF and broadcast in October 2006.

[5] Massaquoi's second work was only published in German.

[6] The title of the Master's thesis is "Hans J. Massaquoi's Autobiographies and Transatlantic Identities" (2005).

of culture's changing processes.[7] Fisher Fishkin, in her Presidential Address to the American Studies Association (12 November 2004), pointed out that the

> goal of American studies is not exporting and championing an arrogant, pro-American nationalism but understanding the multiple meanings of America and American culture in all their complexity. Today American studies scholars increasingly recognize that the understanding requires looking beyond the nation's borders, and understanding how the nation is seen from vantage points beyond its borders. (20)

American studies is becoming a broad field of research that incorporates realms which are tangential to its topics and which might lie outside of America's borders; therefore, African-German literature is part of American studies as well. Also, the Atlantic space plays a prominent role in this new understanding of American studies, hence the birth of transatlantic studies. Especially for the scope of this research, the Atlantic, more precisely what Gilroy depicts as the Black Atlantic, is a crucial factor for finding one's roots and for the development of (African) diasporic identities.

In this dissertation, my main interest lies in the investigation and comparative analysis of contemporary life writings of African-Americans and African-Germans.[8] The African-American life writings are Marita Golden's *Migrations of the Heart: An Autobiography*, Barack Obama's *Dreams from My Father: A Story of Race and Inheritance*, and Saidiya Hartman's *Lose Your Mother: A Journey Along the Atlantic Slave Route*. The African-German life writings comprise Ika Hügel-Marshall's *Daheim unterwegs: Ein deutsches Leben*, Thomas Usleber's *Die Farben unter meiner Haut: Autobiographische Aufzeichnungen*, and Hans J. Massaquoi's *Destined to Witness: Growing Up Black in Nazi Germany*. One of the most pressing questions I address in the analysis is, obviously, whether African-Germans follow in the literary footsteps of the African-American tradition, or if they establish their own literary tradition by deviating from African (-American) literary norms and contents. Then, what is the intention of African-American and of African-German life writing? Who is being addressed and what do these works achieve? Do the authors across the African diaspora share similar goals and are they inevitably connected to each other by way of shared experiences? In what respects do their lives and writings differ? Do they learn from one another, or do they develop new forms of life writing detached from each other? What is the influence of their African and African-American roots for their lives and their identity formation? How do the

---

[7] See Welsch's article on "Transculturality."

[8] I use the term life writing according to the definition of Smith and Watson, who "understand *life writing* as a general term for writing of diverse kinds that takes a life as its subject" (*Reading* 3) to refer to different sub-genres, including auto/biography, memoirs, historical self-references, etc.

acts of life writing and community formation correlate with their identity quests? These and other questions will be addressed throughout the dissertation.

In Chapter Two, I lay the theoretical framework for the later analysis. Here, I scrutinize major discourses in the field of autobiography and African-American criticism while simultaneously developing my own tools and key concepts, such as *performative constructedness*, memory and un/truth and others, for the subsequent study. Together with the concepts, Chapter Two provides the theoretically contingent theses for the later analysis.

The main body of the analysis comprises Chapters Three, Four, and the comparative as well as result-oriented Chapter Five. Within these chapters, I raise more sub-theses that are addressed in their respective sections. In Chapter Three, I first analyze the three contemporary African-American life writings (Obama's, Golden's and Hartman's) with regard to recurring motifs and aspects such as silence and racism; at the same time, I study the works against the backdrop of the tradition of the slave narrative (e.g., the speakerly text) as well as aspects of change. A prominent issue in this context is the one of silence as part of communal discourse: How did or does silence still influence African-American culture and history? In addition, many African-Americans seem to have been or still are entangled in the web of white Western individuality while at the same time trying to follow the black code of community life. Writing becomes one of many outlets to deal on the one hand with this oppositional strain history and society inflict on them and on the other hand to process the search for their roots, i.e., for their identity.

Three contemporary African-German works (Massaquoi's, Usleber's, Hügel-Marshall's) form the basis for analysis in Chapter Four, which follows a similar structure as Chapter Three so that the initial differences and similarities become apparent. Not many African-German life writings exist; those that have been published have only attracted little attention and have not been researched much. Looking at the experiences the authors recount gives the reader a better insight into the lives and problems of the minority of African-Germans in contemporary Germany. In this chapter, I scrutinize in how far an African-German community, culture, and literary tradition is beginning to form by analyzing the content of the works and the literary means the authors employ, such as Hügel-Marshall's dialectic racist discussion. One question that needs to be asked in this context is whether African-Germans take the African-American experience and literary tradition as their blueprint or whether African-Germans cut their own path.

Chapter Five juxtaposes the six writings by pairing African-American and African-German works and looking at issues that are significant and exemplary within the African diaspora and for identity formation, such as individualism and community, wholeness and catharsis. This chapter provides many results and insights for questions of common, i.e., shared or differing experiences of Africans in the diaspora. What connects Africans in the diaspora? What separates them?

Ultimately, Chapter Six recaptures major findings and gives an outlook for further research.

Chapter Two: Theoretical Framework and Theses – Autobiography Theory and Criticism

Chapter Two generates the basis for this thesis because it provides major theoretical paradigms. In addition, in this chapter I develop my own set of key concepts for the subsequent analysis and give the main theses for this dissertation. First, I consider autobiography theory in its evolutionary context before moving on to contemporary understandings of the field. Then I turn to postcolonial approaches and African-American literary criticism.

2.1 Brief History: The Beginnings and the Second Wave

For the scope of this study, it is not necessary to go into great detail about the history of autobiographical writing and theory. However, in order to understand contemporary theories and writings one should be aware of the major historical paradigms in this field. Thus, one has to at least mention the beginnings of autobiographical writing. This is not a simple task. Scholars still argue about which work is the first autobiography, depending on whether one considers it necessary that the term "autobiography" itself is used in the title or not and which autobiographical characteristics are evident. Nevertheless, the art of writing down one's life is, indeed, ancient, no matter the form and no matter whether the term "autobiography" was used or not.[9] Olney claims that Scargill wrote the first autobiography in 1834. He then continues to list numerous autobiographies dating back to Plato, which all could be considered the first autobiography (Olney, "Autobiography" 5-27). Most often, Augustine's *Confessions* (c. 397-400) is said to be the first "true" autobiography, and Marcus sees a crucial link between this view and the notion that "autobiography is in essence an aspect of Christian Western civilization" (2). Most major autobiography critics agree; Gusdorf describes it as such:

> If Augustine's *Confessions* offer us a brilliantly successful landmark right at the beginning, one nevertheless recognizes

---

[9] In fact, the term "autobiography" did not enter the English language before 1797 (Gunzenhauser), and the term itself, most scholars believe, was "coined by the nineteenth-century poet Robert Southey in 1809 when he was describing the work of a Portuguese poet, Francisco Vieura" (Anderson 7). Anderson acknowledges that there might have been earlier usages of the term (7). As for this research, autobiographical writings of the eighteenth and nineteenth centuries (and earlier centuries) as well as the rare, scattered first attempts at an autobiography theory of those times are not of interest. Many earlier writings, however, do have autobiographical traits, even if there was no term yet to describe autobiography. Such examples include Pindar, Sappho, Herodotus, and others (Gunzenhauser). Moreover, even in modern and contemporary times it is often contested what autobiography is; Olney says, "It leaves us at least with the perception that what is autobiography to one observer is history or philosophy, psychology, or lyric poetry, sociology or metaphysics to another" ("Autobiography" 5).

immediately that this is a late phenomenon in Western culture, coming at the moment when the Christian contribution was grafted onto classical traditions. Moreover, it would seem that autobiography is not to be found outside of our cultural area; one would say that it expresses a concern peculiar to Western man [. . .]. (29)

Gusdorf makes an important observation, namely that autobiography is an "invention" of Western Christian culture, in which the individual may need to live in peace with himself or herself in order to be in unison with the divine spirit.[10] Testimonies and conversion literature were common practice in Europe from Augustine to Bunyan, whose works were also the forerunners of autobiographies written in the USA.[11] Through the European Enlightenment, religious testimonies and conversion literature—which focus on the religious act and the "model servant of God" (Gunzenhauser)—saw a gradual transformation. As Smith and Watson claim, "social and philosophical transformations from the seventeenth through the early twentieth centuries contributed in new ways to the formation of the Western subject as an accomplished and exceptional individual" and the autobiography "has been a master narrative of Western rationality, progress, and superiority" (*Reading* 112-13). Most see Montaigne's *Essais* of 1595 as the "defining moment in the history of autobiography" because it is the beginning of autobiographers emphasizing their individual selves (Gunzenhauser). Soon, though, secularization, individualistic societies, capitalism, colonization and decolonization expanded and diversified this formerly Western literary tradition.

In contrast to the ancient practice of writing autobiographically, its theory and criticism are very recent academic preoccupations; autobiography was considered to be the dark continent of literature.[12] There were some early critics in the nineteenth century, but more important and influential criticism (especially for modern criticism and the purposes of this study) started later, in the twentieth century. In the first half of the twentieth century, the emerging critics' debate revolved around defining this literary method and genre. Many scholars see the advent of modern autobiographical theorizing in Georg Misch's *History of Autobiography in Antiquity* of 1907.[13] Misch defines autobiography as "the description (*graphia*) of an individual human life (*bios*) by the individual himself (*autos*)" (5). This basic definition has made its entry into many

---

[10] Many Western scholars neglect the fact that there are also other, important autobiography traditions like the Chinese tradition, for instance.

[11] Religious counterparts in America were Thomas Shepard's autobiography and Samuel Sewall's diary, among many others.

[12] Stephen A. Shapiro published an article with the title: "The Dark Continent of Literature: Autobiography," *Comparative Literature Studies 5* (1968): 421-54.

[13] Misch was influenced by his teacher, German historian Wilhelm Dilthey, who was also his father-in-law. Dilthey also produced an early definition of the genre of autobiography (Smith and Watson, *Reading* 112-13).

dictionaries and has been altered only slightly. Later critics also specified it along the lines of Starobinski's definition that autobiography is a "biography of a person written by himself" (73).

Jumping to mid-century, Olney claims in his "Autobiography and the Cultural Moment" that Georges Gusdorf's work "Conditions et limites de l'autobiographie" of 1956 was the starting point of a continuous and serious autobiography studies (19), which Smith and Watson designate the second wave (*Reading* 22). The new approaches saw "a shift of attention from *bios* to *autos*— from the life to the self" (Olney, "Autobiography" 19). Although Olney acknowledges many of the early names in autobiography criticism,[14] he sees Gusdorf as an influential critic at the turn of the century, impacting many critics to come (8-9).[15] In his essay, Gusdorf reasons, as quoted above, that autobiography is a product of Western culture and many later autobiography critics took issue with his argumentation. Moreover, his idea of autobiography revolves around it being a second chance for the author "to fix his own image" (30) and of "reconstructing the unity of a life across time" (37). Thus, as early as 1956, Gusdorf already accredited the aspect of autobiography's constructedness, which is still being debated today. In his "Autobiography and the Cultural Moment," Olney points out the similarities between his own early work *Metaphors of Self* (1972) and Gusdorf's essay. Olney is in accordance with Gusdorf when he observes that "one discovers a creative, patterned construction that operates from and in the present over a past made coherent in the recall of memory" (Olney, *Metaphors* 37). *Metaphors of Self* starts out to explore the concept of self, i.e., whether it has an "essential quality," which he dubs "oneness" (24), or it is "constantly evolving, transforming" (29). From that point on Olney establishes his theory of *Metaphors of Self*:

> An Autobiography, if one places it in relation to the life from which it comes, is more than a history of the past and more than a book currently circulating in the world; it is also, intentionally or not, a monument of the self as it is becoming, a metaphor of the self at the summary moment of composition. (35)

Apart from the above-sketched critics, among the well known involved in this second wave are also Francis R. Hart, William Spengemann, Wayne Shumaker, Karl Joachim Weintraub and many others. Smith and Watson skillfully summarize the second wave of autobiography critics as having "opened up the discussion of autobiographical narrating by insisting on its status as an act of

---

[14] Olney lists other autobiography critics from the beginning of the twentieth century until the publication of Gusdorf's essay (8-9). Others, such as Timothy D. Adams, see Roy Pascal's *Design and Truth in Autobiography* of 1960 as the starting point of modern autobiography theory (Adams 1).

[15] In turn, Gusdorf's work was influenced by the historian Wilhelm Dilthey and his disciple Georg Misch.

creation rather than mere transcription of the past," which paved the way "to elevate autobiography to the status of a literary genre" (*Reading* 128). While sidestepping the complexities of the generic discussions[16] of autobiography, one has to mention that the debate over whether or not autobiography should be acknowledged as a genre has finally come to an end, namely to acknowledge autobiography as a genre. Therefore, I also treat autobiography[17] as a literary genre, because it distinguishes itself from biographical as well as fictional writing and it does not fit into any other literary category.[18]

2.2 Contemporary Approaches and Key Concepts for this Study

General/Third Wave

There are many contemporary approaches to autobiographical theory; for this study, I compile what I believe have been influential works in this field (especially in American academia) since the 1970s. In order to establish a framework for this study, I bring these theorists' thoughts and my own together by organizing them around key concepts. They provide a paradigm for the subsequent analysis.

Theorists had first focused on the *bios* before having turned their attention to the *autos* of *autobiography*. This new consideration seems to be on the language and the writing, the *graphie* of autobiographical writing. Gunn points out that it "is by means of language (*graphie*) that self both displays itself and has access to depth; it is also through language that self achieves and acknowledges its *bios*" (9). Hence, we can say that the third and most recent wave of autobiography theorizing, which started in the 1970s, has a "new emphasis on *graphia*" (Smith and Watson, *Reading* 137).

> Readers now ask whether there are practices of graphing the *autos* and framing its *bios* that are particular to texts that perform self-reference, be they written, imaged, spoken, and/or figured. Emergent theorizing of the autobiographical at interdisciplinary boundaries suggests new ways to engage the canon of autobiography and the larger field of life narrative, including other media of self-presentation. (Smith and Watson, *Reading* 137)

---

[16] For further details on classic generic discussions, see the groundbreaking work of Elizabeth W. Bruss, *Autobiographical Acts: The Changing Situation of a Literary Genre* (1976).

[17] *Autobiography* is oftentimes used synonymously with other terms such as *life writing, life narrative* etc. In this dissertation, life writing is the umbrella term for many different forms of autobiographies.

[18] Paul de Man's essay "Autobiography as De-Facement" of 1979 is well known for its controversial views on autobiography theory and its generic discussions, in particular on the instability of the self.

This description of the new outlook of autobiography theory illustrates what was touched upon before, namely the performativity and constructedness of autobiographies introduced by Olney (and Gusdorf), who influenced the transition of the second to the third wave of autobiography criticism.

Performative Constructedness

Nowadays, life writings are no longer seen as factual blueprints of a person's life; instead, they are attributed a more creative function, i.e., the author not only recreates but also creates his past while writing it down. First, the terms performativity and constructedness need to be examined briefly. *Performativity* stems from *performance*, and a dictionary on theater language defines performance as "1. A showing of a dramatic, dance, or musical entertainment. 2. A performer's execution of his or her acting assignment" ("Performance"). On the basis of this definition one could say that the author also performs by writing his life. In addition, performativity—closely linked to speech act theory and feminist theory[19]—in autobiography depicts "autobiographical occasions as dynamic sites for the performance of identities constitutive of subjectivity" (Smith and Watson, *Reading* 143). In this context, and from a common-sense perspective, one would consider that constructedness means that the story we read is, to some extent, a creation of the author's memory and arbitrariness, bearing some truth and probably some conscious or unconscious fictionality. Taking both terms together, I claim that an autobiographer performs his or her own script of life as created in the cutting rooms of memory and will.

Formerly, autobiography was deemed to be an accurate account of past events in a person's life. But can an autobiography written in retrospect and from a single, subjective point of view ever provide a "true" account of events in the past? Even historians, with whom autobiographers are often compared, struggle with writing from an objective viewpoint because they cannot, of course, separate themselves from their subjectivity, i.e., how they perceive events and how they react to past happenings as individuals. For them, being aware of their subjectivity and taking it into account is the first and, probably, the only step they can take towards a more objective viewpoint. How, then, should an autobiographer step outside of his or her own being in order to write about this exact same being objectively? Obviously, he or she cannot. The way we see and the way we want to see our lives cannot be "neutralized." Therefore, "[i]t is obvious that the narrative of a life cannot be simply the image-double of that life" (Gusdorf 40). What is it then? What can it be? In former autobiography theory, autobiography was seen as a self-expressive act, but nowadays autobiography critics identify the "autobiographical speaker [as] a performative

---

[19] John L. Austin, P. F. Strawson, and John R. Searle are among many others who contributed to the research field of speech acts in linguistics and language philosophy. For feminist theory see Judith Butler's works such as *Gender Trouble: Feminism and the Subversion of Identity* (1990), *Bodies That Matter: On the Discursive Limits of Sex* (1993), or *Excitable Speech: A Politics of the Performative* (1997).

subject" (Smith, "Performativity" 17). Autobiography is a written (re)construction of those events that we remember and want to share. It is not only what we remember, which is highly selective; it is also that we influence our memory and mold it so that it fits our self-image. The way we portray ourselves (performance) and the way we *are* in combination with *how we want to be seen* (construction) is what I call the performative constructedness of autobiography.

It is not extremely remarkable that autobiography criticism has started to channel its energy towards an analysis of the creativity and creation of autobiographies in a time of blockbusters, virtual communities and blogospheres, as well as media hoaxes.[20] The question is, where does autobiography fit between truth and fiction in a virtualized and globalized world? This question cannot be answered generally for all autobiographies because the degree of performative constructedness changes from one piece to the next. Gusdorf and Olney have laid the groundwork for this inquiry, as stated above. American pact theorist Elizabeth W. Bruss's work *Autobiographical Acts: The Changing Situation of a Literary Genre* of 1976 is a representative work of generic discussions on autobiographies. She claims that "[a]utobiography is a personal performance, an action that exemplifies the character of the agent responsible for that action and how it is performed (Bruss, "Eye for I" 300). For me, autobiography is the written account of an unfinished *product* (the self) still in the *processing* of selective "true" and fictional remembering, as well as an *act* of artistic expression and therapeutic processes. It is not a real-time, factual or necessarily "true" account. The stories of the past are recreated *and* created by the author, and they are mediated by the present situation[21] and by the sign system called language.[22] Thus, through the autobiographical act of writing (*graphia*) do the *autos* and *bios* come to life. Reminiscent of and going beyond de Saussure, Olney describes the autobiographical act as such: "The self expresses itself by the metaphors it creates and projects, and we know it by those metaphors; but it did not exist as it now does and as it now is before creating its metaphors" (34). And Gusdorf goes a step further saying that "the human being is always a making, a doing; memoirs look to an essence beyond existence, and in manifesting it they serve to create it" (47). These definitions come close to my definition of performative constructedness: the being and writing of one's self by selective memory,

---

[20] Examples might be *The Hitler Diaries* or the autobiography of Howard Hughes, which was written without his knowledge by Clifford Irving and Richard Suskind, who later had to face charges of fraud.

[21] Starobinski notices that "[t]he self-referential value of style thus refers back to the moment of writing, to the contemporary 'me.' But this contemporary self-reference may appear as an obstacle to the accurate grasp and transcription of past events" (74).

[22] For more information on Ferdinand de Saussure's theory of semiotics see his major work *Course in General Linguistics*.

present being and performance as well as constructed outlooks into the future – one is always in the process of remaking.

The notion of a created past influenced by the present is only half of the story. Autobiographers not only perform a re/creation of the past, they also shape and influence their present and future through the autobiographical act. Gusdorf rightly claims that by "becoming conscious of the past one alters the present" (47). This is an extremely important aspect for an autobiographer's intention and his or her identity formation. Autobiographers often try to become whole, i.e., to heal identity wounds and find their selves. More recently, Eakin has contributed much to this discussion. In one of his works he claims that "[n]arrative and identity are performed simultaneously [. . .] in a single act of self-narration; the self in question is a self defined by and transacted in narrative process" (*How* 101). His ideas overlap with my own understanding of the effects of the performative constructedness of autobiography, which not only impacts the past but also the present and future.

> Thus the act of composition may be conceived as a mediating term in the autobiographical enterprise, reaching back into the past not merely to recapture but to repeat the psychological rhythms of identity formation, and reaching forward into the future to fix the structure of this identity in a permanent self-made existence as literary text. (Eakin, *Fictions* 226)

Autobiographers are creatively recapturing their past experiences through writing about them, thereby also "straightening" not only the past, but the present and future as well. Eakin's newest work, *Living Autobiographically: How We Create Identity in Narrative*, underlines the notion of the author's (past, present, and prospective) self-fashioning through writing, a dynamic amalgamation of the author's self and his narrative.

Memory and Un/Truth

"All forms of life writing are dependent on memory" (Sheringham).

Autobiography is not solely a form of an intentionally constructed composition. To understand why autobiographies are not simply "true," objective histories of someone's life, one has to comprehend how a human's memory functions, how it remembers, and how it forgets and/or alters. In this context, we have to add to autobiography theory up-to-date neuroscientific and psychological memory research, which has found stunning results as to how human memory works. Many scholars nowadays see memory as a constructive network of multiple modes of storing and recalling past events. Especially when considering personal information, scientists have found out that due to emotions felt during the actual event, a precise remembering of that event is highly improbable, because past emotions and the constructive networking of the memory in its relation to the present situation/emotion alter the mnemonic experience (Schmidt 380). Schmidt, in the original, says:

> Es liegt auf der Hand, daß dieser Prozeß der Muster-Vervollständigung derart vielfältigen gedächtnisinternen wie -externen Einflüssen unterliegt, daß von einer exakten Erinnerung an eine Situation oder ein Geschehnis nur in seltensten Grenzfällen auszugehen ist. Im Regelfall leistet das Gehirn eine komplexe und wie gesagt konstruktive Arbeit, die die Erinnerung mit Bezug auf die jeweilige Gegenwart neu gestaltet. (380)

James Olney, in his *Memory and Narrative*, relies on those contemporary findings on memory from neuroscience, neurology, neurobiology, theoretical neurophysiology, psychology, psychiatry, and journalism (347). He states that they all have shown "how the amygdala, the hippocampus, and the hypothalamus—indeed, the entire limbic system, which is the center of emotional activity and response in the brain—are implicated in every act of memory;" and, linguists assert that "language is as closely bound up with and by emotion as is memory itself" (347). Emotions, therefore, lie at the core of autobiographical memory and writing, and are the reason why we remember. Those emotions also distinguish between what we remember and what we forget, while simultaneously deciding how we remember as well.

In his article "Memory," Sheringham explains that "the office of memory is to gather, preserve, and unify." "For the last few decades psychologists have viewed human memory as an analogue of computer memory with its encoding, storage, and retrieval of information [. . .], neglecting the different natures of the informational, sensory, emotional, and phenomenological qualities of memory" (Rubin 47). Thus, human remembering is much more complicated than a computer file and, as mentioned above, it is highly dependent on emotions. The process of remembering starts out with the actual perception of an event. Our senses capture the phenomena on their respective levels, i.e., colors in the framework of a color memory, sounds in a sound memory, etc. (Fried 136). If an autobiographer wants to actually recall this encoded representation of the past event, he or she needs to reconstruct the components of the stored information step by step. It is obvious that this sequential processing entails numerous alterations, and the person remembering himself or herself also alters the remembered phenomenon due to his or her changed present situation and condition in life (Reimer 27-28). Olney claims that "there is no perception and no cognition that is not altered by the intervention of memory. Before a perception can be registered in consciousness and thus become to us a perception, time will have passed and thrown it into memory, where other memories will affect and transform it" (*Memory* 339). Apart from remembering the past in light of the present, the autobiographer is also prone to *forgetting*, *suppressing*, and *altering* past events. *Forgetting* should not be judged as only negative. It is part of enabling our memory to function at all, because in order to deal with the immense amount of sensations we take in, our memory must sort out unimportant as well as negatively laden information (Fried 113-14).[23]

This study surveys literature dealing with racism, fragmented biracial identities, and traumatic experiences such as World War II in Massaquoi's *Destined to Witness*. People who cope with those kinds of issues often *suppress* certain memories thereof in order to deal with their psychological trauma. However, the memory lies hidden beneath the surface and can break through at any time. Others may want to talk about their trauma, which supports their healing process. Thus, writing down one's traumatic memories, in this case including the experiences of racism and World War II, has often been argued to be an effective strategy for healing, not only in psychotherapy but in literary theory as well.[24] Consequently, there have been numerous attempts to benefit from a symbiotic analysis of trauma narratives involving autobiography criticism, or at least trauma narrative principles and psychoanalytical models, dating back to Freud, Piaget, and others (Kaminer 481-86; Holm-Hadulla 360-64). In autobiography criticism and theory, many theorists have come to the point to grant autobiographical accounts a self-therapeutic function and mission (Hornung, "Autobiography" 222). Chandler observes that "[a]utobiographical strategies" are very similar to therapeutic measures (6).

> As healing gestures, in fact, autobiographies are doubly metaphoric since they not only translate the act of healing into literary terms, they also, in their various narrative techniques, imply particular images of the healing process, i.e., purging, restoring, realigning. (6)

Altering one's memories (memory distortion) can have different origins as well as different purposes. Echterhoff calls it "false memory syndrome" (165) and Schacter identifies it as the sin of bias and distinguishes five types (138-39). The first type, consistency and change biases, occurs when we reconstructed the image in a way that it either resembles or greatly differs from the past. Next there are hindsight biases, which "reveal that recollections of past events are filtered by current knowledge" (139). Egocentric biases depict that we tend to focus on relating everything to ourselves. And lastly, stereotypical biases enforce our view of the world through the memories we recall, be they

---

[23] Fried, in the original, claims the following: "[Vergessen] ist der komplementäre Teil des Erinnerns, so sinnvoll und notwendig wie dieses. Je besser vergessen wird, desto wirksamer wird das tatsächlich Erinnerte. Auch das Vergessen dient demnach dem Überleben" (113-14).

[24] This does not mean that even if an individual decides to recall his or her memories and to write them down, he or she will do/not do something because he or she can still be prone to suppressing and altering certain memories.

conscious or unconscious (139). All these biases are—to differing degrees—inherent in every recollection of memory, and also especially in autobiographies. As a result, life writings should neither be understood as a factual recollection of an individual's history nor as an overall fictional story. The autobiographical "truth" lies somewhere in between, because numerous processes, such as the biases just described, shape autobiographical memory.

As an outcome, memories are never "true" or accurate in an objective sense. Olney raises the question: "'Accurate with regard to what?'" (*Memory* 371). Everything a human perceives is subjective, relational, and temporarily mediated, so that it is difficult to determine which remembered instance, or rather the perception thereof, is actually the most accurate, i.e., which comes closest to reality. Here, then, the problems of how to define reality would open up the field for infinite discussion. True (what humans associate with it) or not, Sturrock believes that "whatever an autobiographer writes, however wild or deceitful, cannot but count as testimony. It is impossible, that is, for an autobiographer not to be autobiographical" (52). It then comes down to the point where "the untruths [the life writing] tells may be as rich, or richer, in significance than the truths" (Sturrock 52). When analyzing a life writing, one can only check the truthfulness to a certain extent; for example, one can verify historical data, witness accounts etc.,[25] so that in some instances one can figure out the degree of veracity. In some other instances the truthfulness will remain obscure. Truthfulness might not be as revealing as lies or some other altered accounts (when detected or at least assumed), which renders autobiography criticism much more complex, diversified, but also at times limited. Adams claims that autobiography is not "meant to be taken as historically accurate but as metaphorically authentic" (ix), just as Olney speaks of metaphors of self. Adams continues that narrative truth and personal myth—moreover, the lying of the autobiographer—take a paramount position to truth, and "once [those stories are] turned into language and written down, become[ ] personal truth without much consideration for [their] literal accuracy" because veracity is always subjective (171). Even Gusdorf, as one of the first to see it this way, claims that "in autobiography the truth of facts is subordinate to the truth of the man, for it is first of all the man who is in question" (43). Nevertheless, truth does play a vital role in autobiography because, as a genre, it must be separable from fictional texts. Lejeune,[26] while trying to define autobiography as a genre by distinguishing it from fiction through *le pacte autobiographique* (3-30), also provides a salient statement on veracity. Truth, or the intention to come to terms with one's own, underlies this pact between the author and the reader, which renders a text autobiographical. In the forward of Eakin's *On Autobiography*, which is an English-language collection of Lejeune's essays, Eakin puts it thus:

---

[25] However, even when scrutinizing accounts of witnesses and historians, one has to keep in mind that they, too, are prone to the exact same memory processes, biases, and emotional issues as anyone else.

[26] Lejeune is considered the founding father of the so-called pact theory.

> Lejeune's solution to the thorny problem of establishing a boundary between factual and fictional modes of discourse was his concept of *le pacte autobiographique*. In effect, the autobiographical pact is a form of contract between author and reader in which the autobiographer explicitly commits himself or herself not to some impossible historical exactitude but rather to the sincere effort to come to terms with and to understand his or her own life. (ix)

Thus, underlying autobiography is a sense of truth, which is understood in the way that it is a personal truth. The autobiographer should commit himself or herself seriously to dealing with his or her self and life. This dealing with one's life may include conscious or unconscious lying or altering of events, which could then be seen as a form of acting, thus a form of performative constructedness. At this point we can answer Olney's question: "Accurate with regard to what?" The autobiography needs to be accurate with regard to the author's sincere effort to a personal sense of truth while constructing his or her own identity.

In conclusion to the debate on personal memory and truth, these terms are not to be seen as absolute bases for an assessment of life writings. They might function as indicators of performative constructedness and the narrative plotting of identity formation. Memory and truth are at times interdependent, mutually constituting, and at other times totally separate. Whatever memories the author shares with his or her readers, however accurate or inaccurate, they can be used to analyze the figural meaning and the metaphorical authenticity of the text and the author's self, but not to measure an objective truth. This is what I call autobiographical memory. Truth is a highly problematic term to define. What can be true for one person does not necessarily hold up to the measurement of someone else. Truth is subjective, relative and, therefore, elusive and should not ultimately serve to categorize life writings or even disqualify a text from being autobiographical. I am in accordance with the scholars' views mentioned above and conclude this debate by quoting Eakin. "Autobiographical truth is not a fixed but an evolving content in an intricate process of self-discovery and self-creation" (Eakin, *Fictions* 3). Moreover, I add that autobiographical truth is highly intertwined with and dependent on our emotions in and of memories.

Above, we have looked at the individualistic level of memory (and its truth). Human beings, though, never live totally isolated but are part of a society or community. Halbwachs, as early as the 1940s, researched collective memory and claimed, "No memory is possible outside frameworks used by people living in society to determine and retrieve their recollections" (43). Whereas Halbwachs sees only a social component to memory, which he calls collective memory, Assmann expands this view to a cultural memory (1). He distinguishes between a communicative memory, which complies with the requirements of Halbwachs, namely "to describe the social aspect of individual memory" (Assmann 3), and a collective/bonding memory, which "is to transmit a collective identity" (7). Every single person partakes in a specific culture and undergoes socialization according to that culture. This intrinsically shapes the individual while all individuals shape their surroundings as well, so that a collective/cultural memory[27] is formed. In this study, cultural memory is crucial for the identity of every individual, but especially for the identity formation of biracial individuals.

For biracial individuals who grow up in one culture, not knowing the other culture their genealogy reflects, the collective memory of this missing culture, might remain obscure. They only know half the story. "Memorials, days of remembrance with the corresponding ceremonies and rituals (such as wreath-laying), flags, songs, and slogans [which] are the typical media of this form [i.e., collective/cultural memory] of commemoration" are one-sided and biased for people of the African diaspora living in western countries, forgetting the cultural heritage of the "other" part of their genealogy (Assmann 7). Cultural memory of all parts of one's background, though, is important for a feeling of belonging.

> It is a projection on the part of the collective that wishes to remember and of the individual who remembers in order to belong. Both the collective and the individual turn to the archive of cultural traditions, the arsenal of symbolic forms, the 'imaginary' of myths and images, of the 'great stories,' sagas and legends, scenes and constellations that live or can be reactivated in the treasure stores of a people. (Assmann 7)

If the link to one's own people is disconnected, then one cannot participate in this cultural/collective memory and, consequently, one cannot belong because "communication is for communicative memory [what] tradition is for cultural memory" (Assmann 8). If one lives in a Western culture whose traditions differ from those in Africa or any other place of one's genealogical background, one is automatically cut off from the traditions of the "other half," its cultural memory and belonging. However, since biracial genealogy is made up of two different cultures, if one is detached from one culture one feels alienated from oneself, as many hyphenated selves claim. Collective, i.e, cultural memory, therefore, plays an integral part in this investigation because the Africans of the diaspora try to fill their missing cultural memory by traveling to the countries from which the "other" half of their genealogy stems. We need to ask questions concerning the nature of the collective memory the author is part of such as: In which culture has the author been socialized and what are the implications for the collective/cultural memory, hence the vantage point of his or her writing? Halbwachs claims that "the mind reconstructs its memories under the pressure

---

[27] Some sociopsychological researchers draw a fine line between collective and cultural memory. For this study, such a subtle distinction is not necessary, because I believe that the collective memory is made up of cultural memory and vice versa. The terms will be used synonymously.

of society" (51), which would entail major effects on the autobiographical memories and writings of African-German and African-American authors. We also need to search for the following: Which cultural memory is missing from his or her writing? And if he or she is trying to retrieve the "other half" of his or her genealogical cultural memory, how does he or she do so? Are there implications for his or her writing and for his or her identity formation?

The Four A's: Authorship and Agency, Authority and Authenticity

The above-mentioned concepts, which I call the four A's, are inseparable due to their referential nature in autobiographies: The *author* is the *agent* who negotiates his *authority* over the subjective, *authentic* autobiographical writing. Lejeune and Eakin have come up with models to prove that "autobiography is nothing if not a referential art, and the self or subject is its principal referent" (Eakin, *Touching* 3). Lejeune's autobiographical pact[28] establishes a contract between the author, who is the referent,[29] and the reader (125), and he introduces the interconnected identity of author, narrator, and protagonist (5-8 and 14-26). I mostly agree with Lejeune, but one must not neglect the mediation that takes place, namely that the *author* writes the *narrator*, who recounts the stories of a past *protagonist*. Consequently, my definition is that what we read is a manifold mediation: Through the eyes of the "present" author the reader meets the narrator, who, mediated through memory (and emotion), language, time, and culture, tells the stories of a past person, the protagonist of the storyline, who is a recreation as much as a creation of the author, narrator, and his or her cultural paradigms. This notion comes close to Eakin's approach to "autobiography's referential aesthetic" (*How* 4) by means of considering the autobiographer's self in "its relation with others" (*How* 43). Thus, referentiality and relationality are the core concepts underlying the four A's.[30] In our case, authorship depicts the referent and writer of the autobiography. We will neglect such forms as forged autobiographies, collaborative autobiographies, etc., but do acknowledge that the author's accounts are based on his culturally conditioned self and thus, although the author (including the narrator and the protagonist of the autobiography) is its primary referent, the figural "authorship of autobiography is tacitly plural" (Adams 12).

The autobiographer fulfills several roles, all present in his identity, which are symbiotic in the referentiality of autobiography, "a position entailing the

---

[28] Elizabeth Bruss is the prominent American pact theorist after Lejeune (Couser, "Authority in Autobiography" 36-37).

[29] I am aware that the terms *referent*, *truth*, and *authenticity* are all associated with the notion of reality and stem from different theoretical schools. Those schools are neglected in this study, even though I borrow their terms. *Referent* is used here to denote the author, narrator, and protagonist; *truth* is seen in its relation to fiction; and *authenticity* is meant to describe the relation of the content to the author and his or her personal and communal truth.

[30] Lejeune explores problems of referentiality in collaborative autobiographies and thus authorship, authority, and authenticity in his chapter "Autobiography of Those Who Do Not Write" (185-215).

agency of the autobiographer" (Smith, Thomas). What is agency in this sense? My definition of agency is the author's actual extra-textual representation for a particular cause, which can be followed through the written account of the protagonist's actions. In the texts at hand, the authors employ their power to come to terms with specific topics, often related to a social issue, community struggle, or identity development. Thomas Smith, in his article "Agency" skillfully summarizes the notion of autobiographical agency:

> Autobiographies effectively reveal agency or the desire for agency because they show how meanings are created for people, how people create meanings for themselves, and how people engage the world around them. Thus, autobiography is well suited to support arguments on behalf of people who have been oppressed or traditionally silenced.

When it comes to ethnic authors, they attempt to achieve not only a personal goal that usually comprises their self-discovery and identity development, but also to support the (minority) group's greater, oftentimes political and/or social goals. In the later analysis, I call the personal and communal goals *internal activism* or *motivation* because the author turns toward himself and toward his or her community. The *external activism* targets the (white) society around them. Thus, the author becomes the agent for his or her own person and the voice for his or her fellow comrades. One can ask questions such as: In how far does the author portray himself or herself as an agent for his or her ethnic group's causes? How does he or she practice his or her agency? By speaking out for the oppressed and by portraying an alternative perspective, the author *transliterates* history, i.e., he or she makes possible a more complete view of past events, including the voices of the silenced. *Transliteration*, in its traditional sense, means to change letters of one alphabet (for example Chinese characters) into the corresponding letters of another alphabet, so that one is able to understand the words. I give the term a new meaning by stating that individuals, who are now speaking out and filling in the gaps of historiography actually *transliterate* history, meaning translating and adding new aspects to historical "facts." Thus the lives and experiences of formerly silent/silenced individuals become part of the accepted canon of historical events, which can then be understood from a different perspective as well.

The last two concepts of the four A's, namely authority and authenticity, are "of interest primarily with regard to autobiographical genres" (Couser, "Authenticity"), i.e., the discussion whether there exists a genre of autobiography and whether or not a written account deserves the label of autobiography. Couser juxtaposes the two recent competing theories when it comes to authority ("Authority in Autobiography" 39-42). First of all, authority is usually associated with veracity, that is the truthfulness of autobiography, by looking at the "relation between the text and the extra-textual world" (Couser,

"Authenticity"). Correspondence theory,[31] with its branches of empiricists, pact theorists (Lejeune, Bruss), and expressivists (Sturrock), propagates this view (Couser, "Authority in Autobiography" 40). Also readers themselves often naïvely assume that what they read mirrors the actual past of the author, which they see as pivotal to granting the author his or her authority.[32] Poststructuralist theorists have challenged this view because they see the self as a mere linguistic structure (Couser, "Authority in Autobiography" 41). I claim that authority is neither a mere textual construct, nor is it a paramount goal of autobiographical writing to narrate objective biographical and historical truth (if that is achievable at all). It is impossible and hindering for autobiography criticism to fully recover that truth or untruth. Nevertheless, there is a contract between author and reader as described by the pact theorists; however, I believe this pact does not fully account for authority, and that it is rather one element of a diverse matrix.

It remains a difficult task to pinpoint the (un)truthfulness of autobiography because authority in autobiography seems to be solely derived from "personal experience, from memory and subjectivity—that is, from self-identity," into which no other person can immerse other than the autobiographer himself or herself (Couser, "Authority"). Gusdorf is often quoted as the purist or literalist with regard to authority, since he claims that "no one can know better than I what I have thought" (35). But is this truly so? Is authority only dependent on the personal truth of the author? As with many other contemporary critics, I do not focus on figuring out the falseness or truthfulness, and I do not believe what Sturrock claims, namely that "'authoritative' in fact means (is synonymous with) 'autobiographical'" (52). I do see the value of the contract between author and reader as introduced by Lejeune and Bruss. However, authority is not only a product of signing the autobiographical pact and making a *sincere* attempt at recollecting one's memories. The problem remains that one cannot fully be able to detect and eliminate potential deceits on the side of the writer, which is frustrating but inescapable. Couser, on the basis of Bakhtin's dialogical theory,[33] introduces a new way of viewing autobiographical authority:

> Authority is located neither in correspondence to an extratextual reality nor in the self-determining agency of language; rather, it is negotiated in the engagement of contending parties and voices in

---

[31] Correspondence Theory, also called the Correspondence Theory of Truth, promotes the idea that "truth consists in a relation to reality" (David).

[32] Just the fact that the writer actually wrote down his or her past experiences does not always grant him/her authority. The limits of authority can be seen when considering female autobiographies and their struggle for authority. Smith claims that the "conception of selfhood is decidedly male identified" (*Poetics* 39). During slavery and after emancipation in the USA, autobiographical accounts by slaves, or rather ex-slaves, often needed white, male Anglo-Saxon advocates to provide them with the authority to be taken seriously, published, and read (Meer; Couser, "Authority in Autobiography" 45).

[33] See Mikhail Bakhtin's *The Dialogic Imagination* for further details.

the world. In sum, authority may be best viewed as culturally negotiated, rather than as inherent in, or necessarily absent from, autobiographical texts. It does not reside exclusively in the correspondence between the text and the facts or the text and the self; rather, it is something to be contested and established by the autobiographer and others—collaborators, editors, critics, biographers, historians, and lay readers. (Couser, "Authority")

Consequently, I treat autobiographical authority as a concept that can neither be derived merely from the real world of the protagonist, outside of the text (related to the correspondence theory as proposed by the pact theorists as Lejeune and Bruss), nor from only its textual immanence (as put forth by poststructuralist theories). I agree with Couser[34] (and ultimately with Bakhtin) that the prerogative of authority is a negotiation between the author, his or her cultural embedding, and the reader. However, I include the above-mentioned extra-textual and intra-textual components as well. This makes my definition broader, treating autobiographical authority as a sometimes elusive principle always fluctuating within the matrix of extra-textual reality, veracity, intra-textual language agency, and the negotiation between culture, author, and recipient. When trying to evaluate the authority of an autobiographical author, one has to take all of these issues into consideration.[35]

The matter of authenticity, in my view, is not to be mistaken for authority and veracity. Authentic is a word that is commonly used to describe the genuine origin of something or someone. Authenticity in autobiography also relies on this notion. Couser claims that "authenticity is essentially a matter of the relation between the text and its putative source—provenance" ("Authenticity"). Simply put, the text is authentic when the author himself or herself has actually written the text culturally embedded in his or her own voice. Starobinski puts it thus: "No matter how doubtful the facts related, the text will at least present an 'authentic' image of the man who 'held the pen'" (75). Authenticity, then, "concerns how writing represents or mediates identity" (Couser, "Authenticity"). Thus, when analyzing autobiographies, we try to find out the real author of the text, his or her origins, and in how far his or her identity might be visible through the writing, in order to evaluate its authenticity. The analyst must be careful, though, not to apply presumptions and biases as to how a text of a specific ethnic background "should" or does typically look like. Couser claims

---

[34] More on this topic can be found in Couser's *Altered Egos*, where he juxtaposes contesting theoretical approaches on the subject of identity and authority in autobiographies.

[35] Gunn puts it eloquently when she describes it thusly:
>Truth lies in the story's *sufficiency*: in its capacity to make sense of experience told, shared, and even made newly possible for both the teller and the hearer of the story. Just as the authorship of autobiography is tacitly plural, so the truth of autobiography is to be found, not in the "facts" of the story itself, but in the relational space *between* the story and its reader. (143)

that the "concern for 'authenticity' may inadvertently serve to hold the 'exotic' subject at a distance, to constrain him or her to the role of the 'Other'" ("Authority in Autobiography" 46-47). One should rather try to find proof as to what influences the author in his or her authenticity, whether it comes naturally or whether he or she attempts to sound authentic in order to achieve not only authenticity but also authority (which, indeed, is often derived from authenticity as well).

Autobiography and Identity/the Self

There would be no writing about the self without the self. Brockmeier and Carbaugh even claim that "such a complex and fleeting construction as human identity—the self in time—can only exist as a narrative construction" (15). But let us examine the basics first. Identity issues lie at the center of many, if not all, life writings. The discussion as to how to define or make transparent the self is ancient, indeed. The last four decades, however, saw a tremendous frequency of discussion about identity and the self[36] in various disciplines. I do not want to resuscitate the wide range of controversy in all its facets here.[37] The overall discussion, however, left an impression on autobiography studies, and autobiography criticism left its imprint on the discussion in return; thus, it is inevitable to portray a brief synopsis. This synopsis, though, will be limited to the points where autobiography criticism and identity discussion intersect in academic discourse.

The main issue at hand was and is the "gist" of identity, i.e., the central discussion on its process-related versus its essential or substantial nature in autobiographical studies.[38] Brockmeier draws a very clear picture of the debate. The first notion he discusses is the "essence" of identity, which is considered to be stable and which cannot be changed over time; it "represents continuity" ("Identity"). This self is unitary and its substance will remain the same. Brockmeier claims that considering "the 'essence' of the self in such temporal terms is specific to [. . .] Western culture of the modern age" ("Identity"). Olney discusses the essential quality of self in his early work *Metaphors of Self*. He goes back to Heraclitus, who assumes that a "oneness of the self" exists (6). He continues:

> The natural scientist may refer to the 'individual' while the poet refers to the 'self,' the theologian may attribute uniqueness to 'soul'

---

[36] The terms *identity* and *self* are used synonymously here, as in most of the literature.

[37] Autobiography studies were and are highly influenced by psychological approaches and their theorists. Their trains of thought are, therefore, immanent in the following discussion of identity.

[38] The discussion on the processual versus the essential nature of identity is not exclusively one of autobiography studies, but can be found in many other fields as well. I concentrate on what literary critics, specifically autobiography scholars, have said on this topic because "we find that many of the disciplines that have concerned themselves with identity employ a theory or theories of their own" (Eakin, *Touching* 75).

and the biologist to 'genes,' but they are all agreed on the essential: that the individual self, because of soul and/or genes, experiences an unrepeated and unrepeatable being. (21)

So far, scholars from different fields have found terms denominating the same "thing," which is referred to as identity or the self in this study. These scholars, like Spengemann and Lundquist in earlier autobiography criticism, contributed an essential quality to the self (Eakin, *Touching* 73). Olney acknowledges the contributions of Hopkins, who holds that "'Self is the intrinsic oneness of a thing,'" but is critical as to what the implications are (Hopkins 146). Olney asks: "But this raises a corollary question: to what extent is the self a continuous entity? and, is 'oneness' absolute?" (24). He expands this view of the self by neglecting to look directly at the self. Instead, we should look at "an experience of self" (29), which he later calls the metaphors of self.[39] Olney still favors the essential nature of identity, which was promoted by the so-called Gestalt psychologists,[40] when he claims that "none of us could have been born a *tabula rasa*" (32) and so the "order-producing capacity must be innate" (33). This traditional view of a unified, essentialized, substantial self has been overcome today.

> The search for models alternative to that of the unitary self, after all, provided a major project for modernism throughout much of the 20th century. [. . .] Their [the various theorists'] combined influence even before mid-century was directing us away from the unitary self and towards models of multidimensionality and nontransparency. (Ohlsen)

Leaving out deconstructivist notions of the self, this other aspect of the controversy, then, depicts the construction, the process-related idea of identity. In this view, "leading a life is conceived of as the making of an identity in the same way that, [. . .] in Shakespeare's histories and tragedies references to historical memory serve to shape an English national identity" (Brockmeier, "Identity"). This angle of identity discourse implicates that humans do *not* have a core self which is unmodifiable and fixed throughout their lives. One's identity is rather an ongoing, ever-changing process, which, in turn, makes it difficult to define or grasp such a fluctuating and elusive concept as identity in this sense. Eakin explains this phenomenon as "continuous identities developing over the course of a lifetime, [which] has become an established article of faith for both autobiographers and their readers" (*Touching* 74). The question of a solution to

---

[39] Olney's book was written in the 1960s and reflects the status of scholarship at that time.

[40] For more details consult the works of some of the representatives of this approach (proponents of the Gestalt theory date back to Goethe, Kant, and Mach; psychologists concerned with this approach are Ehrenfels, Wertheimer, and Husserl, among others).

this dilemma, however, emerges: Is the self, then, substantial, i.e., fixed, or is it always in transition?

A new perspective in autobiography studies has taken the place of the former dichotomic controversy as described above. This new perspective has been introduced by postmodern theorists who see autobiography as "a site of identity production" (Gilmore, "Introduction" 4), which challenges the outdated discourse of an essentialized versus a process-related identity. Autobiography critics took up this new thread and believe that "the very idea of human identity—perhaps we can even say, the very possibility of human identity—is tied to the very notion of narrative and narrativity" (Brockmeier and Carbaugh 15). Thus is my definition of identity as a product in process, just as I claimed earlier that writing autobiographically is; they are both incomplete. But there is a unifying aspect underlying this idea and that is narration. Brockmeier claims that "it is through the many forms of discourse that we order our experiences, memories, desires, and concerns in an autobiographical perspective. Narrating them, we reconstruct and interpret these events along the lines of genre or other narrative conventions provided by culture" ("Identity"). In this way, narration means consistency. Thus, identity or the self is both unified through narration, though never complete(d). Autobiographical identity, then, for me is similar to what I stated in the section on the four A's. Autobiographical identity is the symbiosis of the author, the narrator, and the protagonist, which are, however, all intertwined differently depending on temporality and cultural embeddedness. This referential nature shows that we, as humans, act from within different roles at different times. The roles of the autobiographic identities are, nevertheless, interconnected due to the experiences they share, and in the case of life writings, the experiences that are narrated. The experiences render the narration the continuity in a human being's identity definition and formation.[41]

Identity is, as can be seen, a pervasive and dominating principle. Especially when discussing postcolonial, ethnic, and gender-specific issues does it become paramount. Thus, in order to complete the picture, the subsequent chapter must illuminate identity notions from the particular angles of the above-mentioned approaches.

2.3 Postcolonial Approaches: Brief Introduction

In his essay "Autobiography and the Cultural Moment," Olney asks why it was specifically from the 1950s up to the publication of his work in 1980 that autobiographies were produced so numerously, and why it was that moment in time that autobiography theory and criticism began to emerge and develop.[42] The first reason for this development he mentions is that "autobiography has

---

[41] The form of the narration, whether conversations, letters, blogs, e-mails, diaries, or autobiographies, is not in the center of attention for the purposes of this study.

[42] This was the case especially in the United States of America and among postcolonial writers.

become the focalizing literature for various 'studies' that otherwise have little by way of a defining, organizing center to them" (13). He enumerates American studies, black studies, women's studies, and African studies, which are, not surprisingly, at the core of this dissertation and at the center of postcolonial studies.[43] Many other scholars have recognized the same tendencies. Bergland, for instance, acknowledges that "autobiographical studies focused on ethnic groups and [that] women have especially proliferated in the last two decades in the wake of feminist scholarship and the burgeoning field of ethnic studies" (130). As Olney points out, many see the birth of postcolonialism and ethnic studies, as well as the simultaneous increase of interest in autobiography studies, occuring since the fall of the British Empire.

> Its [postcolonialism's] subjects include universality, difference, nationalism, postmodernism, representation and resistance, ethnicity, feminism, language, education, history, place, and production. As diverse as these topics appear to be, all of them draw attention to one of postcolonialism's major concerns: highlighting the struggle that occurs when one culture is dominated by another. (Bressler 201)

When mentioning postcolonialism[44], I want to draw the connection between African-American criticism, which underlies the analysis in the next chapter, and the above-mentioned postcolonical approach in its intersection with autobiographical studies and identity issues.

2.4 Postcolonial Identity

In a globalized age one has to consider postcolonial criticism when scrutinizing contemporary literature written by a member of a minority and/or ethnic group. Due to the heterogeneous nature of literature flooding the book markets and written by formerly colonized people, suppressed subjects, and other subaltern individuals (to borrow the term from Spivak), what is dubbed "postcolonial" is not necessarily limited to authors formerly "colonized" in the

---

[43] As an example why autobiography plays such a vital role in these fields, we just need to take a look at black studies because their "programs have been organized around autobiography" (Olney, "Autobiography" 15). Similar reasons are true for the other fields mentioned; identity is an important aspect of those scholarly fields, and identity finds it manifestation in autobiography more than in any other literary form.

[44] A first attempt to define the term postcolonialism was undertaken by Ashcroft, et al. in *The Empire Writes Back: Theory and Practice in Post-Colonial Literatures* of 1989. "We use the term 'postcolonial' [. . .] to cover all the culture affected by the imperial process from the moment of colonization to the present day. This is because there is a continuity of preoccupations throughout the historical process initiated by European imperial aggression" (2).

literal sense.[45] The term rather includes deprived groups of people who were (and - some would agree - still are) subdued by a Western society. This umbrella term is, therefore, controversial and some critics dissent from this view due to the heterogeneity of literature subsumed under this term. Also, many argue that postcolonialism is not an appropriate term because they believe that a new form of dependence has taken the place of colonialism and therefore consider the new age *neo*colonial (Huddart).[46] I see the problematic nature of the term postcolonialism, though I continue to use it and refer to Smith and Watson, who define postcolonial literature as "the cultural productions of subjects marginalized by virtue of their race and/or ethnicity" ("Criticism").[47] Among many other scholars, there is the often referred to "Holy Trinity" of postcolonial theorists: Edward W. Said, Gayatri C. Spivak, and Homi K. Bhabha (Huddart). These critics have more or less established and shaped postcolonial approaches. Said's *Orientalism* shows the cultural ramifications of imperialism; Spivak's numerous works engage in postcolonial discourses with deconstructivist, Marxist, and feminist points of view; and Bhabha's *The Location of Culture* and other works try to explain Western urges for colonization and domination, while simultaneously breaking up Western binary oppositions and introducing his notion of *hybridity*.

At this point, I turn directly to the juxtaposition of postcolonial theory, autobiography theory, and identity politics. There seems to be no better site to voice one's personal issues than in life writing. Thus, autobiographical writing is the place for ethnic individuals to speak up against and resist Western imperialism and ideologies. "Autobiography is now a key element in new understandings of cultural identity and coalition politics. Yet many recent critics have found the 'genre' of autobiography to be irrevocably tainted by its Eurocentric, masculinist, individualist assumption" (Marcus 293). This claim definitely bears truth and one should always keep in mind that ethnic autobiographies suffer from those mentioned limitations and/or influences. However, life writings have been used to establish a counter-dialogue and counter-discourse to the dominant one in order to understand the "cultural Other," who is a person "negatively constructed in the dominant symbolic order: not-male, not-white, not-American" or generally not-Western and/or not-

---

[45] Most often, India's independence and Commonwealth literature are seen as the starting point of postcolonialism (Bressler 200). The term itself first appeared in Ashcroft, et al. *The Empire Writes Back: Theory and Practice in Post-Colonial Literatures* (1989). The authors of this work are Australian scholars, and one has to mention that they mostly neglect to investigate African-American literature.

[46] In addition, even the spelling of the term itself is as varied as the field of study. For the debate on the spelling and its subsequent meaning, see Bressler 201.

[47] Whereas so-called race theorists such as Gobineau and others believed in the natural hierarchy of different human races, it has nowadays been proven that *race* is not a biological or natural fact but rather a social construct; "there is no such thing as a 'black,' or 'white,' or 'Asian' gene" (Wright, *Becoming* 1). This implies that all humans are equal because there are no different human races. The term *race* is today often used synonymously with ethnicity.

civilized (Bergland 133). The texts at hand are written by some form of "cultural Other" and try to find a voice to resist the dominating culture and its stigmatization and discrimination, though by slightly varied means and to differing extents, as their later analyses will show.

One example of a life writing technique by a "cultural Other" is what I call the dialectic racist discussion Hügel-Marshall employs. When she writes about an action or thought, her writing—and thus her action or thought—is oftentimes interrupted by derogative comments of family, friends, or people on the street. Just like she, the reader is annoyed by the interjected statements which are comprised of racist or simply prejudiced comments. Hügel-Marshall has had to fight against all sorts of antagonisms every single day. She uses a back-and-forth style, the dialectic racist discussion, to fight the odds. Even though many people criticize her, after having listened to their talk, Hügel-Marshall takes up what she left off to do before their comments. This technique is reminiscent of the African-American speakerly text, which is treated in the following subchapter.

Those "othered" individuals attempt to break restraining chains and find their own spaces and voices.[48] This is part of their coming of age and constitutes their identity formation through narration, as mentioned earlier. Identity issues in postcolonial terms are, mostly, questions of who one is and where one belongs in cultural terms, hence cultural identity. Thus, autobiography is "a site of identity production" (Gilmore, "Introduction" 4), and this is especially true and valuable for postcolonial subjects.[49] Why is that so? Having lived a suppressed life, having been "othered," deprived and ostracized, having been socialized in the dominant, and sometimes in the subordinate culture, often results in a complex yet fragmented self. The question of who one is and where one belongs is paramount for the "othered" individuals. Writing down one's life, one's pain, and one's dreams supports one's coming to terms with who one is, thus forming an identity through narration. What is most unbearable for many is the tension between their "two souls" of the dominant and subordinate cultures they grew up in, for instance, Indian and British, American and African-American cultures. One important question to be examined is: Has an African-German subculture emerged like the African-American one?

It is this binary opposition of being both yet not fully belonging to either culture that seems to rip the selves of the African diaspora apart. Bhabha wants to overcome this binary opposition; he states that postcolonial scholars "propose forms of contestatory subjectivities that are empowered in the act of erasing the politics of binary opposition" (256). To do so is to emphasize that the hyphenated identity is hybrid and that this hybridity, once accepted, combines

---

[48] The question of agency is very important to postcolonial approaches. The postcolonial subject becomes the agent who makes possible "another history, an alternative way of knowing the Other" (Williams and Chrisman 8).

[49] Gilroy acknowledges that artistic expression by formerly subdued individuals, such as in music or autobiographies, provides a new stage for a counter dialogue (40).

the strength of all cultures without the necessity of strictly belonging to only one, i.e., to avoid "necessary or eternal belongingness" (Hall qtd. in Bhabha 256). Bhabha considers hybridity to be *"neither the One* [. . .] *nor the Other* [. . .] *but something else besides"* (41). From the autobiographies at hand, I analyze the following: Are Africans in the diaspora achieving a status that they define and own themselves, like *being something else besides*? Are African-Germans still "othered" while African-Americans have passed this phase and moved on to something else besides?

One's identity is not one specific thing or another, but it needs to be negotiated at all times. Fischer suggests that "such a process of assuming an ethnic identity is an insistence on a pluralist, multidimensional, or multifaceted concept of self: one can be many different things" (196); only then can we truly leave behind or overcome boundaries or binary oppositions of whatever kind. I want to conclude this paragraph by quoting Hall, who skillfully summarizes a postcolonial definition of identity, which he places in the context of culture:

> Cultural identity [. . .] is a matter of 'becoming' as well as of 'being'. It belongs to the future as much as to the past. It is not something which already exists, transcending place, time, history and culture. Cultural identities come from somewhere, have histories. But, like everything which is historical, they undergo constant transformation. (394)

Hall talks about the past and the future, and my understanding of autobiography is tied to this idea, namely the author re/creates the past in order also to shape his or her future, and he or she does it by writing, i.e., by the autobiographical act, in the present. Writing is the negotiation of one's life, or as defined earlier, the performative constructedness of autobiographies. In addition, Hall's quotation also exemplifies the elusive nature of a postcolonial, hybrid identity as well as its transformation over time. Gilroy also sees the "instability and mutability of identities which are always unfinished, always being remade" (xi). Thus, I also consider (postcolonial) identities to be floating across time, place, and culture, while on their way to find a definition that is not fixed but mirrors one's being in that one short moment in time and space before one changes again into something new. Writing down this development in autobiographical form seems to be the appropriate way for one's own re/production and re/negotiation. Narration is the consistency in this unruly path of life.

2.5 African-American Criticism[50]

<u>The Black Atlantic</u>

African-American criticism has often been subsumed under postcolonialism. However, African-American criticism was not sparked by postcolonialism but tentatively coincided with it in the latter half of the twentieth century. In 1985, Henry L. Gates was the guest editor of a special issue of *Critical Inquiry* in which influential critics of the postcolonial and post-structuralist/deconstructivist school met African-American scholars. The contributors include Said, Bhabha, Spivak, Derrida, and Gates (Gruesser 3). "This special issue represents a key moment of confluence for a variety of theoretical and critical approaches to literature and culture, especially postcolonial and African-American Studies" (Gruesser 3). The Atlantic as the space of the slave trade and of other voluntary and involuntary migration is often seen as the bridge between postcolonialism and African-American criticism. It is the Atlantic ocean that both theoretical approaches share as a space of trauma, history, and identity (re)negotiation (see also Paul Gilroy's *The Black Atlantic*). This dissertation, therefore, stresses the importance of lives and identities re/negotiated in life writings that seem to float adrift in the transatlantic space. Moreover, African-American studies are associated with postcolonialism because African-American history is marked by deportation, racism, deprivation, minority struggles, and so forth. Also, the "character of African-American arts is communal rather than individualistic, their psychology is repudiative rather than accommodative of racism, and their tradition is oral-musical rather than textual: they possess their own values styles, customs, themes, techniques, and genres" which draws a clear line to a Western view (Leitch 26).[51]

Formerly, African-American literature had mainly been analyzed "through the lens of the dominant culture, a lens that, for the most part, was focused based on one color—white, the dominant element in the binary opposition white/black as Derrida would state it" (Bressler 206). However, if such a subculture emerges, one needs to find appropriate means to interpret it rather than applying the tools of the dominant culture. African-Americans have long been "theory-resistant," and Gates sees the reason for this in the fact that any theory was a "*Western* theory" (*Figures* 27; italics in original). Gates, West, and Stepto, who are prominent examples of influential contemporary African-American scholars and critics, provide in their respective works a scheme of an

---

[50] This dissertation focuses on contemporary literature as well as contemporary criticism. Therefore, I do not trace back the entire historical evolution of African-American criticism to the *black aesthetic movement* or the well-known *Harlem Renaissance*, but draw on current discourses.

[51] However, Gates argues against repudiative notions as put forth by Baker, Stepto, and others.

African-American tradition of criticism. I mainly draw from Gates's vast oeuvre as an initial African-American theoretical framework.

In order to see the differences between other postcolonial issues and the African-American (and African-German) topic, one needs to highlight their specifics. Postcolonial subjects in India, for instance, live in the country they are born in (which is also the country of their ancestors and original culture), look like their fellow countrymen, but are socialized within dichotomic cultures, the one of the (former) oppressor/colonizers, i.e., the British, as well as the one of their own country (India). Their cultural identity is split due to direct colonization; they do not necessarily know from which cultural repertoire to choose. Descendants of slaves in America or descendants of people of African descent who were forced to migrate to a different country or continent face slightly different issues.[52] African-Americans who descend from people originally deported from Africa grow up and are socialized in the Western world. Nevertheless, a transformed version of their African heritage continues to live on in music (jazz, rap, hip hop), black vernacular, and other cultural customs. A direct contact zone with the African heritage, though, does not exist anymore; everything African-Americans nowadays know about their African heritage has been mediated through time, space, language, racism, trauma, and American/Western traditions. Their socialization, in comparison with other postcolonial people, is mainly that of mainstream American culture. The tension and identity problems they face stem from the racism and deprivation they have had to endure for centuries.[53]

African Oral Tradition at the Interface with White Literary Tradition

African-Americans continue an altered form of the oral tradition from Africa, where so-called *griots* preserve the history of the community. Owomoyela resists this idea and claims that Africans and Africans in the diaspora have taken on the route from folklore to literature. This means that Africans adopt the Western ideology that folklore with its oral tradition results in backwardness, and so they become literate according to the Western tradition and betray their roots; they rather opt for scripture than for orality (275-83). In the USA, African-Americans have formed a sort of subculture with magazines (*Jet*, *Ebony*, *O*), television talk shows (*Oprah*, *Montel*), music (rap, R&B, hip hop),[54] and even TV networks for a mainly black audience (BET, BBTV). Their identity struggle focuses on being American *and* being black, not totally losing

---

[52] I neglect the generation of immigrants because the texts at hand do not deal with this issue at large.

[53] Certainly, one has to add that African-Americans did not suffer exclusively, but that they encountered positive aspects in America as well.

[54] In recent years many scholars have devoted their attention to black music such as rap. As an example, Brown argues that Tupac Shakur's *Greatest Hits* Album is essentially a form of black musical autobiography, which follows African-American cultural values such as the oral tradition (Brown 558-73).

their ties to their African heritage, though transforming it continually so that it fits a modern, Western image and lifestyle. Whereas the cultural memory of both cultures is still prevalent in some postcolonial societies, African-Americans have to work hard to preserve some mediated form of their African cultural memory, which was partly destroyed and interrupted by the middle passage and slavery.

Going back to the Black Atlantic and in time to the beginning of an African-American culture, we need to ask: How could former slaves and ex-slaves in the USA voice their issues? They had to leave behind their original names, their mother tongues, their folklore (i.e., the way in which they knew how to pass on knowledge and memory, namely through an oral tradition), learn English, and above all, learn to write (if they were allowed to). Formal writing among slaves began with "the five autobiographical slave narratives published in English between 1760 and 1798" (Gates, *Figures* 4). Many Westerners saw the main requirement for progress and civilization in writing (Owomoyela 277). Gates answers the question why the "creative writing of the African [was] of such importance to the eighteenth century's debate over slavery," by claiming that writing "was taken to be the visible sign of reason" (*Signifying* 129). To write was considered to be human. However, scholars found out that Egyptians knew how to write before Europeans or other Westerners, and that other African societies were not "backward" even if they did not use writing (Owomoyela 277-83). Diedrich acknowledges as well that the slaves brought to America came from cultures with highly developed literary traditions. They brought traditions, such as the practice of the *griots* and folk tales, with them and those were the means that aided them to keep their collective memory alive (Diedrich 416). It is perverse that African-Americans had to adopt Western ways of writing in order to prove that they were human beings, civilized, and equal at that.

The slave narrative in the USA was the first form of writing by Africans, who were deported to America. It was a unifying force and it helped establish an African-American community and tradition. African-Americans had to find a way to communicate their existence for the sake of feeling alive, and with it they initiated their long struggle for acceptance. Gates claims that the slave narrative helped them to "*write themselves into being*" (*Loose* 57). The

> production of literature was taken to be the central arena in which persons of African descent could, or could not, establish and redefine their status within the human community. Black people, the evidence suggests, had to represent themselves as 'speaking subjects' before they could even begin to destroy their status as objects, as commodities, within Western culture. (Gates, *Signifying* 129)

I claim that contemporary African-American life writings have their origin in the oral African-American tradition dating back to the early slave narratives or literary productions by slaves in general, including poems such as Phillis Wheatly's "On Being Brought from Africa to America."[55] Still today, African-Americans talk, sing, and also write themselves into being in order to be accepted as equal citizens in the USA. Nevertheless, I want to trace back those traditions and investigate whether there are new, "non-black" or other tendencies in their writings that digress from the tradition of the slave narrative. Moreover, I want to find out whether contemporary life writings still pursue a variant of the goal of an "African-American exceptionalism" promoted by Garvey and explained by Gilroy, i.e., whether the African-American experience and particularly African-American literary tradition serve as guiding forces for other Africans in the diaspora, in our case for African-German life writing. However, African-Germans do not have such a literary tradition and the question of whether African-Germans find a similar unifying factor as in slave narratives or not must be investigated.

One needs to ask: Of what exactly is this tradition of slave narratives and African-American criticism made? What are the specifics? According to Gates, it is the "common experience, or, more accurately, the shared sense of a common experience" (*Signifying* 128), which entails a certain blackness of the text, i.e., tropes that signify this "'concord of sensibilities' shared by persons of African descent in the Western hemisphere" (128). Overall, it is the genuine voice of the author of African descent who struggles with "the tension between the black vernacular and the literate white text, between the spoken and the written word, between the oral and the printed forms of literary discourse" and thus creates what Gates terms the "Talking Book" (*Signifying* 130-31). The African-American, stemming from the African diaspora, has to transform his or her oral tradition into a form of writing that is accepted by a white audience as well. However, he or she is able to preserve the oral tradition by special means of narration, such as can be seen in "the speakerly text, in which third and first person, oral and written voices, oscillate freely within one structure, as in Zora Neale Hurston's *Their Eyes Were Watching God*. These tensions are figured in the myths of Esu and the Monkey" (Gates, *Signifying* 22). Thus, African-American literary tradition is rooted in its oral African heritage. Baker claims that the oral, collectivistic and repudiative aspects of African-American culture separate it from white American culture (qtd. in Gates, "Preface" 250). Gates counters Baker and "argues that black American writing is not simply a repudiation of assertions of black inferiority that either imitates white literature or refutes its assumptions, nor is it a reflection of distinctive black essence" (Gruesser 12).

---

[55] In my claim I follow Gates's idea that the "literature of the slave, published in English between 1760 and 1865, is the most obvious site to excavate the origins of the Afro-American literary tradition. [. . .] [I]t is to the literature of the black slave that the critic must turn to identify the beginning of the Afro-American literary tradition" (*Signifying* 127).

Whereas Baker sees black criticism stemming from white discourses, Gates roots his argument in a counter discourse based on a trope inherent in African tradition and literature. He believes that African-American criticism is not rooted in white discourse and does not react to it. Gates claims that it stems from the African trope called the signifyin(g) monkey, who "stands as the figure of an oral writing within black vernacular language rituals," i.e., "of a black rhetoric in the Afro-American speech community" (*Signifying* 52 and 53). Thus, he sees "black literature [as] a verbal art like other verbal arts" ("Preface" 254).[56] The signifyin(g) monkey conflates with various black tricksters such as the "divine trickster figure of Yoruba mythology, Esu-Elegbara" (*Signifying* 5). The monkey's and the trickster's function is mainly interpretation for "both are doctors of interpretation" (*Signifying* 20).[57] Esu is seen as the god of indeterminacy and thus "Esu is our metaphor for the uncertainties of explication, for the open-endedness of every literary text" (*Signifying* 21). Esu's interpretation of texts relies on a process that is never-ending. The relation between the Esu(-Elegbara) and the signifyin(g) monkey, according to Gates, is as follows: "If Esu stands for discourse upon a text, then his Pan-African kinsman, the signifying monkey, stands for the rhetorical strategies of which each literary text consists" and so the signifying language of the monkey becomes the sign of the African-American tradition (*Signifying* 21).

In *Figures in Black* Gates stresses the importance of black figurative language, relations of form and content, and "the arbitrary relationships between the sign and its referent. Finally, we must begin to understand the nature of intertextuality, that is, the non-thematic manner by which texts—poems and novels—respond to other texts" (41).[58] For Gates,

> Signifyin(g) is a uniquely black rhetorical concept, entirely textual or linguistic, by which a second statement or figure repeats, or tropes, or reverses the first. Its use as figure for intertextuality allows us to understand literary revision without resource to thematic, biographical, or Oedipal slayings at the crossroads; [. . .]. Indeed, the very concept of Signifyin(g) can exist only in the realm of the intertextual relation. (*Figures* 49)

It is obvious that Gates follows in the footsteps of poststructuralists (and hence deconstruction), stressing linguistic importance and, above all, the instability of

---

[56] How can one detect Gates's black trope of signifyin(g) in a text? First of all, signifying is how a text refers, or rather responds, to another text (Gruesser 14). In *The Signifying Monkey*, Gates enumerates the rhetorical tropes that can be subsumed under s*ignifying*: metaphor, metonymy, synecdoche, irony, hyperbole, litotes, and metalepsis, aporia, chiasmus, catechresis (52).

[57] Please consult *The Signifying Monkey* for the various background myths underlying Gates's arguments.

[58] Here, I certainly add autobiographical writing to the list of texts he names.

language while neglecting the content. I agree with Gates's idea that signifying, derived from the African trickster Esu-Elegbara, underlies African-American culture and literature.

However, I disagree with Gates when it comes to analyzing only intertextuality and ignoring the message. I believe that the content and the textual realms actually supplement each other in African-American literature and culture. In addition, I see where Baker's argument of a white influence comes from, because being born into a white society, being socialized in that society, one cannot but be influenced by that white culture; it is inevitable. However, that does not mean that one cannot consciously resist this very influence. Thus, I choose the middle ground here. I use "Signifyin(g) [as] the black trope of tropes" in the way that I investigate the intertextuality of the works, but I expand this notion insofar as to include the thematic concerns and possible white influences of life writing as well. I take a hybrid route again, combining Baker's repudiative and sense-making view as well as Gates's signifying and rhetorical concept. Contrary to Gates, in my view the African-American tradition is inevitably rooted in two conflicting cultures: the white one and the black one. The black rhetoric and tradition survived constant white pressure and influences, which transformed the tradition over time. The analysis shows how the traces of this black culture survived and transformed. It was in order to be acknowledged as equal human beings that former African slaves had to learn how to write in English and had to adopt Western literary forms.

<u>Western Individualism versus African Communalism in Diaspora Life Writing</u>

I pointed out that materialist and capitalist tendencies as well as individualism molded modern Western autobiographical writing. Thus, it is especially this individual self that constitutes the center of attention in life writing. When African-Americans learned to read and write they were unconsciously educated in this rather Christian, Western tradition of writing about the self. However, people of African descent do not stem from such an individualistic society as the one they were forcibly relocated/translocated to. Their original societies in Africa emphasize(d) communal belonging and collective identity. Chinosole points out that

> [a]ll autobiographies center on the self, and Black autobiographical writing is no exception to this practice. However, Afrikan [sic] meanings of the self overlap with and depart from European-derived meanings. In the autobiographies of Benjamin Franklin and Jean-Jacques Rousseau, the self is lodged in the discourse of individualism. [. . .] In response to the dominant discourse of individualism, beginning with ex-slave narratives, Afrikan [sic] autobiographical writing directed at Western readership has been two-tiered: individual and group. The group self represents both

collective (political group) and communal (cultural group) expression. (155)

I believe that when analyzing African-American life writings one can trace both traditions. There are certainly Western notions of individualism inherent, consciously and unconsciously, as well as attempts at re/finding and re/affirming collective tendencies. Overall, autobiography, then, becomes a form of individual survival and communal political action for them. Again, I do not rely on an either/or definition but rather establish, once more, a hybrid framework, which I believe most suitable for the critique of African-American literature. In the subsequent analysis I focus on tracing both aspects, i.e., the individual and the collective notion, in the selected African-American works. What will be interesting to find out is whether or not the same is true for the selected African-German works because of their disparate backgrounds and differing contemporary situation.

The case of African-Germans is different. Slavery, abolitionism, the Civil Rights Movement, and so forth were not part of their struggle. Germans from African descent[59] are not as numerous in Germany as African-Americans are in the USA. They do not share a common heritage and struggle and have only recently begun to emerge to find their voice. For most of them, they have been raised to be German, yet a number of Germans have not accepted them as "real" Germans due to their skin color. Oftentimes, they do not have a cultural memory of their African ancestry because they themselves as well as their ancestors did not have a community that preserved traditions and customs. Also, some African-Germans are of German and African origin, some are of German and African-American origin. They often lack the link to their "other" half of their genealogical background while simultaneously not fully "owning" their German side of their being. Their historical, social, cultural, and emotional dislocation from a communal memory, shared traditions, feelings of belonging as well as their non-acceptance in society provide for the identity issues they face. However, a cultural memory is important for everyone to establish a feeling of community and belonging, which is needed to have a sense of who one is and where one belongs. African-Germans often lack both, the cultural memory/tradition of their African side as well as a feeling of belonging in their native German society.

Before the age of cyberspace and worldwide networking, a great number of African-Germans lived isolated lives while being scattered throughout Germany. Only after the fall of the Berlin Wall and new floods of immigrants into Germany did the discourse on African-Germans intensify. The Internet and new ways of communication and meeting have accelerated the process in the past decade and contributed to a new African-German sense of community.

---

[59] Most African-Germans are either so-called *Besatzungskinder*, i.e., they are the children of former or contemporary African-American and African-French troops stationed in Germany, or they are (descendants of) African immigrants.

African-German literature was born when Audre Lorde visited Berlin and gave classes to African-Germans. The question whether the African-American tradition of life writing was and is used as the archetype for African-German autobiographical writing is what I also investigate in the subsequent chapters.

Chapter Three: Roots en Route – African-American Life Writings

All three African-American authors discussed here travel to Africa and try to immerse into their pasts as well. Obama, Hartman, and Golden write about their lives and paths to find out who they are and how it has come to be this way. The journeys into the past and to Africa help them in their quests to define themselves and are the reasons why this chapter is called "Roots en Route." In order to be able to follow and understand their writings about the routes to their roots and back, one needs to illuminate the historical backdrop against which the African-American writers here re/create their stories. Thus the first subchapter is about slave narratives and the African-American tradition of life writing. In what follows, I introduce the selection of works and their significance for the scope of this project. Then, I analyze the works in depth with regard to specific aspects dealing with political agency as continuity, communal and individual fights against the silencing of racial and other issues, as well as the ways of writing that support the authors' means to shape their own lives.

3.1 A Brief Contemplation on Slave Narratives and the African-American Tradition of Life Writing

As with all literary epochs, critics also attempt to categorize African-American life writings, which begin with the era of the slave narrative. The first example of African-American life writing is *The Narrative of the Uncommon Sufferings and Surprizing Deliverance of Briton Hammon, a Negro Man* of 1760, followed by Olaudah Equiano's famous *The Interesting Narrative of the Life of Olaudah Equiano, or Gustavus Vassa, the African*. Many researchers see the peak of slave narratives from circa 1831 to 1872. The main concern of these texts was to undermine the institution of human commodification and to "become a person." Slave narratives more or less follow a strict pattern of outline, style, and topic, as to emphasize the importance of the matter. The subsequent period of black autobiographies in America begins right at the start of the twentieth century with Booker T. Washington's controversial *Up From Slavery* (1901) and his debate with W.E.B. Du Bois's *The Souls of Black Folk* (1903). This phase is characterized by two opposite views: (i) desegregationist attempts by Du Bois and the NAACP versus (ii) the view of Booker T. Washington and his followers. They were in favor of a form of independence through craftsmanship. Also, the Harlem Renaissance initiated a new awareness of black life and success in the city. This second period is no longer marked by the unity which was inherent in slave narratives, but by a new sense of opposing directions that could be taken. More and more, authors become preoccupied with questions of identity, which is also displayed in the quality of writings (form, style, content are all differing; see Johnson, Redding, and Hughes, among others). The fifties and sixties sound the bell for the Civil Rights Movement and its subsequent Black Power phase. The latter reintroduces revolutionary aspects of the Civil War and, therefore, black autobiographies become more militant and seem to take on a similar role as former slave narratives, namely as strong political agents (for example: Malcolm X's autobiography). The works at hand are taken from the most modern era of black autobiography, a phase comprising the 1970s and 1980s. This period of black life writing is characterized by various tendencies, which the selected works represent.

Olney once claimed that the sole motivation of slave narratives was to show "the reality of slavery and the necessity of abolishing it" (Olney, "'I Was Born'" 156). Can one claim, then, that contemporary African-American life writings have only slightly changed their motivation to show the reality of racism and the necessity of abolishing it? Previously, writing in English for (ex-)slaves had been "political, implicitly or explicitly, regardless of its intent or its subject" (Gates, *Signifying* 132). This notion emphasizes the highly important aspect of agency stemming from slave narratives then and now, i.e., telling the "truth" and resisting oppression (Olney, "'I Was Born'"156). Slaves wrote themselves into being because writing meant to be human and civilized; their writing, however, served "higher," i.e., more collectivistic or communal, goals of resistance and abolitionism. I believe that the story of the individual struggle of (ex-)slaves—and Olney suggests that even though there are numerous stories, they are all the same ("'I Was Born'"148)—was also used by abolitionists, for it served as a proof for the need to prohibit slavery. The unity of form of slave narratives seems to be imperative vis-à-vis the enemy, namely slave owners. Slaves, ex-slaves, and abolitionists had to stand united against this cruel form of human trade and exploitation, not only in physical, but also in literary terms. Nonetheless, the slave or ex-slave still profited from his or her writing because he or she was taken more seriously.[60] Moreover, one important aspect is that this form of life writing, even though its outline and style was highly influenced by a white Western tradition, still preserved what Gates and others point out to be an African trait, namely to write from and for a more communal viewpoint rather than stressing individualism. Olney laments the sameness of slave narratives and that their sole goal was the abolition of slavery. Hence, one can claim that slave narratives preserved African communalism and that they, through the shared experiences and the similarities in writing, promoted a sense of togetherness.

The question whether contemporary African-American life writings only promote anti-racism, as raised above, would be a narrow-minded view and exclude a more personal intention on the side of the authors. Today, African-American life writings, of course, still follow in the footsteps of their forerunners, the slave narratives, insofar as they share a black responsibility of political agency, as do most ethnic life writings. Dudley points out that "[s]lave narratives established many themes intrinsic to subsequent African-American

---

[60] However, the author's existence and the truthfulness of the story always had to be guaranteed by white benefactors who acknowledged the author's identity, authenticity, and skills by writing a preface or a testimonial (for instance, see Frederick Douglass's *Narrative of the Life of Frederick Douglass: An American Slave*).

life writing," i.e., to make public the wrongdoings of slavery and to fight for equality (Dudley). Nevertheless, they do also have more intentions than merely to point out that racism is still flourishing in many societies (although racism and its implications are at the core of these texts since ethnic life writings are written from within power relations). Many contemporary life writings display an array of themes apart from racism. Some of those themes include black success stories (politicians, artists, and other accomplished individuals), self-help books, classical memoirs, and so on. A common thread seems to run through many of the contemporary African-American life writings. This thread has evolved over time and consists of the quest for an African aspect of identity, the search of an emotional home away from a mere geographical home, as well as the endeavor to succeed in life. Accordingly, I see the first and foremost difference of slave narratives and contemporary African-American life writings as such: Whereas the purpose of slave narratives lay in illustrating the cruelties of slavery to serve the aim of abolishing it—and simultaneously to write oneself into being—contemporary life writings focus more on the individual, whose aspiration it is to paint a picture of his or her black life in America in order to see a clearer picture of himself or herself and to find a more rounded sense of identity. It could be said that this development stems from the influence of the Western literary tradition, since white autobiographers tend to focus more on themselves rather than on their communities.

The differences between former slave narratives and contemporary African-American autobiographies, accordingly, are manifold and I only want to mention them briefly due to their obvious nature. Slave narratives dealt with one subject, namely slavery, and were oftentimes outlined in a very similar fashion so as to please a white audience and verify the story (Olney "'I Was Born'" 148-56). Slaves and ex-slaves were preoccupied with achieving and keeping their freedom and could not spend their energy on more personal wishes. Due to societal and technical advances in the USA, African-American life writing has changed significantly in many aspects. First of all, white people do not have to promote black writing any longer, as was the case with slave narratives. Today, African-Americans do not only serve a white literary market but a black, ethnic audience as well. Whereas slave narratives were written by slaves or former slaves, nowadays life writings by African-Americans are written by scholars, politicians, singers, celebrities, and many others, which is, of course, a logical development. Naturally, all this has transformed African-American life writing. Nonetheless, as pointed out, African-Americans still feel obliged to fight for their cause (political agency) and use special African tropes (for example, the talking book or signifying monkey) to convey their messages. One cannot deny that white literary and societal influences have "tampered" with African-American life writing as the analysis will show.

Many books have been published that deal with and analyze slave narratives. It is not my intention to summarize or recount these works or to give specific examples of slave narratives. My goal is to point out briefly the early beginnings of black forms of life writing in the USA and juxtapose their characteristics to contemporary forms in order to determine continuities and variations, or even dissimilarities, within the African-American tradition. This brief analytical conjunction will not only be helpful for the deeper interrogation and understanding of contemporary African-American works, but also for the placement of African-German life writings within the African diaspora in the second part of the analysis of this dissertation. The focus of the subsequent investigation is upon the concepts presented erlier as well as the specific aspects that play an important role in all works, namely silence, racism, sexism, and exoticism.

3.2 Selection and Significance of Contemporary African-American Life Writings

Before continuing with the analysis, I give a brief explanation on the choice of the works to be analyzed. First, I must emphasize that the selection of autobiographies excludes immigration literature, since the backgrounds and topics of these works differ to a considerable extent from the life writings of African-Americans born and raised in the USA. The first of the selected African-American autobiographies from the latest period, Marita Golden's *Migrations of the Heart* was written in 1983 and displays African-American disorientation after the Black Power Movement. The search for one's African roots—one's home away from home—by the children of the Civil Rights and Black Power Movements plays an overarching role in the narratives. Moreover, Golden belongs to a new, at that time growing, group of autobiographers: women. Other famous black female writers of the time are Maya Angelou and Audre Lorde.

Barack Obama's *Dreams from My Father*[61] of 1995 is partly a "typical" African-American success story, one of many that can be found on the shelves of a Barnes & Noble bookstore. However, this life writing differs from other celebrity memoirs[62] in its newly acquired importance as the autobiography of a president, but also in its eloquence and quality of reflection that many other memoirs lack. Unlike *Dreams from My Father*, ghostwriters often write these kinds of celebrity memoirs, or the person of interest creates it together with the help of a professional writer. Also, the audiences for which they are written play a crucial role for content and style of these works. Oftentimes readers are looking for an easily read success story and not for a book of high literary quality; and Obama's life writing, though a "typical" black success story, is of rather higher literary quality.

The third of the selected autobiographies is Saidiya Hartman's *Lose Your Mother* of 2007, which exemplifies the scholarly yet personal writings of black

---

[61] In this paper I use quotes from Obama's *Dreams* and not from his *Audacity*. Therefore, I omit the parenthetical reference to *Dreams* where redundant.

[62] For instance, Sidney Poitier's *The Measure of a Man: A Spiritual Autobiography*.

academics. Characteristic of works by black scholars is that the narrators undeniably have a personal interest in the subject they research; however, they maintain a professional approach.

Whether these works delineate the interests and specifics of the decade they were written in, or whether all three differing yet similar writings characterize this entire new period and happen simultaneously (i.e., stand for the multiplicity of directions, interests, and possibilities), are topics of this analysis. Yet, it has become clear that today there are more forms of African-American life writings than ever before, and their topics are as wide or wider than any other ethnic group's life writings. The reader comes to ask himself or herself that if contemporary African-American life writings are so diverse, is there still some aspect that connects them? Are there still patterns that can be traced back to slave narratives or even to Africa? Is there an African (-American) tradition visible in today's works? Dudley has a general answer to this question, which I share:

> African-American life writing uses forms and themes found in both American and other national literatures. The spiritual autobiography, the story of a rise to fame and fortune from humble beginnings, the account of the artist's coming of age and realization of his or her vocation—these are not uniquely African-American. But blacks *have* contributed one new form to world literature. The classic slave narrative perhaps best summarizes the impulses behind African-American life writing: to assert one's full humanity and to call upon America to make good its promises to grant all citizens freedom to fashion and live lives of their own choosing. (Dudley)

According to Dudley, the African-American literary tradition, especially life writing, has evolved out of a mixture of the Western literary tradition and black forms of writing. The latter finds expression in special African-American writing techniques such as the speakerly text/talking book and the signifying monkey, which Gates has explored and which stem from an African tradition of community, orality, figurative signs, and political agency. These techniques especially render African-American life writings unique. I chose different forms of African-American life writing to pay tribute to the existing wide variety in this literary field, which the following individual introductions emphasize.

3.2.1 Marita Golden's *Migrations of the Heart: An Autobiography* (1983)

Marita Golden and her works are not quite as famous as Maya Angelou's or Audre Lorde's, but they are at least as important for black contemporary women in the USA. Golden was born in Washington, D.C. in 1950 as the daughter of a taxi driver father and boarding house owner mother. *Migrations* (1983) is her first work to be published, even though she had initially started out to write a novel. Many other novels and non-fiction works followed, among them: *A Woman's Place* (novel, 1986), *Long Distance Life* (novel, 1989), and *Saving Our Sons: Raising Black Children in a Turbulent World* (a personal account of raising her son, 1994).

In her first autobiographical work, *Migrations,* she portrays herself as a woman who is, on the one hand, a self-sufficient and determined person in a modern yet still partly racist America. On the other hand, she is looking for guidance and a feeling of belonging when moving to Nigeria with her newlywed Nigerian husband Femi Ajayi, to whom she submits herself. She turns her back on the USA and hopes to find a new, better life as a black American woman among blacks in Africa. Unfortunately, "becoming" an African among Africans is not easy, even impossible, and she flees the continent to, ironically, "return home" to the USA. The title of the book mirrors the story insofar as her genealogical restlessness and her journey to Nigeria are inseparably intertwined with her love life and coming of age—thus its full title: *Migrations of the Heart: An Autobiography*. Her work was published in 1983, which is the era of new forms of African-American autobiographical writings as well as the emergence of many influential black women writers in the USA. Heritage travel, as sparked by Alex Haley's *Roots* (1974), has long become an important means for many African-Americans to retrace their roots and to attempt to reconnect to Africa.

There are a number of reasons why I chose her work over the writings of others. First of all, Maya Angelou's and other African-American women writers' life writings have been studied time and again. However, Marita Golden has also contributed a lot to the lives of black women in the USA as a journalist and a writer. Not surprisingly, her first work was her autobiography, which was published during a very interesting time period, and it captures the atmosphere of that time but also that of the late 1970s. It was during the aftermath of the Civil Rights era and Black Power Movement when she decided to emigrate. This time period is marked by new feminist tendencies in literature and culture. Moreover, her work exemplifies the role of heritage travel, which Golden plays to the extreme when she becomes an expatriate in Nigeria—i.e., choosing the African culture over the (African-) American one. Also, her work is acutely important due to her literary background: Golden is the "real" African-American of the three African-American writers that comprise this study (both her mother and father were African-Americans), and she is the only one who is a professional writer. Obama had a white mother and an African father, and he is a lawyer and a politician. Saidiya Hartman's mother was a descendant of several generations of slaves and her father was a police officer, who was a first generation immigrant from a small island off the coast of Venezuela (Jensen). Hartman is a professor, scholar, and teacher. Thus, it will be interesting to compare Golden's literary craftsmanship with that of the other two authors.

3.2.2 Barack Obama's *Dreams from My Father: A Story of Race and Inheritance* (1995/2004)

While a Democrat State Senator, Obama gave an important speech in Chicago in 2002, entitled "Against Going to War with Iraq," and the famous keynote address to the Democratic Convention in 2004. Due to his political ambitions, it is no coincidence that his autobiography, including his keynote address, was republished in 2004. It was a time when he gained more and more popularity and two years before he published his personal political creed in *The Audacity of Hope: Thoughts on Reclaiming the American Dream* (2006). In hindsight, it seems as if Barack Obama had intended to run for president between 2004 and 2006 and already then had been carefully preparing his campaign.

Obama is not the "typical" African-American with an ancestry linked to slavery. He is the son of a white mother from Kansas, who has Native-American heritage as well, and a father from Kenya, who met his mother as a student in Hawaii, where they were living at that time. Obama was born in Hawaii in 1961. During his life, he has undertaken many "explorations" and "experiments:" growing up in multicultural Hawaii but within a homogeneous white family after his parents split; acculturating to a new life with his Muslim stepfather, half-sister, and mother in Indonesia; subsequently returning to Hawaii and suffering from his identity insecurities; studying at Columbia in New York; becoming a relentless community organizer in Chicago; searching for his family and roots in Kenya; and studying law before becoming a successful politician for the Democratic Party. Obama is not a person that can be easily categorized because of the manifold facets of his genealogy, his diverse interests, his openness to all questions of faith and cultures, and his life motto of *change*, which also became the political slogan of his presidential campaign.

Obama's work is the second one I chose. It was published in 1995 and, as he points out in his introduction, he intended to write a different book, but somehow it became an autobiography—even though he was very young (as were all three African-American writers when writing down their young lives). He started to write after graduating from law school. A graduation is always a point of departure, to start anew, to re-orientate, to maybe reinvent oneself, even if only in writing. Again, one reason for choosing this work was also the time it had been written and published in: the 1990s. The 1980s (Golden) and 90s (Obama) under Presidents Ronald Reagan and George Bush, Sr., were characterized by radical political changes which led to a "Verschlechterung der ökonomischen und politischen Situation der Minoritäten" and to a "Debatte um *race*, *class*, und *gender*" (Hornung, "Postmoderne" 361).

"[A]utobiography is the product of a specific culture" (Eakin, *Touching* 72) and the American culture of the 1980s and 90s became more and more preoccupied with questions of a postmodern, multicultural society. Accordingly, the literary scene of the 1980s witnessed a flood of autobiographies (Hornung,

"Autobiography" 221), especially a "florescence of ethnic autobiography" (Fischer 194). During the 1980s and 90s, ethnic minorities tried to gain literary acceptance within the dominant white literary culture of America. African-Americans in particular wanted to free themselves from their "Objektrolle" through literary emancipation (Georgi-Findlay, Diedrich, and Bus 433). Golden and Obama grew up and came of age during these times, which makes their works all the more important. In addition, Obama was to become the third black senator since Reconstruction, which renders his life writing one of many African-American success memoirs that began to flood the bookstores in the 1990s. Yet, his writing differs from other success stories because he writes himself, is a very skilled writer, and his content is dense and complex. His new popularity and celebrity status as president puts even more emphasis on his autobiography, which can be interpreted in terms of the hopes and dreams of a nation. His life writing is important to display the contemporary atmosphere and importance of and for American society, culture, and the entire world.

Another reason to analyze his work is his uncommon and diverse genealogy. He represents the "new" ethnic USA due to his white, Native-American, and African background. His life's story also includes crucial elements such as geographical wanderings, community work, and trips to Kenya. Hence, could his life writing be seen as the manifestation of a new era of life writing? Is his book a transition from the "classic" African-American autobiography, the fight against slavery and racism and one's coming of age, and the subsequent modern African-American success story, to a new model of uncovering the past in unsentimental, unromantic, and realistic ways? I think that Obama's and others' life writings of the time have evolved into a new form, a form that is represented by what I consider an innovative, almost revolutionary life writing: Saidiya Hartman's *Lose Your Mother*.

3.2.3 Saidiya Hartman's *Lose Your Mother: A Journey Along the Atlantic Slave Route* (2007)

Saidiya Hartman, now Professor of English and Comparative Literature and Women's and Gender Studies at Columbia University, was born Valarie Hartman. During her sophomore year in college, she decided to rename herself, i.e., to give herself the Swahili name of Saidiya, which means helper (Hartman 8). The reason she shares this story of renaming herself becomes clear when reading her autobiographical account. There is no appropriate "label" for this new form of life writing yet; maybe one could dub it a travel ethnography with testimonial traits because it is neither a classic autobiography nor a traditional travel account nor scholarly research book. Her work is similar to other works that combine historical facts with personal accounts, travel encounters with personal interests and points of view, and academic techniques of research with private thoughts and emotions. Her work, however, differs greatly from preceding works using techniques similar to those found in Melville's *Moby*

Dick, or in works by transcendentalists like Thoreau; instead of adhering to romantic or divine notions of the world, Hartman draws a clear line between reality and nostalgia. The different techniques in Hartman are also much more skillfully woven together and result in a form of life writing that represents her scholarly interest as a historian as well as her individual quests to come to terms with her identity and her African-American community's past.

Hartman recounts her experiences traveling to and living in Ghana for academic purposes. She retraces the Atlantic slave route in search of the long dead and forgotten enslaved ancestors of African-Americans. Undoing the unnaming is one of her goals. She attempts to rewrite history insofar as to find an alternative story, a story that gives the slaves back their names in order to make them human again. Hartman is able to make them come to life, if only through her imagination and a vivid description on paper. Imagination and fictionality are necessary for reproduction of fragmentary stories. Pandey argues that "the historian needs to struggle to recover 'marginal' voices and memories, forgotten dreams and signs of resistance, if history is to be anything more than a celebratory account of the march of certain victorious concepts and powers like the nation-state, bureaucratic rationalism, capitalism, science and progress" (214). Thus, some parts of Hartman's work become imaginative counter-histories and so her narrative reminds one of so-called neo-slave narratives.[63] Nevertheless, Hartman, though mostly unsentimental and drawn to realism, becomes more and more disappointed when encountering African ignorance toward slavery. In order to redeem the lost souls (and herself), she decides to take a different route. Instead of participating in the quick "returning home" rituals that many African-American tourists hope to find their salvation in, and instead of searching for African royals and kings, Hartman chooses to look for the commoners, the lost souls, and the cruelties done to them. At the end of her journey, when she returns to the States, she is disappointed because she has been unable to meet Africans willing to talk openly and without distorted views about the slavery of the past. She realizes that Africans on the continent and Africans in the diaspora do not necessarily share the same past, or rather the same memory of what had happened in the past, which she had hoped to find and use as a bridge across the Atlantic, and as the meaning to the hyphen between African and American of her own identity.

Hartman's book of 2007 must be part of this study, for it seems to pave the way to a new era of thought and life writing in the African-American tradition. First of all, her life writing reflects on her personal genealogy as well as America's slave past from within a new vantage point: from living and researching in Africa, she looks back upon African and American history and

---

[63] A neo-slave narrative is considerd to be a contemporary work dealing with slavery, oftentimes novels. Neo-slave narratives use different methods and sources to create the story, like imagination and historical accounts. Examples of neo-slave narratives are Toni Morrison's *Beloved*, Octavia E. Butler's *Kindred*, or David Anthony Durham's *Walk Through Darkness*.

tries to make sense of her and other African-Americans' lives back in the USA. The story is told from the point of view of her academic but also personal endeavors in Ghana, which provides for a special in-depth viewpoint. Moreover, it is neither a spiritual autobiography, nor a celebrity memoir or "typical" African-American self-help book in the form of a success story; and above all it is *not* a romanticized or sentimental account of going back to one's roots in Africa. Hartman most often succeeds in keeping a clear vision as to what she is looking for, and her expectations remain realistic although often unfulfilled. Thus, her work represents the deconstruction of romantic notions about Africa and African-American salvation. In comparison, Hartman travels to Africa out of academic interest *and* personal longings, whereas Golden marries an African man and briefly lives in Nigeria before her intentions fail. Obama travels to Kenya to meet the African part of his family and hence retraces his roots. Hartman's work exemplifies the new direction of African-American thought in the new millennium, namely an unromantic debate of the role of Africa in the search for one's identity.

3.3 Political Agency and Activism as Continuity? Analysis of *Migrations, Dreams from My Father*, and *Lose Your Mother*

The African-American literary tradition is one of shared concerns and values, of militant and nonviolent protests, of hopes and shattered dreams. African-Americans have always used the medium of the written text to fight for their rights since the day slaves learned the oppressors' language and their tools for persuasion. One of those tools was writing, for which they partly neglected their African oral folklore. To succeed on the enemy's ground, one has to know his rules and master his tools. Therefore, from the early African-American writings, the so-called slave narratives, a tradition of political and social protest has shaped African-American discourse and literature up until today. I claim that even though the form and style of this political activism has changed over time and in consonance with the respective zeitgeist, it is still clearly visible in contemporary life writings, even if to differing degrees. African-American writers still perform their roles as political representatives to promote the cause of African-Americans, which clearly serves as the connecting and continuous factor within the African-American community and African diaspora. However, I deduce that the addressees of the messages in African-American life writings nowadays are less and less white audiences, racists, and other adversaries but more and more African-Americans themselves and their beliefs. Today, African-Americans speak to their own people in order to de-romanticize their hopes and to make them see clearer. In that sense, African-Americans hope that their brothers and sisters start working towards their own success instead of dwelling on the negative aspects of being a descendant of slaves, which might entail any kinds of disadvantages; this approach is rather realistic and optimistic than pessimistic. Still, of course, African-Americans are in discourse with a white audience as well, and they still attack white hierarchies and discrimination, but I claim that the political agency and activism that focused on a rather external-targeted criticism in the past has now been complemented with a pragmatic, realistic internal ethnic motivation.

The motivation for this advocacy has not changed much; the motivation still is to free African-Americans from all inequalities and from racial, societal, and all other imaginable constraints in order to become successful. This motivational issue is linked to the familiar dispute, or rather tense relationship, between ideas of traditional African communalism and collectivity versus white, Western individuality. When studying African-American life writings, it becomes obvious that African-Americans had to learn to deal with these conflicting concepts; of course, slaves wrote to free themselves (individually), but also to a great extent to help the entire abolitionist movement (communally). Nowadays, African-Americans often write about their success in life, but their accomplishments are then used to demonstrate and advertise the possibilities for uplifting the African-American community. Thus, African-Americans have learned to juggle with the Western literary tradition of individualism on the one hand, and the need to serve African-American people by addressing communal aspects on the other. This shows that African-Americans are socialized in two, at times conflicting, societies: the white and the black one, and, therefore, political activism is a continuous factor in African-American life writing. This activism, though, has evolved, and a new era of life writings encourages a more pragmatic external *and* internal motivation. In the following, I dissect the motivation of each author, how African-Americans cope with the tension of individualism and collectivity in their respective works, and how they act as political agents. The analysis aims to investigate the differences, evolutions, and continuities between the tradition and the contemporary works at hand.

3.3.1 Communal and Individual Issues at the Interface with Political Motivation: The Fight Against Silence

Communal issues are analyzed by looking at how the authors write about their concerns and for the advancement of the African-American community, often by means characteristic of the African-American literary tradition, such as intertextuality, signifying, or the speakerly text/talking book. Individual issues are part of the motivation of the authors and are, of course, connected to the struggles and concerns of their community. Both communal and individual interests are part of political activism displayed in the works. This activism, as claimed before, evolves from mainly targeting outsiders—i.e., everyone outside the African-American community who has participated in discriminating against African-Americans—to addressing more and more oneself and members of the African-American community. This happens in an overall positive way, namely by showing how one can not only survive but be successful in life.

The chronology of the works is important when it comes to investigating political activism. Golden's work was written very close to the Civil Rights era, a time in which African-American anger was targeted at mainstream, white American society. Golden grew up during these turbulent times, and she recounts the day she and her mother heard that Martin Luther King, Jr., was shot. "In that flashing, endless moment that had come on like a seizure, the blood of my belief in America seeped through my flesh and formed a puddle at my feet" (14). Not surprisingly, in her following teenage and college years, Golden joins other African-Americans in movements such as the SNCC, i.e., the Student Nonviolent Coordination Committee, which was one of the primary institutions of the American Civil Rights Movement in the 1960s. However, hers is not the typical activist work of that era, or rather of the preceding era, as were Angelou's or Malcolm X's writings. I chose her autobiography because it exemplifies a transition of African-American thought and activism in life writing. Her coming of age during the Civil Rights Movement and subsequently her travels and life in Nigeria are characterized by the still predominant romanticism of Africa; but she becomes more and more disillusioned and realistic. Her style of writing features devices used in the African-American tradition such as the repetition of symbols, intertextuality, and a metaphoric language.

One of the most important triggers for political action is fighting against *silence*. Thus, silence is a recurring motif in almost all African-American writings and it is most prominent in Golden. She becomes an advocate for speaking up because from the days of her childhood up until adulthood, in her private life as well as in public, silence was a means to cover up problems, a way to an easy peace pact; however, the price for this peace pact was losing one's integrity and beliefs. The first time she mentions silence is when she describes the troubled relationship of her parents (8). Moreover, in the aftermath of her mother's death silence determines the relationship between herself and her father (27). It seems as if silence is an accepted form of communication within the power relations of her and within any other (African-) American family: the wife is not allowed to articulate her concerns so that the family peace can be kept. Is this silence a mere gender-related issue, i.e., a form of male dominance, or is there also a cultural or even genealogical background to it?

From the problems of her family life, the motif then moves on to her love life with an African man, Femi, when first language becomes a barrier (56-57) and then cultural differences contribute to the silencing of problems, for Femi is unable to talk about his feelings with Marita (58). Soon it becomes clear to Golden that silence has a double burden for a woman. She has learned in her family that women have to be quiet in order to keep the peace within the home, and it is a means in the Nigerian tradition to keep the peace on both a personal level and, even more importantly and consequently, on a familial, communal level. When Tope, Femi's brother, marries Nike in an arranged marriage,

> the others congratulate them [Tope and Nike[64]] on the silence emanating their lives. The man who conducted the naming ceremony explained to me, "Where there is disharmony in one marriage, there will be disharmony in all. For we are wives and husbands together. Now that they have found themselves, my wife can respect me again. (62)

Slowly, it dawns on the reader that silence is misused as a foul peace treaty between unequal partners, like wife and husband in Nigeria or black and white in many parts of the world. The hierarchy in power relations equips the powerful with the might to mute the powerless.

From her personal hurtful encounters of silencing, she enters a new stage, namely that of African communal cultural differences. As a skilled writer, this recurring motif also prepares her coming of age. When she joins her husband in Nigeria, the silence in their marriage explodes into a bigger concept of cultural differences and a political agenda for Golden (102; 178). Through her female friends and her own life she finds out that women are subdued and silenced by men, but, above all, that this measure serves the higher goal of an allegedly peaceful community in the USA and even more so in Nigeria. Golden learns her lesson, when again and again Femi reminds her that family, thus kinship, stands above the individual, i.e., her and, besides, women are not regarded as individuals in Nigeria anyways (176). In the end, she finds an outlet for her voice in writing a novel, although she will never finish or publish it (130). Writing becomes her way to stay sane and to speak out what she is forbidden to say, which is analog to writing this autobiography, namely speaking the unspeakable, fighting for women's rights, un-silencing her past (relationships in her family) and de-romanticizing Africa.

The development of her political agenda becomes apparent when in the first part of the work, Golden turns to radical Black Power groups. Her anger is mainly turned towards white, Western society and the veil of silence this society enforces. Especially after the murder of Martin Luther King, Jr., the African-American community is figuratively and literally stripped of speech (14) and Golden tries to re-conquer the arena of powerful words and, in her early life, actions by joining radical groups. Her anger is directed at whites; she says, for instance, "I almost forgave them [her teachers at college] for being white" (18), and, "[s]ince there would be no love in our revolution, I turned to hate" (20). This hate is targeted at those responsible for the horrible slave past, the lynchings, and discrimination (20). It is clearly an outwardly targeted political activism, which has been characteristic of the African-American tradition. To speak up and to fight for one's rights, against the muteness of society and white racism, becomes her external political activism—a fight against unfair power relations between black and white.

---

[64] The passage is about the naming ceremony of their twins and precedes the quarreling and fighting of their young marriage.

Early in the work, however, she also starts to direct some of her energy towards a positive motivation of her Africanness and a well-meant criticism of internal African-American sexism and racism. She attempts to elope and free herself of her parents' grip on her. In addition, she wants to get away from her parents' way of silently adapting to the status quo, like white dominance and white beauty standards, as well as internalized sexism and racism. Her mother "warned me against wearing browns or yellows and reds, assuring me they would turn on me like an ugly secret revealed. And every summer I was admonished not to play in the sun, ''cause you gonna have to get a light husband anyway, for the sake of your children'" (20-21). In addition, her father prohibits Marita from wearing her make-up and Afro proudly (23). Golden, early on, starts to see the double standards *within* the African-American community and wants to become a role model, thus her internal political agenda develops simultaneously with the outward political activism in the story. In comparison, slave narratives broke the societal silence and the authors acted as political agents. Former authors' activism was mainly triggered by extrinsic factors and they targeted their agenda towards an often hostile exterior society. In the history of the USA phases of silence and utterance alternated. After each step towards equality had been made (abolition of the slave trade, abolition of slavery, black suffrage, etc.), it had been assumed that there would be a return to silence as a foul form of a peaceful compromise—only until the next outburst came and African-Americans became organized once again to re/discover their voices. This is why I see Golden's work as being in a transitional phase from a former, more extrinsically generated and externally addressed criticism to also intrinsically caused issues of African-American interest, which entails that the political agenda of African-American works shifts to address also inequalities *within* the community and *between* cultures.

Stylistically, Golden employs African-American literary tools to contest the white literary text by interlacing her work with orality, e.g., black vernacular conversations in order to drive out the muteness. None of the contemporary works at hand go as far as the speakerly text, exemplified in Zora Neale Hurston's *Their Eyes Were Watching God*, but they still make use of a more adjusted form of this African-American literary device. Golden's use of this orality highlights the importance of male-female relationships within the African-American community and can best be shown by the following quotation, when Golden echoes a conversation she had with her best friend Wanda:

> *Me*: Jive nigguhs, all they do is rap. What's wrong with the brothers?
> *Wanda*: Askin, "Sistuh, can you *love* a black man?"
> *Me*: Hey, brother, can you *understand* a black woman?
> *Us*: Laughter so close to tears it hurt. (22; italics/emphasis in original)

Thus, communal problems are interlaced with societal constraints and personal issues because Golden has just come out of a "ruined love affair" (22). Golden skillfully displays the differences between men and women, black and white, orality and literacy, by discussing these issues while simultaneously making use of the black vernacular and the concept of signifying. She uses the African-Americans' "own language" to criticize them: Golden complains about the culture of the black man ("all they do is rap") and criticizes the differences between female emotions and male ignorance. By speaking out about what bothers her, even if it is only a dialog with her best friend and not a real conversation with a black "brother," she breaks free and claims her voice as a black woman in the USA. Moreover, by hinting at rap music, and by playing the game of answering a question with another question, Golden follows the tradition of African-American signifying, which also reminds the reader of the concept of "doin' the dozens,"[65] i.e., competing head-to-head for verbal ability and wit, though Golden does it in a much milder and non-humiliating form. It is also sometimes referred to as "playing the dozens," which is a way to communicate something implicitly and Golden aims at an African-American internal reform.

Silence also plays a role in Obama's *Dreams*. The motif, though, is less apparent as it is in Golden's autobiography because Golden, as a woman of the 80s, still has to claim her voice, i.e., fight for her recognition and to be heard as a black woman. Obama, as the son of a white mother and a black father growing up in Hawaii obviously did not face the same hindrances as Golden. Nonetheless, his use of the motif of silence is, on the one hand, marked by racism and, on the other hand, by the muteness radiating from the relationship of his mother and stepfather and from his virtually non-existent relationship to his estranged father. As a nine-year-old boy, he discovers the race factor for the first time while waiting for his mother at the embassy in Indonesia, where they were living at that time. He is looking through a copy of *Life* magazine when he learns of a black man who had tried to whiten his skin in order to pass for white, but the chemicals had made his skin look sick (29-30). Obama is shocked by this story and by the fact that there are thousands of blacks who try to do the same. Until that day, Obama had lived a sheltered life in Hawaii and in Indonesia, far away from black urban life and racism. Right there and then, he becomes aware of racial differences and does not know what to make of it and where he stands in this picture. He writes,

> I felt my face and neck get hot. My stomach knotted, the type began to blur on the page. Did my mother know about this? What about

---

[65] For example, rappers compete against each other by way of improvising rap songs directed against their competitor, often by humiliating the competitor or his or her family members. Today, this form of music and competition, especially the language thereof, is often criticized, even by blacks themselves, as a form of internal criticism. They most often condemn terms like "nigger," which are taken out of their historical context (Saloy).

her boss—why was he so calm, reading through his reports a few feet down the hall? I had a desperate urge to jump out of my seat, to show them what I had learned, to demand some explanation or assurance. But something held me back. As in a dream, I had no voice for my newfound fear. By the time my mother came to take me home, my face wore a smile and the magazines were back in their proper place. The room, the air, was quiet as before. (30)

This instance certainly paves the way for Obama's coming of age as an African-American later on in his life and, of course, in his autobiographical act. However true or fictionalized this memory of his is, it shows that at some point Obama encountered an internal conflict triggered by a racial awareness unknown to him before. It is the moment that Mercer describes as such: "identity only becomes an issue when it is in crisis, when something assumed to be fixed, coherent and stable is displaced by the experience of doubt and uncertainty" (503). Obama is certainly too young to grasp the magnitude of this discovery, but this instance lays the ground for further identity investigations and his narrative outline. Strikingly, Obama does not react with a childlike naïveté by simply addressing this concern, because he feels the underlying complexity of this problematic issue and hopes to keep the peace and find peace himself by keeping his mouth shut. He explicitly says that he "had no voice"— for he first needs to find a community and to learn the vocabulary to address this issue. Therefore, for now he adapts to the foul peace pact like everyone else. "The room, the air, was as quiet as before" (30). The recounting of this episode is an outcry against the wrongdoings of humanity, i.e., the destructive values set forth by a white society which were adapted and internalized by blacks and led to identity crises and self-destructive measures as the one above. Silence, then, is used to do "business as usual." Obama, here, obviously uses both ways of political criticism, namely internal (How can blacks do this to themselves?) and external (Why is the white standard the right one?).

Strikingly, contrary to the mentioning of silence in Golden, where she first encounters the silence within her family before starting to fight against societal silence, Obama is first thrown off guard by societal racism and the muteness that it entails as described above. Yet in the following, it is also the silence that has been creeping into the relationship of his mother and stepfather that becomes an issue worth mentioning in the autobiography. Even though his stepfather Lolo is a modern and tolerant man, his failures as opposed to his wife's success bring about an implicit gender-based conflict, which can only be kept in check by not talking about it. Obama observes the parental problems as such: "In fact, it seemed as though he barely spoke to her at all, only out of necessity or when spoken to, and even then only of the task at hand, repairing a leak or planning a trip to visit some distant cousin" (42). "Whenever she asked him what was wrong, he would gently rebuff her, saying he was just tired. It was as if he had come to mistrust words somehow. Words, and the sentiments words carried" (43). In Golden and Obama, women suffer from the silence in their marriages; thus both Golden and Obama, by raising the subject, indict the (African-) American community of this tradition of silencing. Also, Obama here prepares his autobiographical act well, i.e., his narrative plotting becomes apparent for he, later on in life and in the story, will become the person who will use words to make a change as a student and community organizer, and subsequently he will study law and become the President of the USA. Therefore, by revealing this troublesome neglect of communication and by working against the silence through writing a book (Golden and Obama) and becoming a politician (Obama), the authors' inward criticism gets a positive motivation and successful role models. It is a new era of practicable internal (and external) criticism and motivation, as opposed to the mainly outward political agency of slave narratives.

One day when talking to Regina, Obama has a moment of revelation when he believes that after his freshman year at college and many identity trials and errors, he finally overcomes his speechlessness.

> Strange how a single conversation can change you. [. . .] I know that after what seemed like a long absence, I had felt my voice returning to me that afternoon with Regina. It remained shaky afterward, subject to distortion. But entering sophomore year I could feel it growing stronger, sturdier, that constant, honest portion of myself, a bridge between my future and my past. (105)

He loses his voice vis-à-vis racial issues as a nine-year-old and witnesses how adults deal with problems by silencing them. Moreover, he endures identity struggles in his first year of college (96-105). All this and a meaningful conversation with Regina trigger Obama's new belief in his voice and words. In the following, he tells the story when he is a politically active student and helps to organize a rally where he is to give a speech. This instance is another example of narrative plotting and how both Obama and Golden perform and construct themselves as developing characters in their works. Obama's conversation with Regina and the subsequent speech constitute a point of revelation comparable to when Golden starts to write her novel after having lost her first baby. Thus, after a period of disappointment and failure, words become meaningful and a way to shape oneself, even one's destiny.

Afterwards, while preparing for a rally, Obama demonstrates how he reclaims his voice as a representative for the African-American community. "I noticed that people had begun to listen to my opinions. It was a discovery that made me hungry for words. Not words to hide behind but words that could carry a message, support an idea. [. . .] I thought my voice wouldn't fail me" and it does not (105). Even the Frisbee players, who did not come for the rally, stop playing when Obama begins to speak (106-7). Consciously or unconsciously, the way Obama portrays this event reminds one of how the writers of slave narratives must have felt when they realized that there was actually an audience, a white one at that, interested in what they had to tell. Even though he himself is disappointed in his performance, everyone else thinks it was great. Regina tells him to be less egoistic and more communal:

> Well, let me tell you something, Mr. Obama. It's not just about you. It's never just about you. It's about people who need your help. Children who are depending on you. They're not interested in your irony or your sophistication or your ego getting bruised. And neither am I. (109)

This episode, on the one hand, shows the young, strong Obama, "hungry for words" and ready to change the world and, on the other hand, a young, disoriented Obama who is still trying to figure out who he is. He acknowledges that the fear of not knowing who he is and where he belongs still has a tight grip on him (111). Thus, this process of finding one's voice is inevitably interlaced with the process of finding out who one is; and this process had just begun for Obama. For the most part of the book then, silence is no longer a big issue. At the very end of the work, however, it becomes a symbol full of meaning once again when Obama visits his father's grave in Africa. He talks to his dead father and tells him that there was no shame in his fears.

> There was only shame in the silence fear had produced. It was the silence that betrayed us. If it weren't for that silence, your grandfather might have told your father that he could never escape himself, or re-create himself alone. Your father might have taught those same lessons to you.[66] (429)

Foremost, here Obama represents a political activism against a silence within families, a silence that prohibits that a meaningful father-son relationship can develop. It is a silence in a family that easily and most certainly spreads out into the community and vice versa. Thus, Obama here criticizes the practices of his African family and mainly directs his political activism against inward silence. Implicitly, though, Obama also reproaches the dominant white American culture because through the hierarchies established and fears produced within it, its contribution to the foul peace treaty is paramount.

Strikingly, although Obama never really establishes a relationship with his biological father, it is his father's talent of speaking that Obama inherits. Between father and son, and between Obama and his African family background, silence dominates. When time comes to speak up and talk about

---

[66] It is doubtful that Obama is able to remember the entire emotional conversation as recounted. As made clear in the theory chapter, autobiographers construct their lives' stories in a performative way, meaning they use their selective memory as well as conscious and unconscious fictionality to create them (see chapter 2).

important issues, though, Obama, just like his father, becomes a great orator who is able to cast a spell over his audience. Early on in *Dreams from My Father*, his grandparents go into raptures over Obama's father's way of talking with eloquence and authority. "For whenever he spoke [. . .] I would see a sudden change take place in the family. [. . .] It was as if his presence had summoned the spirit of earlier times" (67). When as a student Obama is about to give a speech at a political rally, he remembers this talent of his father and wishes it were also his. "I started to remember my father's visit to Miss Hefty's class; the look on Coretta's face that day; the power of my father's words to transform. If I could just find the right words, I had thought to myself" (106). And he does find the right words and the right tone—he overcomes racialized silence and speaks up against apartheid in South Africa that day.

During his presidential campaign, his oral talent becomes the center of attention for the media as well. As President, the media show great interest in his talent, and the *Financial Times Weekend* titled in 2009, "Man of his words" referring to his father's talent as well. In the above-mentioned article in the *Financial Times*, the unnamed author discusses the importance of Obama's oratory to his success and claims that "Obama is not just a fine orator: he is consciously putting oratory at the centre of his political being" and, obviously, this strategy is a winning one, for Obama becomes President of the United States of America. By overcoming the silence within his family and within the African-American community does Obama shape his being and fight against racism.

His political activism against whites that are racist, thus his external activism, happens at approximately the same time in his life as in Golden's, namely during his school and college years. Understandably, in high school and college everyone faces identity questions, but for black people racial issues are added to already confusing identity developments. Golden goes to college in continental, urban USA in the late 60s, and Obama goes to high school in Hawaii in the mid-seventies and to college in the late 70s. Though time and place are different, the struggles are similar, even though Golden's struggle is more radical during the Civil Rights Movement. Golden employs similar techniques, as shown above, when she recites the conversation with her friend Wanda. Obama makes use of the speakerly text. He remembers a conversation with a black friend, Ray, about being turned down by a white girl and about race policies on the basketball team. Again, as in Golden's story, Obama and Ray do not have this conversation with the real addressees, i.e., the white girl and the basketball coach, but they do not remain silent either; it is a mediated silence. They break the silence and talk about their problems with each other because they are not yet able to communicate the issues openly and directly. Obama, even though his writing is obviously influenced by a white, Western tradition and by his law-studies, now and then follows the African-American literary tradition, as in this case:

[Obama:] "Just 'cause a girl don't go out with you doesn't make her racist."
[Ray:] "Don't be thick, all right? I'm not just talking about one time. Look, I ask Monica out, she says no. I say okay . . . your shit's not so hot anyway." (73)
Or about the personnel policy on the basketball team:
[Ray:] "Tell me we wouldn't be treated different if we was white. Or Japanese. Or Hawaiian. Or fucking Eskimo." (75)

Ray is demoralized because white girls reject him and the recruitment for the basketball team seems to be color-based as well. Up until then, apart from some minor racial encounters and due to his white family upbringing, Obama has been less critical than Ray and he also, timidly, tries to find a balance between the facts, his black friend's strong opinion, and his own identity and family background. He does not want to betray either one. When in college, Obama follows in the footsteps of Ray's anti-white attitude when he talks bad about another guy, Tim, who goes out with a white girl (102). It is striking that in both Golden's and Obama's works the authors only use the black vernacular when reciting instances of their younger lives.

When looking closely at both life writings, one can discern that external political activism is predominant in the younger years of both authors, and it coincides with the nurturing of the African-American tradition of signifying and its black vernacular, as exemplified by the examples of the conversations the authors share. At a certain point of revelation (Golden's loss of her first baby and Obama's encounter with Regina and his speech), both start to search for their identity, which, strikingly as well, coincides with the point of departure for a more internal political activism. It is this moment when they both begin to grasp the power of words. At this point, Golden starts to write and Obama becomes hungry for words.

Silence is also an aspect that Hartman explores in her new form of life writing. It is not comparable to the motif of silence in the first two works discussed. Hartman's investigation of silence, however, and her attempt to break it is a means to interpret and understand the silence in Golden and Obama. Hartman digs deeper into the concept of silence and its origin. Her political agenda is motivated by her individual quest for the memories of the past, by the wish to break the communal silence, as well as the reversal of external and internal silence.

Unlike Golden and Obama, Hartman avoids telling very personal things, but she does incorporate family tales and connects them to her research and her trip to and stay in Africa. The motif of silence has a deeper meaning in *Lose Your Mother*, for she traces the silence her forefathers had once deliberately chosen to the silence vis-à-vis the slave past in Africa. Thus, silence is inevitably linked to slavery in her work, which also shows that silence in African-American life writings is of high importance and stems from the dark days of slavery. It is this ongoing breaking versus nurturing of silence, this tensed relationship that runs like a thread through African-American history and writings. Her paternal grandparents, who had emigrated from Curaçao to the USA, "erected a wall of half-truths and silence between themselves and the past," and they decided to forget all that lay behind them (15). Hartman, though, "thought the past was a country to which [she] could return;" and this is why she chose to research slavery, "in search of people who left behind no traces" (15). It is a difficult task to search for something that remains mute and unknown. Many black people hope to forget and erase these stories from their memories, but these exact stories are needed, for "[a]ll forms of life writing are dependent on memory" (Sheringham).

Hartman's maternal great-great-grandmother remained silent when asked about slavery by a white interviewer. She claimed to not remember a thing about slavery (15), which triggered Hartman's curiosity. "But her silence stirred my own questions about memory and slavery: What is it we choose to remember about the past and what is it we will to forget? Did my great-great-grandmother believe that forgetting provided the possibility of a new life?" (15). If not for a new life, then she had probably at least hoped for freedom and for being treated humanely. The concealment of the cruel past was the price to pay for a more agreeable life and also for her own sanity because keeping quiet about slavery was also a way to try to forget and leave it behind. In addition, keeping one's mouth shut was much safer in a white, often racist society and therefore many African-Americans followed this path. There are recurrent phases in American history in which silence becomes the peace treaty between black and white. But it is more than that. For some, suppressing the horrible events of the past is a way of coping with it, while others, e.g., Hartman as the descendant of former slaves, try to break the silence by writing and talking about it in order to heal.[67] I claim that all three, Golden, Obama, and Hartman, are the new, contemporary political activists who fight against the silence promoted by a white society, by their own forefathers, and also by contemporary Africans in Africa. Thus, contemporary Africans and former African-Americans chose and some still choose silence to cope with the slave past and to deal with the present situation. Nowadays, many Africans in the diaspora intend to break this silence in order to live a truly equal life and to come to terms with the past; where their ancestors chose and their brethren in Africa still choose silence, they opt for words.

For Hartman, it is this particular silence, the untold stories and unspoken names that make her embark on her journey to Africa and research the past where it had all started. She hopes to break the at times still emerging silence within the African-American community by listening to the stories Africa can tell. Unfortunately, Hartman soon finds out that Africans are even more close-lipped than her ancestors in America. "To revere your forbears was one thing; to speak openly of slave descent was a different matter altogether. Silence was the

---

[67] For more details on healing through writing see chapter 2.

only reasonable position to be assumed by a descendant of slaves" (71). It is still a shame to be a descendant of slaves in Africa and most Africans seem to be unwilling to talk about that part of history. Even when working together with African researchers, she experiences her outsider status:

> A pattern of collegial joking and teasing had developed over the course of our first weeks together. Ninety percent of the remarks began, "You South Africans," "You Nigerians," "You Ghanaians." But when I entered the circle I was greeted by an awkward silence either because my colleagues didn't know what to say or because they feared that I would be insulted if they called attention to my difference, which was charged for all of us, especially in the context of our collective investigation of slavery. My presence tainted the glory of precolonial Africa. I was the disposable offspring of the "African family," the flesh-and-blood reminder of its shame and tragic mistakes. (215)

In the USA it had long been shameful and a stigma to be black because it automatically categorized that person as a son or daughter of former slaves, which is another reason why Hartman's and others' parents chose to remain quiet when it came to tell the stories of the past. "But, as I found out, the line between masters and slaves was no less indelible, even when it wasn't a color line" (73). In Africa, skin color is not a sign of bondage and serfdom; it is rather one's social classification that hints at one's status as a successor of commoners, i.e., most probably slaves, or of merchants or even nobles. Many Africans are still in denial about what happened long ago and most of them reject any sense of responsibility on their side. Thus, silence is the means to keep the peace among the different classes of people, to subdue the pain and the shame, and to try to live a normal life. However, Hartman sees that it is important for African-Americans that Africans take on their share of responsibility or, at least, that African-Americans leave behind their long-held romantic notion of Africa as their savior and home.

Hartman is an African-American writer of the new era, for she really attempts to put all pieces of the puzzle together, even if it hurts and even if it includes accusing one's kin. When in Africa, she more and more realizes that Africa and Africans still have a whole lot to come to terms with and that African-Americans have to leave behind their romantic picture of Africa as their motherland that can and will solve all of their problems. She finds out that the silence cuts deep and that her presumption that "the black world shared a thread of connection or a common chord of memory based upon this, our tragic past" proves inaccurate (73). As the children of slave ancestry and the Civil Rights Movement, Golden, Obama, and Hartman are also children of the diaspora. Detached from the proximity to slavery by generations and geography, they are the ones who decide that it is now their turn and responsibility to break the silence once and for all; and Hartman even goes a step further. She does not only try to break the silence that covers up the cruelties of white people (as did the slave narratives) or the problems within the black family and community in the USA. She even attempts to grasp the importance of a hushed up history in Africa, which is where it all started and which then shaped the lives of so many blacks in the diaspora. Her political agenda does not neglect to point at the wrongdoings of white, Western society, but above all, she wants to de-mystify and de-sanctify Africa, because she sees behind the superficiality of the heritage travels and African-Americans' fruitless attempts to redeem themselves in Africa, for Africa rejects any possibility of guilt. She skillfully combines external and internal political issues, while stressing the latter, for she stresses that internal criticism has been neglected so far.

In Hartman, memory and silence are closely connected. The connection becomes clear when thinking about slaves who were put through rituals to forget their pre-slave past, or about contemporary Africans who refuse to think and talk about slavery. She visits former dungeons and concentrates really hard in order to hear the cries and voices, "but the space was mute" (116). One reason for this, she learns, is that in "every slave society, slave owners attempted to eradicate the slave's memory, that is, to erase all the evidence of an existence before slavery. This was true in Africa as in the Americas. A slave without a past has no life to avenge" (155). In addition, once someone becomes a slave he or she is too ashamed to recall anything associated with his time in bondage. The descendants of slaves are *unable* to recall family genealogies and stories from before the enslavement and are *unwilling* to remember the time of their families' shameful slave past. It is no wonder that Hartman encounters silence in the USA as well as in Africa. The positive aspects have forcefully been deleted from her ancestors' memory and the painful ones were either suppressed, consciously or unconsciously, or forgotten in order for the victims to stay sane and keep their humanity. For Hartman it becomes a paramount goal to fight the silence on all fronts. At least she tries to point out that the silence is not only produced by a white hierarchy (outside of the community, thus outward political activism) but also by one's own shame and, above all, by the co-responsibility of Africans in the slave trade (inward political criticism). Her evaluation of the situation in Africa and America now and then mirrors what I claimed earlier, namely that silence is a foul peace treaty in an unequal relationship every way you look at it. "Silence didn't protect and it never had. All that it offered was a tentative belonging in the master's house" (195). Black-white, female-male, slave-master, no matter what the constellation, silence supports the hierarchy and injustice, which is what all three authors at hand fight against. African-Americans feel that they have to reclaim their voice and regain their memory in order to become equal human beings. As research has shown, talking and writing about the painful past is a means of healing even if it hurts to begin with.

Whereas Golden's style is rather fictional and Obama's writing is characterized by eloquence but also at times by a factual style (probably stemming from his law background), Hartman's book is somewhat unique, for she combines historical facts, new findings, personal stories, travel encounters, and conversations skillfully. Her style changes from one episode to the next without losing its integrity or authentic voice. Golden's and Obama's works are rather obvious coming of age narratives, while Hartman's coming of age is more subtle, for it is not mirrored in a classic success of breaking the silence. Also, her style of writing is influenced by both white and black literary traditions and/or her academic background, for she always backs up her information and often refers to thinkers such as Nkrumah, W.E.B. Du Bois, Malcolm X, and Frantz Fanon (36), or Thomas More, Sigmund Freud, and Karl Marx (46-47), Toni Morrison (80), James Baldwin (88), Frederick Douglass (103), and many more. Her work truly reflects that African-Americans write from a double consciousness, as Du Bois would call it. African-Americans can and do choose their words and stories from the two societies they are part of and are socialized in. Whereas slave narratives had to be verified by white benefactors, it seems that Hartman, as a contemporary African-American author, references a great many figures of both black and white thought, in order to underline her academic background as well as her hybrid identity that has been and is being shaped by a black *and* a white society.

Hartman makes use of intertextuality quite a lot, and it seems as if her Western academic approach has to be counterbalanced by African-American traditional writing tools. She quotes, for instance, from *Uncle Tom's Cabin*, when Topsy cannot answer the question about the origin and whereabouts of her parents and says, "'I jes grew'" (Hartman 194), which underlines the loss of memory, hence family genealogy, due to slavery and silence that lies at the core of Hartman's work. This intertextuality also helps to pick up topics of the past to voice and interpret them again, in order to fight contemporary silence and problems. Hartman also uses signifying when she takes on Langston Hughes's "I, Too, Sing America." She earlier hints at this poem and then writes, "I, too, am the afterlife of slavery" (6), and later, "I, too, was a failed witness" (129), and refers to her visits to the dungeons. In the same fashion, Hartman recounts the story of the slave girl: "I too am trying to save the girl, not from death or sickness or a tyrant but from oblivion"[68] (137). Whereas Hughes plays with the double-mindedness of African-Americans and claims his place in American society, Hartman signifies her status as a descendant of slaves and a researcher of slavery and emphasizes her African side more than her American side by playing with Hughes' poem. It is a way to reinvent oneself and to reinterpret history, which stems from the trickster god Esu that Gates describes in his *Signifying Monkey*. She "struggled to connect the dots between then and now and to chart the trajectory between the Gold Coast and Curaçao and

---

[68] Starting on page 136, Hartman tells the story of a slave girl who died on a slave ship. She uses the African-American technique of open-endedness, the free interpretation of the story, for it is unclear what really happened. Therefore, Hartman uses her imagination and tells the story from different perspectives.

Montgomery and Brooklyn" and tries to weave together her own life and family past with the history of all African-Americans (129). Thus, she wants to find the balance between personal and communal interests in her research and quests, and she juggles with her black and white socialization, and the influences of both, the African-American community as well as white American society.

Her writing mirrors her hybridity and intensifies the issues raised in Golden and Obama, for she travels to Africa, to the "cradle" of slavery, and investigates those issues in depth. Slave narratives thrived at banishing the silence about the cruelties of slavery, and theirs was an outward political activism against white racism and domination. It was a personal as well as communal fight for freedom. Of course, contemporary African-American authors continue to fight white tendencies to silence the stories of the past, and their fight perpetuates an external political activism. Moreover, contemporary African-American writers still fight other forms of silence. One of them is the silence one might encounter within their families and which is based on male-dominance. The other one is a communal silence of some elder members who are ashamed and still afraid to talk about the slave past and the writers try to fight this communal form of silence. Fighting these forms of silence requires that the writers also turn inwards, meaning towards their community, to motivate their own people. A number of African-Americans hope to establish a bond between all Africans in the diaspora in their quests, and also hope to reconnect to their kin in Africa. Hartman, though, shows that African-Americans encounter yet another form of silence there, against which she fights her lonely battle. All in all, the political activism that started with the slave narratives is being continued by contemporary authors, if only in modified terms since modern times demand new strategies and new objectives: communal *and* individual, external *and* internal.

3.3.2 Writing to Shape Their Lives: The Route to Success via the Fight Against Racism, Sexism, and Exoticism

While many contemporary African-Americans battle silence and discrimination in order to form their identity, former slaves had to lay the groundwork for this development by writing themselves into the public consciousness, i.e., by proving that they were and should be treated as human beings. Slaves had to prove that they existed first: "'I subscribe myself' – I write myself down in letters, I underwrite my identity and my very being, as indeed I have done in and all through the foregoing narrative that has brought me to this place, this moment, this state of being" (Olney, "'I Was Born'" 157). White (male) autobiographers never had to emphasize their state of being, their existence. Olney gives the example of Franklin,

> who begins not with any claims or proofs that he was born and now really exists but with an explanation of why he has chosen to write

> such a document as the one in hand. With the ex-slave, however, it was his existence and his identity, not his reasons for writing, that were called into question: if the former could be established the latter would be obvious. (155)

Contemporary African-American life writings benefit from the literary naissance of African-Americans through slave narratives. They paved the way for African-Americans, who no longer need to prove that they are indeed human beings, alive, and worth listening to. Before then, I claim, the main objective of African-American life writings, next to abolitionist motivations, was to write the black individual into being, whereas nowadays African-Americans follow a more Western route of shaping one's past, present, and future in the autobiographical act because they live in the West and want to belong. It is not a fight for mere being anymore (which is the first step on the way to becoming a free subject), but rather a fight against being exoticized, racialized, and thus ostracized. African-Americans, accordingly, create their own history and thus attain agency over history as well.

Golden, Obama, and Hartman write down their stories in order to overcome or win against discrimination and to mold their past, present, and future lives as well. Golden's and Obama's stories can be regarded as different examples of classic black success narratives. When looking at the story in a cursory way, Hartman seems to fail in her endeavors. However, in the end her life writing is an atypical success story, for her success lies in the discovery of not being able to relive or change the past, and of leaving behind the inhibiting notion of a romanticized view of Africa. I want to start this part of the analysis by scrutinizing Hartman's work in light of her personal development and success because Hartman focuses on racism in Africa today and its connection to slavery and the slave trade of long ago. Success is oftentimes measured in terms of money, material possessions, or professional achievements. Golden and Obama most certainly are successful in these terms, but moreover they are also thriving in their African-American identity. Hartman's success is one that cannot be measured directly by these stipulations.

Whereas Obama—and to a certain extent Golden as well—mainly tries to comprehend and fight American-style racism and discrimination, Hartman sees that the root of it lies elsewhere, so she embarks on her African journey. To understand her slave ancestry and slavery in general, to cope with her present status as an African-American and to be able to influence the outcome of her future, she takes on the difficult task to go back to where it all began. She hopes to find the answer to her questions in Africa, in her case Ghana. Her approach is manifold: personal, academic (historical), communal, and diasporic. For her, as for anyone else in the diaspora, racism is at the core of the problems she faces, and it is what keeps many diasporic peoples from succeeding in life. Her academic background comes through when she contemplates race and racism; "[t]he simple fact was that we still lived in a world in which racism sorts the haves and have-nots and decides who lives and who dies. Racism, according to Michel Foucault, is the social distribution of death" (129). Hartmann also cites Hannah Arendt: "Race, Hannah Arendt observed, 'is politically speaking, not the beginning of humanity but its end . . . not the natural birth of man but his unnatural death'" (157). These quotations tell the reader a lot about Hartman, her individual quest, and her view of racism. She is a child of a binary social upbringing and education, for she has studied not only black history[69] but also white Western philosophy, as her quotations of Foucault, Arendt, and others show. By alluding to Du Bois, Hartman uses the African-American technique of signifying. In this context, she gives Du Bois's expression a more modern meaning of poverty and wealth, of life and death, and by quoting Foucault and Arendt, Hartman carries it to the extreme by saying that racism is the social distribution of death. Her investigation in Africa is not mainly professionally motivated but stems from her personal quandary as well, because she wants to find the connection between her life and the places her ancestors came from (29). Thus, she is working on finding out who she is and where she wants to be, and, while doing this, racism becomes the obstacle to overcome. Foucault's definition is a very strong one, but it most certainly connects her feelings with the racist slave past in Africa, which was definitely marked by death.

Consequently, Hartman does not focus her attention on the racism she encounters in the USA, but on the racism still prevalent on the African continent. In a white-dominated society as the USA, slaves had to take the first step against racism by writing themselves into being. Hartman, today, goes beyond societal, geographical, and epochal boundaries in order to fight racism. To influence her own individual development she travels to Africa, where people lost their identities when they were turned into commodities, where they had to leave behind their beings, their humanity, for which they had to struggle while in the USA (through slave narratives, for instance). While in Africa and studying slavery, she encounters discrimination between Africans and people of African descent like herself. She wants to get to the root of this racism, to understand it, and to contribute to its elimination. To begin with, Hartman, who hopes to blend into Ghanaian society since she is also black, must discover right away that she is different here, too. Even Ghanaian children can tell that she is not one of them, but an exotic, an *obruni* (stranger).

> As I disembarked from the bus in Elmina, I heard it. It was sharp and clear, as it rang in the air, and clattered in my ear making me recoil. *Obruni*. A stranger. A foreigner from across the sea. Three children gathered at the bus station shouted it, giggling as it erupted from their mouths, tickled to have spotted some extraterrestrial

---

[69] By claiming that racism decides about poor and rich, life and death, she is hinting at Du Bois's famous quotation that "the problem of the Twentieth Century is the problem of the color-line" (Du Bois v).

fallen to earth in Ghana. They summoned me, *"obruni, obruni,"* as if it were a form of *akwaaba* (welcome), reserved just for me. (3)

Instead of gaining acceptance and belonging in Ghana, she is excluded from African kinship as soon as she takes her first steps on African soil. It is the verification of what many African-Americans refuse to accept, namely that a common genealogy and a "black face didn't make [them] kin" (4). Hartman more and more introduces African/Ghanaian terms in her work, which stresses the fact of authenticity but, above all, difference: another country, another language, and another culture.[70] For the children Hartman is the exotic person from America, and for some white Americans she still constitutes the African Other, so she feels that she does not really belong anywhere. Many African-Americans still feel socially excluded from white, mainstream America; at the same time, Hartman and other African-Americans are excluded from real African kinship. African-Americans, like other Africans in the diaspora, are often treated as exotics wherever they go. But admittedly for Hartman, Africans are very different as well.

Her colleagues do not include Hartman in their jokes and, more importantly, they do not think that she is one of them. "No matter how expansive the category 'sister,' I always fell outside its embrace" (217). Although these Africans are also scholars and study slavery, even they cannot overcome their perception of Hartman as the descendant of slaves. On the one hand, they are unsure whether they will hurt her by joking about her background. On the other hand, they are reminded of their horrible past, which they have difficulty confronting. In addition, her very presence seems to make them feel guilty. The obviousness of her slave ancestry is a *corpus delicti*, a shameful fact Africans cannot cope with. Especially when Hartman fights the silence tooth and nail by continually asking about slavery and who is of slave ancestry in the places they visit, a question prohibited by law, she does not make (m)any friends. She asks the chief of Salagwura:

> "What about the slaves of Salaga? Are there people in town who are the descendants of slaves?" The chief stiffened upon hearing my question. He spoke with pursed lips and Muhammad translated. "It is still difficult for us to speak of slavery. One cannot point a finger and say he or she is a slave. It is prohibited to do so." (193)

The Africans she encounters reject any responsibility in the slave trade and do not want to be reminded of that time. Even when Hartman presses on the question of *who* sold the slaves, a schoolteacher and guide tells her that it was the white men and that Africans were only middle men in the trade. Hartman objects the statement that European traders did not reach Salaga until 1876

---

[70] All authors at hand use African vocabulary to render their texts authentic, which is also a way to pay tribute to the African-American literary tradition of the spoken word.

(188). Nevertheless, everyone nowadays knows exactly who is of slave ancestry and who is not, so that there is an underlying racism among Africans, between the descendants of the commoners (slaves) and nobles (masters and traders). The Africans she meets only want to tell the glorious stories of kingdoms and nobles, and they do not wish to be reminded of the slave past. What makes matters worse is that in

> Ghana, slavery wasn't a rallying cry against the crimes of the West or the evils of white men; to the contrary, it shattered any illusions of a unanimity of sentiment in the black world and exposed the fragility and precariousness of the grand collective *we* that had yet to be actualized (75).

This finding underlines the fragmentation and internal discrimination within the African/Ghanaian society. African-Americans view Africa as *one* community; however, Africa is made up of different countries and innumerable tribes, which are very heterogeneous and oftentimes at odds or even warlike with one another. "African people represented no unanimity of sentiment or common purpose or recognizable collectivity but rather heterogeneous and embattled social groups" (Hartman 230). This fact contributes to the identity problems of the *African* in *African-Americans*. For Hartman, figuring this out and writing about it, she can leave any romantic notions behind, which hinder so many African-Americans in their true identity formation and of taking charge of their lives. Her research and the autobiographical act support her individual shaping by neglecting long-held illusions of the African-American community.

When discussing racism and exoticism, one must say that, on the one hand, many Africans detest African-Americans like Hartman, because Africans view them as rich people from America and do not understand that they come in search of a shameful past. The majority of Africans think that African-Americans should be happy with what they have and many would trade their situation: "In Ghana, they joked that if a slave ship bound for America docked off the coast today so many Ghanaians would volunteer for the passage that they would stampede one another trying to get on board" (170). African-Americans who come to Africa hope to find their roots and calm their identity quandaries, whereas Africans long for the life that they think African-Americans lead in the New World. Hartman writes that "[she] had fled to their world and the boys yearned to escape to [hers]" (89). African-Americans, especially the expatriates who settled in Ghana, are considered "black *white* men. Every brick and pillar [of their houses] testified to the impossibility of returning and to the imprudence of believing in origins and trying to recover them" (102). Moreover, Africans try to profit from heritage tourism and are "selling" African-Americans once again. Wherever she goes, Ghanaians pressure her to come back and spend money in Ghana. The chief of Salagwura "welcomed us to Salaga and invited us to think of it as our home. 'You must come again many times'" (192). It is almost perverse that there are Africans who deny Africans in the diaspora any feeling of belonging and kinship, but when it comes to money, all of a sudden, African-American visitors are supposed to view the very place where their ancestors were sold as their home, just in order to bring more heritage pilgrims there and make money.

> If in the era of the trade the enslaved had been forced to forget mother, now their descendants were being encouraged to do the impossible and reclaim her. In the 1990s, Ghana discovered that remembering the suffering of slaves might not be such a bad thing after all, if for no other reason than it was profitable. (162)

However, Hartman detects the reasons for this and thus does not follow the trend of nostalgia for lost times and homes as do other African-Americans, for she experiences that there is "no common chord of memory, no bedrock of shared sentiment" (171).

In addition, Ghanaian children already know which buttons to press when dealing with African-American tourists, because Africans "were used to Americans with identity problems" (154), and so they play on this weakness. At specific sights, children gather and shout: "'Sister!' 'One Africa!' 'Slavery separated us'" (84), and they hand out letters that feign kinship, ask for contact, and in the end demand money and other materialistic things (84-85). Racism is also visible in the children's letters since they still think of African-Americans as slaves. "Through their letters, they were trying to call me back from *donkorland*" (157). By *donkorland* or *odonkorland*, they hint at the slave past because the "word for 'slave' in Akan that comes closest to what we mean by the term in the West is *odonkor*. It refers to someone who is bought and sold in the market, a commodity" (86). This is a twofold, internal racism that Hartman experiences. First, commoners were sold into bondage because of their low social status. Then today African-Americans, who come in search of their roots in order to redeem them, are "sold" once again by the still existing African profit-thinkers because Africans detest them for their seemingly better status in the USA. Africans try to rub some of the fortune off of their denied kin's skin from across the sea. Hartman, by telling those stories without being blinded by romanticism, hopes to see behind it all and use her discoveries to come to terms with her own self, even if it means to uncover those cruelties. It is also a double alienation or double betrayal. The first one lies in the fact that African-Americans were forcefully alienated from Africa and their own identities and became slaves. The second act of betrayal is that as soon as their descendants return to Africa and want to claim their Africanness, they have to negate their very past (as descendents of slaves) in order to belong.

Throughout her work, Hartman regularly reflects on her experiences and right away transforms them into a meaning for her own self.

> Every generation confronts the task of choosing its past. Inheritances are chosen as much as they are passed on. The past depends less on "what happened then" than on the desires and discontents of the present. [. . .] The hope is that return could resolve the old dilemmas, make a victory out of defeat, and engender a new order. And the disappointment is that there is no going back to a former condition. Loss remakes you. Return is as much about the world to which you no longer belong as it is about the one in which you have yet to make a home. [. . .] It is to lose your mother, always. (100)

Thus, Hartman becomes an African-American agent for new perspectives. She leaves behind any nostalgia and false hopes, and therein lies her personal "success"—which is also a more or less revolutionary act in African-American thought. She now knows how Africans think and act and how this affects African-American history and life. Therefore, her political activism focuses on trying to open up a dialog to maybe, eventually, change racialized views, while not succumbing to a romantic, unrealistic vision of Africa. She faces reality in order to make progress. She does not want to stand still any longer by keeping up the false desires of the African-American community. It is as if saying: You can go home but you cannot stay[71] or, like the title of Thomas Wolfe's novel, *You Can't Go Home Again*. By candidly writing about a shameful past and by doggedly scrutinizing the status quo in Africa, Hartman chooses to tell the truth about the past in Africa. The discoveries help her to understand her identity in the present, and by disclosing African and African-American impossibilities she actively shapes her future and, possibly, that of her African-American community as well. Thus, she refuses that others determine her story and her being. I want to conclude by citing Hartman's outlook and personal conviction:

> At the end of the journey, I knew that Africa wasn't dead to me, nor was it just a grave. My future was entangled with it, just as it was entangled with every other place on the globe where people were struggling to live and hoping to thrive. The fugitive's dream exceeded the borders of the continent; it was a dream of the world house. If I learned anything in Gwolu, it was that old identities sometimes had to be jettisoned in order to invent new ones. Your life just might depend on this capacity for self-fashioning. Naming oneself anew was sometimes the price exacted by the practice of freedom. (233)

---

[71] Although Hartman's emphasis is on Africa, racism there, and how it affects her and other African-Americans' lives, every now and then she links her experiences in Ghana to examples in the USA, which also underscores her personal fight against racism at home and in general.

This finding is Hartman's form of success and thus her work is revolutionary, for it guides African-American life writings into a new era of unsentimental, unromantic, and pragmatic thought and criticism. She openly and directly pronounces that the belief of Africa as home for African-Americans is a mere utopia.

Hartman's trip to Africa as a form of African-American identity formation was only partly provoked by personal issues and foremost conducted in the name of research. Golden's identity formation is triggered by events in her youth, such as the murder of Martin Luther King, Jr. (13-14). She encounters American racism first-hand and her parents inhibit the development of her black pride, for they have internalized white discriminatory standards. As mentioned earlier, Golden decides to fight inequalities and racism when joining black movements and celebrating her Africanness, e.g., by proudly wearing an Afro (23) and celebrating African traditions and styles within her group of friends, who are all members of the SNCC (19). "They taught [her] the new language, how to roll the words on [her] tongue. [. . .] [They] were prepared for war but would witness only skirmishes that left [them] bloodied nevertheless" (19). Moreover, Golden becomes more active and she

> wrote a biweekly column for the *Eagle*, the campus newspaper, in which [she] spread the gospel of black consciousness, sat on a committee to implement a black studies program at A.U., tutored black high school students and wrote bristling black poetry that sizzled on the page. (20)

Even though Golden fights for equality by many means, she already seems a bit disappointed when she hints at the fact that there is no real "war" but merely "skirmishes" that leave them wounded. Soon, "[t]he summer of [her] mother's death was the beginning of a season of mourning. [She] mourned, too, the demise of the movement that had shaped [her]" (29). An historical era comes to an end, and Golden finds herself in an identity vacuum that has been created by the decline of the Civil Rights Movement and the death of her mother, whom she idolized.

Although her mother tried to instill in Golden a sense of feminism and strength when she tells her to soar where she herself has glided and to migrate where she had chosen to nest (26), Golden is lost without a Black Power community and without her mother as a role model. Therefore, she leaves Washington, D.C., and goes to New York City. It is there that Golden becomes even more disillusioned by the USA and its misconceived promises and is more and more drawn to African men and African culture. She is searching to fill the vacuum she finds herself in. First, she needs to fill the cultural gap which her black activist past left behind, and then she needs to bridge the gap her mother's love bequeathed. Inevitably, Femi Ajayi, a Nigerian student, soon becomes Golden's anchor and center of life when he is able to fill both gaps. He can provide her with the African pride and culture she has been longing for all her life, while at the same time being her lover.

From the beginning of their relationship, different forms of racism, as well as sexism, are part of Golden's life. First, Golden's observations and descriptions of Femi enforce the notion of Golden as an almost typical African-American individual, who has been socialized not only in a black environment, but who has been influenced by white views as well. She describes Femi's lovemaking as "fervent, blunt, like being swept up in a hurricane, and he looked upon [her] with the delight of a child, surprised and grateful that [she] was his" (51). On the one hand, it reminds one of a woman of a different era (and culture), who is being possessed in negative but also positive ways. On the other hand, Golden seems to view Femi from a more Western, romanticized standpoint, namely as the savage, unsophisticated African exotic who seduces her, as the quotation above illustrates. Thus, whereas Femi's background makes him possess his woman and exert a culturally conditioned sexism on her, Golden steps into the role of the Western prey that is fascinated by his African otherness. One must point out here that this passage has not been reflected by Golden either as a coincidence or out of ignorance, or, which I believe is the case, that she plots her coming of age, i.e., she makes use of performative constructedness. A bit later, though, she explains to his brother Tope why most Americans have distorted views of Africa, namely by way of "Tarzan movies, Africa jokes, slavery" and so on (52), and Golden does not really include herself in the group of those who have ignorant standpoints. But it is apparent that she herself is not immune to this ignorance. If she begins to perform and construct her identity formation here, it is in order to show that the mystification and romanticization of Africa does not lead to a utopian, nostalgic state of being, as she discovers much later in the story.

Racism and ignorance unfolds on both sides—on the African-American and the African (in this case Golden as the Western part and Femi as the African part). Golden enforces the stereotypes of how people of differing, almost opposing, cultures eye each other. Speaking, i.e., writing it, out is Golden's way of dealing with her past misconceptions and of overcoming her own ignorance. When she attends the African get-together parties of Femi's friends in the USA, his "friends devoured [her] with lavish, open smiles and conversation. They were aggressive but never rude. The women, clustered in a corner of the room away from the men, nursed babies" (52). She becomes the exotic within the circle of his friends, an object of desire, because the traditional female role is docile: stay out of the way of men and take care of domestic duties. After only fifty-two pages it becomes obvious that gender-related issues are of great interest to Golden, even though she does not judge them at this point. Although her mother tried to make her a strong and self-sufficient woman, Golden forces herself into the role of the dutiful woman because it seems to provide her with the security and stability she has lacked since losing the guidance of the movement and of her mother. On the other hand, Africans meet Golden's presence with envy and also racism when they say, "Another American. Where are their men?" (53). In their views, she is the Western American, not African-American, woman who forcefully enters the ranks of "real" Africans and steals their men. Thus, both sides cannot overcome their stereotypes. It is only the love between Golden and Femi that connects the two confrontational, i.e., racist and sexist, worlds.

Due to her upbringing and socialization, sexism and racism are not new to Golden. She encounters the gender hierarchy of her new African friends as something positive, for she at least knows where she stands and what her role is. It gives her a direction, even though it should function as a warning sign; she, however, ignores it. Femi lets her know that he is "the man. [His] job is to be that. Not to cater to and pet [her] in public" (57). As for the racism, she hopes to overcome it. Is she not African herself? If she really tries and learns their language, can she not also be one of them?

> Among these Nigerians I had found a haven. The turbulent waters of my recent past had washed me ashore. Here I would find peace. Here I would find love. [. . .] I only wanted to shape a rebirth of hope. [. . .] Eagerly I strained to understand and meld into a community grounded in a sense of family and connectedness—the ethic that would heal my wounds. (58)

Consequently, Golden follows Femi to Nigeria because she hopes to forget her disturbing family past as well as her often discriminatory environment in America. As with many other African-Americans of that time, she believes that "returning" to Africa will solve her identity problems and that she will find peace and salvation there. Golden, however, does not go there as a tourist, but as a woman who tries to recreate, or rather reinvent, herself—and stay.

In a way, Golden's first visit to Africa mirrors the experiences of Hartman. However, Golden goes there in a time when African-Americans had put all their eggs into one basket. Golden and others see Africa as the savior—and thus her story is misty-eyed and romanticized, unlike Hartman's. Writing down her emotions that have been stirred by her observations, though, is part of her autobiographical act, for the narrative and her identity formation are performed simultaneously.

> To set foot on the continent that we no longer called home but that, in a historical sense, had birthed us, had become a necessary pilgrimage. A way of discovering who, indeed, we were. In the sixties Africa was a symbol and source of pride and regeneration. (65)

They went "back to the empires of Timbuktu and Mali, village life, Swahili, noble kings and tribal tongues" (65). It is the notion that African-Americans want to find out who they are by visiting Africa and listening to the glorious stories. Most of them return to the US satisfied because they do not want to hear the truth. It is the same truth that Hartman tries to uncover, which has nothing to do with the stories of noble kingdoms and a glorious past, though they remain indeed major motivations. However, there is a slight hint at the fact that Golden, even though still very much romanticizing, does acknowledge darker sides, too. "Hungrily we read, exchanged and discussed the books that revealed Africa's resilient cultures, its plunder at the hands of white conquerors, and its betrayal by its own sons" (65). She also hears the children calling her "'oyingbo, oyingbo,' 'foreigner, foreigner'" in Yoruba when she stays with Femi's family in Nigeria (79). This is a similar experience to the one of Hartman. If one neglects parts that belong to the whole picture, one cannot lastingly find peace, one cannot overcome racism in order to shape one's own life.

Landing in Ghana, her stopover, she finds that exoticism is two-fold. In America, African-Americans are oftentimes still regarded as the exotics, the others, the ones with an inherited slave ancestry. In Ghana, African-American tourists are also the descendents of slaves but moreover the rich exotics, the rich Westerners, and are even considered to be white. Vice versa, to the eyes of an African-American, Ghana and its inhabitants are exotic. "As the plane descended into Kotoka International Airport in Accra, the land below astonished. Reached out with palm tree arms, nestled us against its red clay breast" (67). Moreover, Golden looks "out the window at a panorama that was exotic and serene" (69). It is striking that Golden, when meeting Femi, describes her African lover similarly by talking about his palms, that "were the color of brownish-red clay" (50), and his appearance, which was solemn, strong, different, and enticing to her, just like the land in front of her. Golden is trying to combine the search for her self with the search for love on the ground she thinks will make her whole: Africa, with its breasts welcoming her home to the motherland (67). She skillfully uses the African-American stylistic device of repeating and reinterpreting certain terms, which then take on symbolic meaning, just like the terms "breasts" and "red clay." This is very typical of signifying, and the term "red clay" comes up at different times in the autobiography. Red clay is the association many people have when thinking of African soil and the structure of dwellings. When still in the USA, Golden already sees the continent and its exotic landscape reflected in the palms of Femi's hand. Later on, she actually sets foot on this special soil. In addition, red is the color of love and of the heart, and Golden attempts to find love in Africa and fill the empty spot in her heart of a feeling of belonging. Clay, the particular texture of it as a binding agent, represents family bonds and kinship for Golden in Africa; she wants to be part of this ancient human family. Clay is the oldest form of construction material and just as Africans build the homes for themselves and their kin, Golden wants to construct her own life in Africa, after trying to overcome racism, sexism, and exoticism. There is something, however, she does not take into consideration. When using wet clay, it can still be molded; when it is dry, it is solid as rock. Thus, when in the USA, Femi adapted a bit to her American way of living, and his strong character was "softer" and his friends accepted Golden after a while. This reminds one of wet clay that can still be formed and be penetrated. In Africa, the sun makes the red clay very hard, and so kinship, i.e., belonging, soon will prove to be impermeable for a Westerner like her.

During her first visit and later on when she moves to Nigeria, Golden gives accounts of the many instances that show how racism, sexism, and exoticism are also part of African society, and how her hope to find peace there and overcome all this must inevitably fail. For a long time, however, Golden nurtures the illusion of belonging, finding her black self, and happiness in Africa. She tries her best to learn Yoruba, to fulfill all duties of a woman in Nigerian society and family life, and to love Femi more than anyone can. She encounters tribalism and internal racism, but she tries to see the positive aspects of it. For instance, in Nigeria she talks to an American by the name of Calvin who observes, "The tribalism. It's as bad as racism at home. [. . .] [A]nd me—I'm in the middle of it all [as the American]" (76). Golden replies that the middle can be a good place to be in at times. She claims that one "can be protected" when in the middle (76). Calvin counters that one can also get crushed. It is narrative plotting on Golden's part, for she foreshadows what will happen. Golden will find herself in the middle of all that they are discussing here. She will not belong but instead will almost get crushed by her false illusions on the one hand and the cultural and gender-specific expectations of Femi and his family on the other.

Nevertheless, the more Golden tries to conform and live up to the various expectations, the clearer does she see. The shattered identity that had led her to Africa now unfolds and two opposing paths open up, i.e., to either become an obedient, submissive want-to-be Nigerian wife and mother or an enlightened, strength-regaining and self-determined modern African-American woman. Golden begins to reflect why she is in Africa at all. "Never mind the destination. The journey was all that mattered. Still, this potentially deadly rhythm touched my own restless soul. I was there because, like everyone else, I was an explorer looking for the end of my personal rainbow" (83). For the first time, life is not merely about her unconditional, almost superhuman, love for Femi and how to best please him anymore; she discovers that she is more than anything else in search of her self. It seems as if she tries out the different possibilities, like the different colors˙ of the rainbow, to find out who she is and where she belongs. The work becomes less romantic and sentimental when Golden begins to establish herself as an independent woman. The narrative becomes less the *his*tory of her life and more the feminist, coming-into-existence-first-before-coming-of-age *her*story. She is not blinded by love and cultural illusions anymore, and, like Hartman, she sees behind the promises of Africans vis-à-vis African-American tourists. Africans call them sister and brother, but in reality most Africans do not acknowledge this kinship due to the slave ancestry of

African-Americans. However, Africans know that African-Americans come in search of exactly this kinship and so they, as mentioned in the analysis of Hartman, "sell" African-Americans again—and sometimes they do so very bluntly: "'Ah, soul sister, bring money, bring money'" (84).

Two very endearing aspects keep her in Africa, playing along with racial and gender-specific roles. First, it is the irresistible masculinity of society and above all of Femi (84). It must be the strength that is so enticing to her formerly weak and lost soul. Second, it is the "sense of community [that] enveloped [her] during the journey. [. . .] No longer constrained to apologize for the accident of color, [she]'d felt free, for the first time in [her] life, to become whatever else there was inside [her]" (86-87). Before, she did not feel alive. "My devotion was nothing less than a crusade to regain the courage I needed simply to be. So I swore that no matter what, Femi and I would not fail" (87). Golden, in order to find herself, had to come to Africa, where her self-esteem as a black woman would almost be leveled out totally. She is not regarded and not treated as an individual there. Slowly, Golden tries to come alive, to come into being in Africa. As a result, one can say that the function of her autobiography, i.e., the writing of her life and her life itself before, starkly resembles that of slave narratives, but with a feminist twist. Golden writes herself into being, into existence as an African-American woman in the diaspora and in the world. It is a personal quest turned into a feminist one when Golden as a black female writer comes into being, which is similar to former slave authors. Golden, though, takes it a step further. She not only writes herself and other black women into existence, but by taking charge of her life, difficult as it may be, and by choosing what and how to write about her life, she also follows in the new African-American literary footsteps of shaping one's past, present, and future. Golden, maybe more than Hartman and Obama, endures racism, sexism, and exoticism in the USA and on the African continent. She loses her already shaky identity when her mother dies and the movement collapses. Subsequently, she tries to reinvent herself and is willing to give up a lot. In the end, all this misery and drama makes her find her inner strength. She cannot eliminate racism and sexism because one cannot change others[72]—but one can change oneself and choose the life one wants to live, which is exactly what she does in the end.

There is a point when Golden starts to break out of her restraining bonds while in Africa. It is when she discovers that writing is more important to her at that time than having a baby, which is what Femi so desperately yearns for. She begins to write a novel, "inspired by all the people and experiences [she] had known" (131), and the characters "performed the tasks of all good friends—they kept [her] sane. They made [her] whole" (131). She uses performative constructedness when the narrative and her identity develop at the same time. Also, becoming "whole" seems to be unachievable in reality, but novels are

---

[72] The British had left behind a country full of tribalism and internal racism (Golden 111).

created and their structure of having a beginning, a middle, and an end provide at least some form of wholeness. At the time of writing, i.e., creating, this novel while attempting to give birth to a new self, however, her self-determined, free mind is still trapped in her compliant body. She lets her life be extraneously determined by Femi and gives in to his desire to have children, becomes pregnant, and is consequently incapable of writing. Instead of writing and thus giving birth to a virtual new self, she is supposed to give birth to a baby she does not want. "Writing was the only child I wanted then, and I was racked by a sense of guilt because of my inability to nurture it [i.e., the writing]" (160). Soon, she loses the baby—she felt she was not ready for it. Immediately, she

> began to write furiously, with the fervor of a long-awaited eruption. [She] filled page after page with an outpouring the loss of [her] child released. The writing affirmed [her], anointed [her] with a sense of purpose. [. . .] The writing redeemed [her] talent for creation and, as the days passed, made [her] whole once again. (170)

When the baby dies, a weakened Golden and her misleading wishes die with the baby, and a strong Golden is reborn as an African-American woman and writer.[73] She takes charge of her own life as a woman, despite being discriminated against on account of race, gender, and social background; and, in the autobiographical act of sharing her story with an audience, she actively shapes her own life. Golden, whose experiences date back to the seventies, wrote them down in the early eighties, which is the time when many African-Americans held a romantic view of Africa. By moving to Africa and by immersing herself into every-day life, she actually encountered both negative and positive aspects and came out a new person. Sexism was certainly exercised in a more open and powerful way in Africa than in America, which is what accelerated Golden's feminist identity development.

Her experiences and the experiences of other women are what Hartman later took on as the basis for her research and as the starting point to topple the sentimental view of and wishful thinking about Africa, in order to come to a more realistic conclusion. Golden, among other female writers of the era, lay the groundwork for a strong feminist consciousness among African-Americans. This basis serves as the foundation of the subsequent women writers and researchers, who, like their male counterparts, want to be accepted as equal human beings who can control and direct their own life's path. By this act of self-determination and autobiographical writing they, relentlessly, fight against racism, sexism, and exoticism. African-American women do not want to have to prove any longer that they are equal human beings. Today, Marita Golden is a successful author of novels, non-fiction, and essays, and she is an acclaimed

---

[73] This incident is reminiscent of the Western Protestant pattern in literature called (religious) rebirth.

teacher of writing—thus, her very first work, her autobiography, *Migrations of the Heart*, has certainly led to her personal and professional success[74] as well as the progress of black women's rights and status in society.

Barack Obama takes charge of molding his self by writing an autobiography in his thirties. Although he openly reflects on the fact that he himself has tried to "rewrite these stories [of his life], plugging up holes in the narrative, accommodating unwelcome details" and having "selective lapses of memory" (xvi), he tries to avoid most of those hazards in his work but cannot guarantee that none of them entered his autobiography. He claims to have attempted to create an honest account; however, no author, or rather no human being, is immune to portraying the best picture possible of himself. Nonetheless, his autobiography, like Golden's and Hartman's, is a piece of art that bolsters, or even creates, his identity formation and his life's story—its past, present, and future—by narrating the stories that shaped who he is and how he came to be that way. As an African-American, these stories are embedded in experiences of racism and exoticism, just like the stories of the other authors.

When Obama is still a young boy, there are not many instances of racism or identity problems. Although his mother had always tried to instill in him a sense of black pride, it is the story in *Life* magazine, where he finds out that black people try to whiten their skin with chemicals that sparks his racial awareness. "But my vision had been permanently altered. [. . .] I still trusted my mother's love—but I now faced the prospect that her account of the world, and my father's place in it, was somehow incomplete" (52). Up until this event, Obama builds up the basis for his subsequent coming of age, outlining his heritage, his grandparents' background, his parents' short union, his family's move to Indonesia, and his acculturation. All this points to his surroundings and not his self because he is not yet in crisis and, seemingly, his life is in order. He draws a picture of internal quandaries of his white grandparents and his white mother, and talks about the myths surrounding his African father so that the differences, or even the incompatibilities, of that former picture vis-à-vis his newly discovered view become obvious. His childish naïveté vanishes after reading the article and glimpsing the cruelties and realities of the world, especially the ones of racial division and consciousness. Step by step, before his discovery, Obama as the writer shifts the attention from the stories and backgrounds of his family to his own self. The discovery throws him into crisis. It appears as if some form of racial incident must inevitably happen in the life of a black person living in a racist society or even in the world. The discovery is the point where the story sets off and where his individual journey begins. Also, Obama writes down his family history and genealogy as if the act of putting it on paper for everyone to see manifests, once and for all, his hybrid, i.e., multicultural, identity; as if seeing is believing *and* accepting.

---

[74] Golden's website at http://maritagolden.com/ provides information about her, her up-to-date professional biography, and her class schedule.

The distorted racial beauty standards of the article in *Life* magazine does not touch Obama's life directly, but his first day of middle school in Hawaii, supposedly the multicultural and tolerant melting pot of America, will prove to be his first personal encounter with racial humiliation. His uncommon and Muslim name of Barack Obama becomes the target of ridicule when his teacher reads it out loud (59). The inherited racial stereotypes of the teacher and especially of his classmates[75] become apparent when the teacher asks from which tribe his father stems. Someone in the class accompanies the answer with the hooting sound of apes. Moreover, a girl wants to touch Obama's hair, but he does not let her (60). All this is very new for Obama, who, having lived in Indonesia before, has not really encountered discrimination or being othered up until this point. His situation in Hawaii, though, can neither be compared to the much worse racial discrimination in urban America nor to the carefree life he led in Indonesia. However, he, like many other African-Americans, cannot get over the feeling that he does not fully belong (60).

Before finding a community in Hawaii, and later on in urban Chicago, Obama tries to at least make himself more interesting by inventing exotic stories about his family in Africa. It is a way for a little boy, who is thrown off guard by his mixed racial background, to shape his past in order to make his present easier and more pleasant. He, for instance, claims that his father is a prince and his friends find this very enticing (63). While constructing a family background according to his own fantasies, the young Obama simultaneously performs his identity. He even wants to believe these stories, and he hopes to find out that his father's tribe is that of the Nilotic people from Egypt. "I had visions of ancient Egypt, the great kingdoms I had read about, pyramids and pharaohs, Nefertiti and Cleopatra" (64). From readings and the works at hand, it becomes apparent that many African-Americans are longing for a noble past and share this wishful thinking. Golden's father talks about Cleopatra and the Sphinx, whereas Hartman tries to overcome these longings and false hopes. For Obama, Africa is exotic and has a great history; he wants to be part of this great story, but when he finds out that the tribe of his father is made up of farmers, he is very disappointed (64). In addition to this mythic picture of a noble past, the reality Hartman exemplifies in her book about Africa's denial of any responsibility in the slave trade is mirrored in Obama's work. He gives account of what his father tells his class, namely that "many had been enslaved only because of the color of their skin" (70). This shows that his father wants to believe that whites enslaved blacks because of the color of their skin. Hartman, among others, proves that this is too easy an explanation and that actually it was one's social standing in Africa that contributed for the most part to enslavement: African nobles captured African commoners and sold them to other nobles or whites. Of course, it is also true that white people captured black people, regardless of their social status. As Hartman sees it, many Africans, however, do not want to come to

---

[75] The class was mainly white except for Obama and one other black student (60-61).

terms with their own guilt and responsibility vis-à-vis the slave past, for it is more favorable for their conscience and easier to blame whites. Obama and Golden, unlike Hartman, do not reflect on this aspect. They are still too much blinded by their inner longings, even though reality, time and again, catches up with them; and they too want to leave their romantic visions behind.

It seems that up until his father's visit, he has not played much of a role in Obama's life, or at least Obama does not share such thoughts with the reader. So far, the autobiography has mostly been about the other people in his life and less about Obama's troubled or even non-existent relationship with his biological father. One could say that by not mentioning the relationship to his father, Obama wants to stress the absence of a father figure in his life. In addition, thus far, the lack of his father in the narrative does correspond with the title because they are "dreams" from or about his father. But with his father's visit it becomes apparent that the remainder of the book will deal with identity issues, community struggles, and transatlantic family bonds. All these are issues that are triggered by a new sensibility for race relations and family backgrounds. Consequently, the title is filled with meaning by the following stories and events. By beginning to enumerate the negative and positive aspects of his father's visit and by swaying back and forth between wanting him to leave soon versus getting accustomed to him, Obama seems to slowly "build a case" like a lawyer[76], trying to find evidence for a statement of reasons to permit his father being a part of his life (64-70). Obama's identity develops just as the narration unfolds in a performative construction: Obama is back in Hawaii, where he encounters initial identity problems and teasings right before his father arrives. His father's visit further complicates the boy's life and thoughts when Obama is around ten years of age. It is as if his racial problems only become real when Obama meets his biological father and it is this side of his genealogy that entails identity struggles and discrimination for him.

Most urban African-Americans live and act in communities, which is something that Obama lacks in Hawaii in the beginning. He knows that "something wasn't quite right" (82) when he has to face discrimination by himself but can not pinpoint what is not right. When he goes to high school, he meets Ray and other black students and plays on the basketball team, and for the first time he is part of a black community and understands what it is that is not quite right. They are angry because they "were always playing on the white man's court, [. . .] by the white man's rules" (85). Thus, they gather and "teach [Obama] an attitude that didn't just have to do with the sport" (79), and their "confusion and anger would help shape [his] own" (80). Obama lives a life "in-between" two conflicting worlds, one of them the white world at home with his grandparents and mother, and the other one the black one of his friends. This middle position makes it difficult for him to always and fully take the discrimination personally and to blame whites for everything. He differentiates

---

[76] Obama later goes to law school.

between his black friends, his family, and the other bad *"white folks"* (80). During puberty, his black awareness is shaped by his black environment on the basketball team and in his clique, and can be traced by analyzing the language Obama uses to reproduce the conversations among his friends. Obama and his adolescent friends converse by using African-American vernacular, so the pages in the book take on the function of the talking book or speakerly text when Obama recounts those instances without quotation marks.

> We were in goddammned Hawaii. We said what we pleased, ate where we pleased; we sat at the front of the proverbial bus. None of our white friends, guys like Jeff or Scott from the basketball team, treated us any differently than they treated each other. They loved us, and we loved them back. Shit, seemed like half of 'em wanted to be black themselves—or at least Doctor J.
> Well, that's true, Ray would admit.
> Maybe we could afford to give the bad-assed nigger pose a rest. Save it for when we really needed it.
> And Ray would shake his head. A pose, huh? Speak for your own self. (82)

This example shows that Obama is unsure of who this "self" is, and is still not fully immersed in the black community or ready to unleash anger at white people. While he defends white folks, he uses black language to still be part of the black folks. He underlines the latter with his oratorical style while writing his autobiography. Whether his memory recalls this instance as it actually happened or whether Obama purposefully paints a picture of himself as an individual, whose heart beats for a black *and* a white world, cannot be determined. Nevertheless, it shows that Obama is, indeed, a person who has been socialized in opposing communities and has lived a life getting to know both views, which is definitely helpful for him today as a politician to win over both black and white "camps." Additionally, Obama's genealogy differs from the majority of African-Americans in that his background is not part of the history of slavery.

Previous and also subsequent to the above-mentioned conversation, he uses black vernacular many times to display authenticity and to reach his black audience. Simultaneously, though, he portrays himself as swaying back and forth between the black and the white world, unsure of where he belongs, which also stresses his mostly white upbringing. He turns to reading African-American literature, which is what Golden and many other African-Americans claim they do when they are thrown into an identity crisis. They portray themselves as literate, intelligent black individuals, who turn to black books as a source of information, assurance, and rescue. Malcolm X's autobiography is especially enticing to Obama, due to his "repeated acts of self-creation" (86), which is precisely what Obama's autobiographical act does, namely creating and recreating his self. Consequently, he is actively shaping his past life, his present being, and his professional, i.e., political, future by constructing a story that is inclusive for a black *and* white audience. Therefore, on a narrative level, Obama reconciles this dichotomy because he serves a black and a white audience. On a personal level, he is unable to do so and claims that even though he tries to reconcile "the world as [he]'d found it with the terms of [his] birth," he soon learns that "there was no escape to be had" and is left behind disillusioned (85). However, Obama's special status, his in-betweenness, his being neither black (in the traditional African-American sense) nor white, will later provide him with the necessary means of bridging the gap that divides white and black societies as a community organizer in Chicago and, above all, as the first black President of the United States of America.

When Obama moves to the North American continent after having lived in Indonesia and Hawaii, he is the exotic even among African-Americans. Whereas Golden and Hartman belong to the African-American community *per definitionem*, i.e., by their slave ancestry and upbringing, Obama does not have "the certainty of the tribe" (98-99). It is interesting that Obama uses the term "tribe" when explaining how black students stick together on Oxy campus. The term usually describes African kinship so, by hinting at African-American togetherness due to their unique slave past, Obama allusively excludes himself because he cannot be fully immersed into this "tribe." He continues, "But I hadn't grown up in Compton, or Watts. I had nothing to escape from except my own inner doubt. I was more like the black students who had grown up in the suburbs, kids whose parents had already paid the price of escape" (99). Thus, he knows he does not share the same background that has shaped African-American lives, and he does not suffer from discrimination as badly as black urban children or teenagers do. However, there is something that connects him to the African-American community and that is his inner struggle with his identity and genealogy, as well as his doubts about the racialized world. Moreover, the young people from the suburbs, to whom he compares himself, he says, "weren't defined by the color of their skin, they would tell you. They were individuals" (99). This remark is striking for it again underlines the influence not only of the progress and self-definition of the African-American community, but also of the white Western ideal of individualism. This reminds the reader of the tension between the African concept of community and kinship versus the white Western concept of individualism. Here, Obama is an individual, just like the black suburban youth he gives as an example, but he also wants to be part of the African-American community. While being the exotic again, he tries to merge both life concepts.

As a community organizer in Chicago, Obama experiences African-American struggles mostly not first-hand, but as a by-stander who is trying to help. Obama wants to become part of the black community in Chicago and the USA. He wants to share common experiences, which is what Gates describes, with the aim of being included in the community. Thus, Obama's "sacrifice" is to settle for a job for which he is overly qualified and badly underpaid in order to prove his authenticity and integrity, i.e., his sincere commitment to the African-American community. Even though he does not really become one of "them," he at least takes part in their struggles. Obama does not encounter racism or discrimination directed straight at him (or he does not write about it). He shares the stories of discrimination directed at the citizens of the boroughs he takes care of, and so racism remains rather abstract, i.e., indirect, to the reader.[77] Obama, by trying to overcome those injustices in real life and by writing about them, implements imagery to convey how the situation in Chicago is. "Winter came and the city turned monochrome—black trees against gray sky above white earth" (187). Organizing a black urban community is not an easy task, especially for an outsider like Obama. The conditions are harsh for anyone visiting the city because of the stone-cold weather of Chicago in winter. However, Obama is taking on the role as organizer and actively shapes his own life by working against the odds. The black trees are like African-Americans grounded to the place and willing to fight for themselves and their place on earth (187). The gray sky symbolizes the not so clear and for some not so fortunate future vis-à-vis the odds against the "enemy:" the white earth, meaning the white society and the white people in control surrounding them. This image describes the structure of society in Chicago, and many other places in America, and Obama tries to make the best of it for "his" people. As a skilled writer, he employs this image in order to overcome the status quo of unjust power and opportunity allocation, and his individual identity is also being shaped by his unrelenting community work. Obama knows and openly admits that he has never been a victim of racism as badly as other African-Americans have been. Thus, he never felt the urge to prove that he is a human being. By becoming a community organizer, he tries to feel some of their pain. By actively deciding what to do with his own life, he also helps African-Americans take control of their fate. As an author, writing about this becomes a means of giving a positive example to overcome racism.

Racism is a way to categorize human beings into an arbitrary hierarchical order. Obama, though not racist, also categorizes into "brown," "white," and "black" (e.g., 135). Obama's status as the "brown" exotic, neither fully belonging to the white nor the black community, plays a paramount role in his life no matter where he lives or goes. Therefore, after having lived in a white family in Hawaii and a mixed family in Indonesia, after having worked his way into the black community in Chicago, he decides to travel to Africa, to meet his paternal side and come to terms with his exotic, particular "uneasy status: a Westerner not entirely at home in the West, an African on his way to a land full of strangers" (301). By going on this journey he wants to take charge of his being and his fate. He wants to understand his background and otherness in

---

[77] Seemingly, the discrimination against blacks in American suburbs are not only based on skin color but often goes hand in hand with social status. Skin color and social standing are apparently mutually influencing each other.

order to resist categorization by others and to shape his own personality, no matter what the shade his skin is. Like most African-Americans traveling to Africa hope, Obama also wishes that "[i]t'll be just like *Roots*" and that he can "finally fill that emptiness" that he finds when he looks inside himself (302). But, as Golden and Hartman experience as well, reality hits him when he is considered to be an American tourist, even a white one. A merchant tries to make as much money as possible by selling Obama a necklace. "Auma frowned and said something to the man in Swahili. 'He's giving you the wazungu price,' she explained. 'The white man's price'" (310). As in Golden's and Hartman's works, the Africans they meet try to "sell" their former kin again. Even though Obama enjoys the "steady procession of black faces" and "the freedom that comes from not feeling watched" (311), he discovers the truth as well, namely that he will never fully belong here either. He remains neither black nor white, but "brown."

When Obama arrives in Kenya, the land of his father's family, he describes what he sees much in the same way that Golden or Hartman do. They see Africa through the eyes of a Westerner, who views this continent as exotic. African-Americans are, in these terms, not different from white Westerners who visit the continent for the first time and who might have read Conrad's *Heart of Darkness*. Obama gives reference to this work early on, when his white grandfather tells young Obama what he knows about third world countries (31), and when Obama is ashamed or even disgusted by his mother's sentimentalism when watching the movie *Black Orpheus*, where "the reverse image of Conrad's dark savages" is portrayed (124). Also, Obama himself reads *Heart of Darkness* while at college and is mocked by his black friends for reading it (102). Thus, he cannot but apply his biracial concepts, which are indeed binary opposites, when observing the new surroundings in Kenya. "Wide plains stretched out on either side of the road, savannah grass mostly, an occasional thorn tree against the horizon, a landscape that seemed at once ancient and raw" (307). Every traveler is in awe when describing these heretofore-unseen images. The traveler therefore relates what he or she sees to his or her known set of ideas and describes it in these terms. Obama has been mostly socialized in a white Western society and that is the reason why he depicts his view of Kenya - at least in the first parts about Kenya - in the way a tourist would. In addition, he compares Kenya to Indonesia, another third-world country. He remembers "other mornings in Indonesia, with [his] mother and Lolo talking in the front seat, the same smell of burning wood and diesel, the same stillness that lingered at the center of the morning rush" (307). As in Golden, the color red in combination with soil comes up: "back down the road of red earth" (427), which again underlines how African-Americans view Africa, namely as the land of their love, heart, and blood, a land of nostalgic longings. The sentimental views of Obama and other African-Americans are juxtaposed with the distancing views of Africans, i.e., the way Africans distinguish between their kin in Africa and former slaves from America. A great number of Africans regard African-

Americans as exotic white, Western tourists, whereas many African-Americans hope to find a home in Africa, even though Africa is a foreign and exotic country to them. It is a mutual exoticizing and racializing between Africans and African-Americans. By discovering that reality in Africa is different from his ideas and ideals, Obama can take charge of his life's path and discard romantic views of Africa.

Chapter Four: Roots en Route – African-German Life Writing

In the following chapter, I justify my choice of the three African-German works by Hügel-Marshall, Massaquoi, and Usleber and analyze them. As the title of this chapter indicates, the African-German authors dealt with in this doctoral thesis are trying to find their roots by looking elsewhere, by taking geographical and mental journeys, by fighting alone and with others for equal opportunities, and by finally writing themselves into being. At this point, I want to stress that the dichotomous view of a black versus a racist white world is the one mostly portrayed in the works of the authors. Germans are not generally racist, but the experiences of the authors underline the fact that racism is still prevalent to some extent in German society.

4.1 A Brief Contemplation on African-German vis-à-vis African-American Life Writing

African-German Life Writing is still in its infancy. In fact, it only came to life recently, when *Showing Our Colors: Afro-German Women Speak Out* was first published in German in 1986 and in English in 1992.[78] Unlike the long tradition of writing, and especially autobiographical writing of African-American culture, African-Germans started to make use of their literary and public voice approximately two to three decades ago. African-Americans were and still are able to benefit from their African heritage of orality and *griot* storytelling, which have been handed down from one generation to the next. African-American life writing has developed from early slave narratives to more modern forms of African-American autobiographical writing that concern themselves with an increasingly realistic view of their relationship to Africa and with African-American identity. Over hundreds of years of African-American life writing, African-American authors adapted their writings to the predominant discourses and problems of the respective times. Thus, their writings evolved and produced a specific African-American literary tradition of speakerly texts and talking books, a tradition of signifying, political agency, and even self-help books. African-German life writing, in comparison, has just begun to form a small but growing niche of literature within the greater context of mainstream German literature. Unlike African-American writers, the majority of African-German authors cannot draw input or experience from African oral or written heritages due to the prevailing rupture between most African-Germans and their African genealogy. The main exposure to literature of African-Germans was and often still is a white, Western literature.

In addition, African-Germans in the past were not able to establish African-German communities, for in Germany live proportionately fewer

---

[78] Audre Lorde came to the Free University in Berlin in the spring of 1984 to teach poetry. There she met a number of black German women. Later on, some of their works were published in *Showing Our Colors*.

African-Germans than African-Americans in America; and they are scattered about the country. It took initiatives of some African-Germans, as well as the advent of widespread Internet access, to actually find others in order to convene (if only virtually) and to become organized. Much more effort has been and is needed in Germany than in the USA to form a community of not only like-looking but also like-minded people. African-German get-togethers and the creation of smaller communities in the eighties and nineties actually sparked the will to ensure that African-Germans are not only perceived in a visual, which was and still is mostly negative, but also in an auditory and above all positive sense. Thus, by the encouragement and mentorship of Audre Lorde, African-German students in Berlin began to speak out. This was the beginning of the process of writing themselves and their African-German brothers and sisters into being, just like former African-American slaves had done on the American continent hundreds of years ago. The differences, though, are that African-Germans had to rely on their own sense of writing and their mostly white societal and literary background. They did not have any help of inherited African traditions, of a larger community, or of an audience. Audre Lorde, however, inspired African-German life writing by teaching her African-German students how African-Americans write; thus she and her African-American background influenced their writing. The content of African-German literature is preoccupied with the motivation to divert the public focus from skin color and consequently from the otherness of people of African descent. African-Germans want to attract attention to the continuing racism and discrimination by some Germans aimed at them. It is their goal to eliminate this racism. Simultaneously, through the act of speaking, i.e., writing out, and by fighting against this racism, African-Germans want to become fully accepted human beings, citizens in and of German society.

Showing Our Colors marks the beginning of African-German life writing, and after its publication more and more books were published and an increased public presence of and interest in African-Germans could be perceived. It is not surprising that African-Germans and other minorities began to voice their opinions in the 1980s and 1990s. Then, politics of integration slowed down and more and more racism surfaced coinciding with when Helmut Kohl became Germany's Chancellor, *Bundeskanzler*, in 1982, with Germany's reunification in 1990, and with the opening up of Eastern Europe. Even though African-Germans and many other minorities are native citizens of Germany, their different looks in the eyes of some Germans made them feel like foreigners, immigrants, and asylum-seekers. Within this context of a growing foreign-born population and also within a climate of spreading hostility, African-Germans realized that they had to counteract this development. Consequently, African-Germans came out and took on the fight against the newly flickering tendency of racial hatred. Other autobiographical and fictional texts followed *Showing Our Colors* (1992), including Harald Gerunde's *Eine von uns* (2000), Ika Hügel-Marshall's *Daheim unterwegs* (1998), Hans Jürgen Massaquoi's *Destined to*

Witness (1999) and *Hänschen klein, ging allein* . . . , Marie Nejar's *Mach nicht so traurige Augen, weil du ein Negerlein bist* (2007), *Talking Home* by Popoola and Sezen (Ed.) (1999), Thomas Usleber's *Die Farben unter meiner Haut* (2002), and Abini Zöllner's *Schokoladenkind*[79] (2003).[80] In comparison to the consecutive literary epochs of African-American life writing, an African-German tradition of life writing has just recently begun to root and mature. Hence, *Showing Our Colors* and subsequent African-German life writings constitute the first wave or first phase of African-German literary works with a main focus on autobiographical writing.

4.2 Selection and Significance of Contemporary African-German Life Writings

In accordance with the selected African-American works, my selection of African-German life writings also excludes immigration literature because the background and topics of immigrant literature differs considerably from life writings by African-Germans born and raised in Germany. A criterion for the selection of African-German works was the birth date of the author, a generational consideration due to Germany's war history and subsequent occupation. The publication date, in contrast, was one of the criteria for the choice in African-American writings. Massaquoi was born in 1926, Hügel-Marshall was born in 1947, and Usleber in 1960. The latter two belong to the group of the then so-called brown babies or occupation babies (*Besatzungskinder*). It is interesting to see that most of the women in *Showing Our Colors* are about the age of Usleber, some younger, some a bit older. It is striking, however, that the publication of the writings of Audre Lorde's female students preceded the later African-German writings by older Germans of African descent. Arguably, the writings of Lorde's students also presided over many African-German writings to come: Usleber cites from Hügel-Marshall's work, which in turn was inspired and influenced by Audre Lorde and therewith by African-American literature as well as by the African-German and feminist movements.

An important difference between the selected African-American and African-German works is that Golden and Hartman are both professional writers. Golden is a trained author and teacher and Hartman is a scholar who also publishes her research. Obama has written two books and, as a lawyer and politician, is a very eloquent man who even has an entry as a contemporary author in *The Literature Resource Center*. Contrarily, Usleber's and Hügel-Marshall's occupations have nothing to do with professional writing. Massaquoi, on the other hand, has been a journalist and has written two books in

---

[79] Zöllner's work is about her life as an African-German in the former German Democratic Republic (GDR).

[80] There is also an increasing amount of scholarly research being done on the subject of African-German history, culture, and literature.

English and can be considered a professional writer; hence, Massaquoi's background is comparable to the ones of the African-American writers at hand. Therefore, due to his professional background and particular connection to the USA, Massaquoi and his works constitute the link between African-American and African-German life writing; and thus his *Destined to Witness* earns a special status among the chosen African-German works. Most of African-German literature is, however, written by non-professional authors. The autobiographies of Usleber and Hügel-Marshall account for the ratio of books written by untrained African-German writers. This fact resembles the early African-American life writing of slaves and ex-slaves, who were not professional writers either, whereas nowadays African-American life writing is oftentimes characterized by professional authorship.

4.2.1 Ika Hügel-Marshall's *Daheim unterwegs: Ein deutsches Leben* (1998)

Ika Hügel-Marshall's given first name is *Erika* but she changed it to *Ika* later on. She was born in a small town in Bavaria in 1947. Hügel-Marshall is the "result" of a secret love affair of her German mother with a black American soldier stationed nearby. By the time she was born her father had been sent back to the USA because of an illness. Her mother married a white man and one year later Hügel-Marshall's (white) sister was born. Hügel-Marshall is one of the so-called *Besatzungskinder* and in *Das Parlament*[81] of 19 March 1952 the following could be read: "*Eine besondere Gruppe unter den Besatzungskindern bilden die 3 093 Negermischlinge, die ein menschliches und rassistisches Problem besonderer Art darstellen*" (qtd. in Hügel-Marshall 18). The language and viewpoint of this quotation is alarming, keeping in mind that the Nazi regime had been toppled seven years prior. The quotation mirrors reality because Hügel-Marshall suffered under the persistent notion of Aryan purity, and thus her mother was forced to put her into a children's home at age seven. This "home" is where her odyssey begins.

The title of Hügel-Marshall's work, *Daheim unterwegs: Ein deutsches Leben*, indicates that she has been living the life of a nomad. She is someone who is at home nowhere, or does not feel like she has found a *Heimat* even though Germany is the place where she was born and where she lives. Hügel-Marshall's work covers her life in what she perceives as a racist German society and shows how badly she suffers. Her autobiography is an accumulation of chronological examples of discrimination and deprivation and of her accusations vis-à-vis German society; it is an attempt, partly at least, to raise existential and painful questions in a naïve poetic style. The work is less about her sense of life or experiences, for they were imposed on her, and the course of her life was rather unspectacular but painful all the same, namely the horrors of the

---

[81] *Das Parlament* is a political newspaper that mostly deals with German internal politics and provides the reader with (sometimes shortened) versions of political speeches and debates from the German parliament, the *Bundestag*.

children's home, training as a child care worker, being unemployed, marrying a white man and getting divorced, studying and becoming involved with the feminist movement and later on the African-German movement. Her writing revolves more around the injustices and her rage that accumulated over the years. Her autobiographical act releases this pent-up anger and indicts the persons responsible for her suffering.

One of the reasons I chose this work over others is the pain that is still palpable in the text. Hügel-Marshall writes the book about her sufferings as an African-German in order to cure her pain and sorrow, or at least to calm down the figurative blazing inflammations. Moreover, she published the book in 1998 after having been inspired by her friend Audre Lorde, who had taught young female students in Berlin more than a decade earlier how to articulate their concerns. Hügel-Marshall follows in Lorde's and the students' footsteps by writing about her life and her racial humiliation. Her life and writing are definitely influenced by feminist tendencies in Germany since she became part of the women's movement in Germany. In addition, Hügel-Marshall was inspired by a new black movement in Germany, which is mostly represented by other African-German friends, but above all by her African-American friend Audre Lorde. Moreover, by mentioning May Ayim's work on African-German history and racism and by telling her own personal story, Hügel-Marshall wants to contribute to the *transliteration*[82] of German history, i.e., to rewrite or rather correct and append German historiography. *Daheim unterwegs* is a clear denunciation of German discrimination and a declaration of war against racism in Germany and the world. Thus, her autobiography very much reminds the reader of early African-American life writings, namely slave narratives. Hügel-Marshall is not a professional writer; she is just one of the first African-Germans to publicize her hard life in German society. It is a politically motivated work, with which she hopes to achieve public awareness, public apology, and equal opportunities for and acceptance of African-Germans. The goal is to win the fight against racism, to claim what rightfully belongs to her, and to build and recreate her identity. To this end, she also travels to the USA to meet her father and her African-American family.

4.2.2 Hans Jürgen Massaquoi's *Destined to Witness: Growing Up Black in Nazi Germany* (1999)

The stories and fates of African-Germans during the Third Reich and the second half of the twentieth century have been neglected in German and world historiography. Therefore, it is essential to analyze Hans J. Massaquoi's autobiography *Destined to Witness: Growing Up Black in Nazi Germany*, which is a starting point to overcome the lacuna in the dialogue on black Germans in the Nazi era. The autobiography publicizes how an African-German survived

---

[82] For further details on transliteration consult chapter 2.

Nazi rule, endured racial stigmatization in Liberia, and how his endeavors to become a self-directed free subject as a member of the African-American community in the USA unfolded.

Massaquoi neither constitutes the "typical" African immigrant nor the "typical" *Besatzungskind*. His background is rather special, for his grandfather Momolu Massaquoi was Liberian Consul General to Germany in Hamburg in the late 1920s. Massaquoi was born in Hamburg in 1926 as the son of Momolu's oldest son Al-Haj and a German nurse, Bertha. Whereas Usleber and Hügel-Marshall are the more "typical" African-Germans as *Besatzungskinder*, Massaquoi represents another category. He is the "mixed" child of an interracial and intercultural relationship, i.e., of an African diplomat with a German partner. In addition, Massaquoi's course of life provides a special connection to America as well as to Africa, which also differs considerably from the relationship between the other authors and those continents. His work helps to understand the other African-German writings and their authors' search for an identity and for a community. *Destined to Witness* is a conglomeratation of African-American writing techniques and of the story of an African-German during the Nazi era. Massaquoi unites his African-German roots and stories with his African-American identity and sense of community. Thus, Massaquoi's work is less accusatory than the other contemporary African-German works and only minimally politically motivated. The main reason for this is that Massaquoi has lived in the USA for more than half a century and has been embraced by the African-American community. Consequently, his life writing stresses his survival and achievements, which is more of an African-American tradition of a success story, and stands less for a political agenda for African-Germans. Nevertheless, at the end of his work, Massaquoi feels obliged to step in and support other African-Germans in their struggle. In order to pay tribute to the different backgrounds of African-Germans and to the lost or unknown stories about African-Germans during Nazi rule, Massaquoi's work needs to be included.

4.2.3 Thomas Usleber's *Die Farben unter meiner Haut: Autobiographische Aufzeichnungen* (2002)

The racist experiences of Thomas Usleber are most certainly reminiscent of the ones of Hügel-Marshall and reflect the struggles of many *Besatzungskinder*. Usleber was born in Idar-Oberstein in 1960. His father was an African-American army member and his mother a German woman with Hungarian-German roots. The outline of the work is a chronological enumeration of events that outline Usleber's coming of age. He grows up within a poor environment and thus he claims to suffer doubly. His skin color *and* his family's poverty deprive him of social acceptance and opportunities. Even though his teachers assume that Usleber, due to his low social status and skin color, will not further his education, he achieves his *Abitur*, finishes an apprenticeship, and later becomes a civil servant, a *Beamter*, with a successful career. Just like Hügel-Marshall, Usleber also leaves small-town life and longs for a more multicultural life in the city.

Usleber stresses two aspects throughout the work. First, he draws a picture of himself which can best be described as fighting against all odds; he is a man of defiance. Second, he is still very embittered about the racism he encountered and still encounters; and, thus, the tone of the work is, like that of most other African-German writings, critical of and incensed by racism. One aspect is very important, namely that the African-German literary and cultural scene still seems very small. Hügel-Marshall had a close relationship to Audre Lorde and fosters her friendship with other members of the African-German community like Dagmar Schulz, Sara Lennox, and others. Many of those names reappear when reading African-German works or works on them. Usleber had read Hügel-Marshall's book because he cites and mentions her several times. However small, the connection among African-Germans begins to expand and flourish. In the preliminary words to his work, Usleber is said to have written "das erste Buch, in dem ein Mann seiner Generation und seiner Herkunft über seinen Werdegang schreibt" (unattributed quotation, inside cover, n.pag.). This is also an important reason why I chose his work over others: a man of his background and age speaking out for the first time. Even though Massaquoi published his work in 1999, it can be argued that Usleber is the first African-German man of the generation of *Besatzungskinder* to publicize his life. Massaquoi is of a different generation and writes out of a different context because he sees himself as an African-American with German roots (Massaquoi, Hans J. Letter to the author 2), has a different genealogical background, writes in English, and has lived abroad for more than fifty years.

4.3 Political Agency and Activism as the Catalysts for the Formation of an African-German Culture: Analysis of *Daheim unterwegs*, *Destined to Witness*, and *Die Farben unter meiner Haut*

In the following I analyze the works of Hügel-Marshall, Massaquoi, and Usleber with special attention to political agency and activism inherent in the works as the catalysts for the formation of an African-German culture. African-German culture lacks not only a history and tradition, but also a strong lobby. Contemporary African-Germans have begun to get organized and to speak up on their behalf in order to build up a community and form an African-German culture. In this context, it is therefore paramount to have a close look at how politically motivated the authors are and if their forms of activism help to reach the goals of eliminating racism and forming a culture. There are recurring motifs, like silence and writing, in each text that I research by using the tools and concepts developed in Chapter Two of this thesis. Those motifs are linked to the authors' struggle against deprivation and to African-German community-building.

4.3.1 Isolation and Initial Political Motivation: The Fight Against Silence

The aspect of silence in African-German texts differs from the silence in African-American works. In the African-American community silence, on the one hand, was or still is a means to hush up a shameful past, hence an internal silence, i.e., a silence within and toward the community. On the other hand, silence is used to ensure a superficial peace pact between unequal members of a discriminatory society, thus an external silence (between the community members and oftentimes the "outside" world).[83] Additionally, the African-American authors discussed here also experience—and some investigate—silence and racism in Africa and what this entails for their African-American identities. In Germany, African-Germans suffered, and some still suffer, from isolation, i.e., from a lack of community. Without anyone around who shares the same or similar concerns, some African-Germans are subject to racism, without the power and without any form of support to defend themselves by speaking up. Thus, African-German authors stress the overpowering dimension of leading not only a life of deprivation and humiliation due to racism they experience, but also of the isolation which results from it. Consequently, it is essential to note that although silence had long been a tool for survival for African-Germans, nowadays they have the means to meet and contact other African-Germans and have been finding the strength to speak up. African-Germans have therefore found their voice, which they now use to be politically active in the form of resisting white Western silence and oppression. This action can be described as an external political activism.

Daheim unterwegs is not a work in which the reader must read between the lines or look very closely to find hints at the dominating spheres of racism, suffering, silence, and the pain and anger resulting from them. The whole work is one big outcry against the historical silence of a racist society vis-à-vis the assaults against African-Germans and the powerless and voiceless life of African-Germans themselves. Whether Hügel-Marshall intended it or not, the lack of a table of contents and consequently chapter headings hint at the former impossibility to name or publicly speak about African-German suffering. Neither German society nor African-Germans directly spoke about the racism existing in society. Mostly, white Germans did not address such issues because they were not affected by them and some even actively took part in the discrimination; African-Germans were too marginalized and afraid to speak up for their own rights. Thus, by leaving out chapter headings and a table of contents, Hügel-Marshall exemplifies how those Germans, who are referred to as being racist, see her life: as uninteresting and meaningless, or even non-existent. For herself, the lack of chapter headings mirrors how suppressed and isolated her own life had been, and it emphasizes that she and her family have

---

[83] Internal silence targets the inside/the community as a homogeneous group with a shared history of suffering as such, whereas external silence targets others, especially white society.

for too long been quiet about what has happened. The work itself, though, is divided into smaller segments, even if they are not numbered and do not have titles. She recounts her life as a long thread of innumerable assaults against her, which is her way of breaking out of the vicious cycle of silence. Thus, the lack of chapter headings bears a deep significance that can be considered a universal paradigm within African-German history, which symbolizes the notion that many Germans held and some still might hold, namely that African-Germans do not exist.[84] Thus, no words exist to describe anything about them. However, African-Germans are a fact, and they have wrongfully suffered, which is supported by the stories told in African-German life writings. African-Germans try to come into existence by speaking up, even if they do not "make headlines," i.e., do not become the center of attention.

Silence has long been one of the tools of survival for African-Germans, and Hügel-Marshall is no exception. She quickly learns how to behave in the children's home in order to evade punishment.

> Die Angst vor Schlägen, wenn ich etwas Unbedachtes sage oder frage, ist so groß, dass ich lieber meinen Mund halte. Noch schlimmer: Ganz tief in meinem Innern ahne ich, daß ich nie mehr nach Hause darf. Ich frage also erst gar nicht, vielleicht aus Angst, die Antwort nicht ertragen zu können. (25)

In addition to keeping a low profile to avoid getting hit, Hügel-Marshall also does not dare to ask whether she will be allowed to go home soon or not, because she is afraid of the answer. Being quiet is thus a multidimensional means to survive, no matter what the circumstance. "Still sein und stillhalten, wohl wissend, sie lauern begierig auf ein unbedachtes Wort, mit dem ich ihnen eine Rechtfertigung dafür liefere, auf mich einzuschlagen, wenn sie mit ihrer Hilflosigkeit nicht anders umzugehen wissen" (46-47). The white people surrounding her, especially the supervisors in the home, are systematically destroying Hügel-Marshall's already unstable personality. She almost gives up. "Aus dem Gefühl heraus, ein Nichts zu sein, verteidige ich mich nicht mehr, schlage nicht mehr zu" (49). The discrimination culminates at this point. Hügel-Marshall feels worthless and is inhibited from defending herself either verbally or physically, but is in return abused physically and psychologically.

---

[84] Many African-Germans share this experience of not existing in the German consciousness. Massaquoi's teacher, for instance, "took a wet sponge and carefully erased the last remaining empty square, the one that represented [him], thereby graphically emphasizing [his] non-person status" (102). This passage underlines the fact that Massaquoi is not considered a real German boy. The action of erasing his name mirrors and emphasizes prevalent German thinking of the time, namley that "the Afro-German identity is not the *antithesis* in the dialectic of (white) German subjectivity: *it is simply non-existent*" (Wright, "Others-from-Within" 298).

Even during the short visits at home, silence dominates the relationship to the other family members. It is a way for Hügel-Marshall's family to cope with the situation and they mutually accept the status quo, but it is Hügel-Marshall who suffers the most. Her mother simply avoids confrontation and consequences by remaining mute. In addition, when her mother takes Hügel-Marshall to the children's home for the first time, she tells her that she will come back to pick her up in six weeks, which is simply a lie (22-23). When Hügel-Marshall searches for her mother and does not find her, she panics. Schwester Hildegard tells her that her mother "'[. . .] ist schon ganz früh heute morgen mit dem Zug weg'" (24), and Hügel-Marshall asks herself, "Wo ist sie? Warum hat sie mir nicht 'Lebewohl, bis bald' gesagt?" (24). Her mother's decision to leave Hügel-Marshall behind is something she does not want to face, and this is why she leaves without saying good-bye. Hügel-Marshall's mother also avoids confrontation when Hügel-Marshall stays at the family's place for some weeks during vacation. Instead of treating her daughter just like her other white daughter, she excludes Hügel-Marshall from family parties and other gatherings. The family gives in to the prevailing racism of the time and their surroundings and hazards the consequences of Hügel-Marshall being ostracized and discriminated against. However, Hügel-Marshal shows understanding for her mother's behavior: "Ich verstehe sie und ertrage mein Nicht-dabeisein-Können beim Familieneinkauf, bei Familienfesten und Ausflügen. Ihr zuliebe ertrage ich diese Ausgrenzungen" (42). Hügel-Marshall and her mother choose the easy way out in form of a peace pact, comparable to the ones described above in the African-American community, which only functions by means of silence: "Wir sprachen beide kein Wort" (42).

Silence, as can be seen, goes hand in hand with disowning Hügel-Marshall. The relationship to her stepfather and her white stepsister is, therefore, strained as well. "Für meinen Stiefvater habe ich keinen Namen. Er spricht nicht mit mir. [. . .] Mein Stiefvater will sich nicht in der Öffentlichkeit mit mir zeigen, sich nicht dem Gerede der Leute aussetzen" (41). Her stepfather's refusal to use Hügel-Marshall's name, reminds one of the un-naming of slaves in Africa hundreds of years ago. People then believed, or hoped, that a person without a name is not a real person and therefore does not really exist. Furthermore, this passage also brings to mind the many other African-Germans who feel that they are being othered due to their visibility ("Ich bin immer sichtbar" [46][85]), and thus many friends and family members avoid being seen with them publicly. Hügel-Marshall's stepsister even denies being her sister when they are in a disco together. Someone asks her stepsister: "'Ist das eine Freundin von dir, Lisa?' Meine Schwester stellt ruckartig und mit zitternder Hand ihr Glas zurück auf den Tisch und sagt, ohne mich anzusehen: 'Ja.'" (59). The fact that Hügel-Marshall is her sister and belongs to the family is not only silenced but also denied. She is neglected and socially excluded due to her skin

---

[85] The feeling of being visible at all times is something all African-Germans share due to their isolated lives within a white society (Opitz 140, N., Corinna 174).

color. A similar fate develops later on in her life, when Hügel-Marshall marries a white man. When the relationship starts falling apart, Hügel-Marshall is only able to make it work "solange [sie] schweig[t], solange [sie] stillh[ält]" (79). For African-Germans, racism results in their isolation, and silence is the only tool to stay under the radar, to avoid further attention. It is a way of existing without confrontation, although the price is high: isolation and deprivation, a feeling of homelessness and worthlessness. It is a condition and situation that many African-Germans share. There is no safe haven for them, no place to fully belong or feel at home, which is why the book's title is *Daheim unterwegs*, meaning being on the road or in transit although the place should be one's home.

The silence is complemented with what Hügel-Marshall is supposed to accept as truths, *Wahrheiten*: "Alle Weißen sind rassistisch. Sie sind es, weil sie—ebenso wie ich—diese sogenannten Wahrheiten über mich angenommen haben. Man hat ihnen beigebracht, daß Schwarze von Natur aus dumm und minderwertig seien" (47). Hügel-Marshall takes on the language and terms of the racist white people she encounters. She employs *Wahrheiten* in an ironic way, for it is difficult or even impossible to define what is true and what is not, i.e., the term itself is biased and disputable. The fact that white people claim to know the *Wahrheit* is, therefore, ridiculed by Hügel-Marshall and undermined by her own experiences. Hügel-Marshall uses the term again when she says,

> Zusammen singen sie mit mir das Lied von den "Zehn kleinen Negerlein" und spielen mit mir "Wer hat Angst vorm Schwarzen Mann?" – nur mit dem Unterschied, dass ich mit diesen sogenannten Wahrheiten etwas über mich selbst lernen soll. (47)

The term becomes a greater concept later on, when her coming of age has progressed. The term resurfaces as a means to prevent her from meeting other black people:

> Schwarze Menschen sind mir fremd, ich habe Angst vor ihnen, denn es gibt Wahrheiten, auf die mich zu verlassen ich gelernt habe. Ich bin Schwarz, häßlich, unansehnlich, habe wildes Haar, das für keine Frisur geeignet scheint, ich drohe ständig zu verwahrlosen, bin unmoralisch, schmutzig und dumm. All dem will ich nicht gegenübertreten. (86)

Thus, Hügel-Marshall claims that the *Wahrheiten* are actual prejudices and defamations endorsed and enforced by society, sometimes hidden but more often overt and also used in children's songs and plays. Whereas Hügel-Marshall has to keep her mouth shut for her own safety and has internalized the racism directed at her, society intentionally propagates so-called truths, which are, in fact, racial slurs aimed at keeping up the established racial and social hierarchy. As an author, however, she skillfully uses *Wahrheiten* ironically and in different circumstances, which reminds one of the African-American stylistic means of signifying: the indeterminacy of terms and the open-endedness of interpretation (Gates, *Signifying* 21). The questions remain: Who knows the truth? What is truth? Does it even exist? What about her experiences? The friendship to and influence of the African-American Audre Lorde could be the reason for Hügel-Marshall's symbolic use here, and it leaves some room for speculation that African-American life writing functions as a blueprint for African-German life writing.[86]

The quotations above also underline that Hügel-Marshall's self-esteem was very low at that point in her life and that she had to develop her personality, from being oppressed to finding a voice to fight for her rights. She claims that all whites are racists, which is a strong statement. It stresses Hügel-Marshall's agenda, though, of being an agent for African-Germans and for fighting against white dominance and discrimination. Her political motivation is thus directed outwardly, i.e., directed against white, racist people. This can be seen by the strict boundaries she forms while breaking the silence: she talks about a "Schwarze Welt" and a "weiße Welt" (17). It is a simple categorization into black and white, whereas most of the time Hügel-Marshall capitalizes "Schwarz" (black) and uses lower-case letters for "weiß" (white). But she is not consistent in her spelling, which might hint at lingering self-doubts. The capitalization of black is a strong statement, for she wants to pay back a racist society for making black people small. Now she elevates black people and makes them bigger than their white counterparts. Also, her categorization is not one she invented but society's; however, she now uses it in her own right and way. By excluding whites from her own life[87] and by accusing them, she becomes an agent for an outward political agenda of all African-Germans. "Überleben in einer rassistischen Gesellschaft hat für Weiße keine Bedeutung: Sie übersehen ganz einfach, daß es Rassismus gibt" (80). "Es gab nur eine Welt, die weiße Welt, in die ich hineingeboren worden war, eine Schwarze Welt existierte nicht, und es gab nur eine Wirklichkeit, nur eine Wahrheit" (17). Her political awakening coincides with her growing strength to defend herself and speak out. It is a result of two considerations: of growing up and of further education. It is during her last year at *Realschule* that she becomes politically active and speaks out for the first time. The fight against racism is a fight against isolation, silence, racial inequalities, and injustices. Hügel-Marshall is elected to be student council spokeswoman but before the election she has to step on the podium and give a spontaneous speech. She introduces herself and is at first "stotternd, allmählich jedoch weniger aufgeregt" (65). "Ich werde mich immer

---

[86] Further evidence for Lorde's influence on Hügel-Marshall is that at one point in her life Hügel-Marshall also decided to rename herself, from Erika to Ika. Audre Lorde also took charge of her own naming—she was born Audrey Geraldine Lorde—and simply dropped both the *y* from *Audrey* and her middle name. Before her death, she also participated in an African naming ceremony and became Gambda Adisa (Keating 285).

[87] She married a white man but the relationship failed.

dort einsetzen, wo Hilfe und Unterstützung notwendig sind. Und ich werde denen behilflich sein, die ihre Belange nicht lautstark genug vorbringen können" (65). Her words display her newly found self-confidence and her willingness to be the voice for all those who are unable to advance their concerns. She speaks up for herself and others for the first time. "Noch niemals zuvor in meinem Leben habe ich vor so vielen weißen Menschen gestanden. Heute hatte ich den Mut dazu" (66). This situation clearly resembles Obama's first speech during his college years on human rights. Thus, school and education as well as former and continuing wrongdoing have also sensitized Obama, and both he and Hügel-Marshall were prompted to stand up and speak out, to become agents for themselves, others like them, or people in need.

In the following, Hügel-Marshall takes one step at a time to overcome the silence and to fight for her voice and rights. After having been the spokeswoman at school, she still has to learn to discuss problems openly. While at university, she claims that "[sie hat] zuvor nie die Erfahrung gemacht, nach [ihrer] Meinung gefragt zu werden oder Fragen stellen zu dürfen, ohne dafür bestraft zu werden" (70). "[Ihr] politisches Bewußtsein ist erwacht und fordert von [ihr], [sich] der Politik in [ihrem] Land zu stellen" (70). Moreover, she joins the (white) feminist movement in Germany whose motto is "Das Persönliche ist politisch" (81), but she soon has to also fight for ethnic, i.e., black issues within the movement. She again breaks the silence, this time vis-à-vis racism during a meeting of the women's movement but to no avail (82-83). Later, she becomes part of the African-German movement, which is just coming into being at that time. Its political agenda is clear and becomes part of Hügel-Marshall's life:

> Wir Afrodeutschen beginnen, in der BRD unsere eigene Geschichte zu schaffen, sie sichtbar zu machen und weiterzuentwickeln. Haben wir jemals etwas vom Leben Schwarzer in diesem Land, in Deutschland, erfahren? Haben wir jemals etwas davon erfahren, daß der erste afrikanische Student im Jahr 1729 in Halle mit einer juristischen Arbeit über Schwarze in Europa promovierte? (93)

Thus, for Hügel-Marshall and other African-Germans overcoming the silence means not only to fight against everyday racism, but also to rewrite the history of Germany—speaking up becomes the transliteration of German historiography, the filling in of missing gaps. She mentions *Showing Our Colors: Afro-German Women Speak Out* and many new forms of African-German organization (94). It is the combination of the newly acquired tools of education as well as the African-German community that is in the process of building itself up that support Hügel-Marshall's speaking out and political activism. "In Berlin begegnete ich der afroamerikanischen Schriftstellerin, Dichterin und Aktivistin Audre Lorde wieder, nachdem ich sie 1987 in Frankfurt kennengelernt hatte," and a deep friendship develops from there (95). It is Audre Lorde, who unrelentlessly pushes African-German women, especially Hügel-Marshall, to raise their voices. "Sie forderte insbesondere uns Schwarze Frauen auf, unsere Stimmen zu erheben und unsere Rechte und Würde von dieser Gesellschaft einzufordern" (95). "Ihre Worte bleiben mir im Gedächtnis und werden fortan Wegweiser für mein politisches Handeln" and "Audre ermutigt mich und fordert mich gleichzeitig auf, nicht mehr zu schweigen, meine Angst nicht wichtiger zu nehmen als die Wirkung meines Sprechens" (97). The silence is broken and an African-American woman is the inspiration for the movement. The way African-Germans are supported by African-Americans like Audre Lorde makes a comparison to the situation of former slaves in America necessary, who were supported by abolitionists to write down their lives' stories. What is different, apart from time, circumstances, etc., though, is that African-Germans have not had a community or much contact to other African-Germans and thus their isolation contributed to their long-held silence.

Silence was an even more volatile motif during the Nazi era, not only for African-Germans but also for all other so-called non-Aryans. For Massaquoi, silence becomes an overarching maxim that he has to take into consideration at all times if he wants to ensure to be safe from Nazi terror. In comparison to contemporary African-German life, in which African-Germans constantly fight against the hushing up of discriminatory acts against them, Massaquoi has to take double precautions. First, he should not speak out against the Nazis and their rules. Second, he should keep a low profile as a non-Aryan, which includes not to complain about what lies at the core of Nazi philosophy: racism. Speaking up while living under the Nazi regime would equal certain death so it is, therefore, unfeasible and not an option for Massaquoi. He only breaks the silence later on in life, when he is neither isolated nor any longer in danger.

Destined to Witness, accordingly, differs from the other African-German and African-American life writings because silence takes on a very specific meaning for the most part of the book. Additionally, by writing the book many decades after the war and from a new life and vantage point in America, Massaquoi breaks his silence much later in his life as compared to the other African-German authors selected for this study.[88] This is a crucial difference, for Massaquoi looks back upon his life in a different county and during much different times; the other African-German authors are not as old as he is, and they live in Germany, where they have to cope with life. While Massaquoi is in a position in which he can make peace with his past on account of a geographical and temporal lag, the other writers still face specific racial problems Massaquoi can evidently not relate to anymore.

The Nazi regime dominates everyday life and thus Massaquoi's life and story are also always portrayed from that perspective. Germans pit a more general muteness to all things concerning the Nazis against a general outspokenness of, i.e., defamations against, all non-Aryans. One of Massaquoi's

---

[88] This latter group claims—though living in a German society not comparable to Nazi Germany—to still face contemporary forms of racism to some extent.

teachers, Herr Grimmelshäuser, spreads anti-Jewish stories when reading "from *Der Stürmer (The Stormer)*" and other "prominent Nazi Party newspapers" (53). The children "easily believe the scurrilous propaganda" (53). In the following, as a young boy, Massaquoi also starts to hate Jews until his mother has a talk with him and elucidates on the backward and perverse Nazi theory. "'The Nazis don't like Africans either, and they are just as wrong about Jews as they are about Africans'" (58). Massaquoi's mother makes sure that he understands that neither Jews nor Africans have done anything wrong and that the Nazis and Hitler, in their belief to be the better race, are dangerous.

> My mother, noticing my inner turmoil, cautioned me never to talk to anyone about what she had just told me lest both of us get into serious trouble. I gave her my *Ehrenwort* (word of honor) and sealed my promise with a solemn handshake. German boys, it had been drilled into me from as far back as I could remember, never break their *Ehrenwort*, no matter what. My mother took another long, serious look at me that told me she knew her secret was safe with me. (58)

This example demonstrates how successful Nazi propaganda was in making Germans believe that non-Aryans were worth less and needed to be expelled. Moreover, it shows that Germans who detected the propaganda clearly perceived the underlying threat of speaking up against the Nazis and hence kept their mouths shut. The power relations worked in the way that the Nazis used their propaganda while simultaneously displaying their strength and superiority, and the common people either followed their leaders or remained silent.

Not discussing any ambiguity towards the people in power or those privileged in the hierarchy is a universal rule and runs like a thread through Massaquoi's as well as other African-German and African-American works. For instance, Massaquoi hears adults "talk in hushed tones" about the fate of a family friend who was a member of a forbidden party (84). No one dares to discuss this matter publicly, and so they warn each other to not talk about it with others. Massaquoi, by "keeping [his] mouth shut and [his] ears open," learns about the fates of some neighbors as well (108). In addition, no one really talks about his or her political views, especially if one is not a member of the *Nationalsozialistische Deutsche Arbeiterpartei* (*NSDAP*, the Nazi Party). When Massaquoi and his mother stay with relatives in the countryside they find out that "Onkel Karl and Tante Grete had learned to keep their political views to themselves, even from us. They didn't have to tell us to do the same" (211). Silence is an accepted and existential code of conduct. The entire village even ignores the fact that truckloads of presumably Jewish and other non-Aryan people are driven to a place called Kohnstein, which becomes later known as the concentration camp Dora-Mittelbau (213-16). "When I ask Onkel Karl what was going on in the Kohnstein, he merely put his index finger in front of his lips and whispered that whatever it was, it was a top government secret and none of our business" (214). Although Massaquoi and his mother also follow this rule of silence because he is black, Massaquoi accuses Germans of not speaking up.

> Their [the Germans'] monstrous guilt, however, one that will never be erased, is that they let the perks they enjoyed under the Nazis make them blind and deaf to the suffering and annihilation of countless fellow citizens whom the Nazis had branded as undesirable. (105)

In countries with a history of massive racist discrimination, people are often not only blind and deaf – but also tongueless. Not speaking up is a leitmotif within German society that has even survived, in parts, until the present day. African-Germans, by openly talking and writing about their experiences and concealed historical facts, reveal a hidden side of society and history. This side assists African-Germans in redeeming their oppressed lives. Thus, it is an external political activism that is directed at a partly still racist, white Western society from within the African-German community.

After the war, Massaquoi's skin color, not his direct African bloodline, becomes an asset due to the presence of African-American occupation troops in Hamburg. In order to benefit from his new status, Massaquoi makes "the study of English [his] number-one priority" (262). It is this language that helps him to communicate with the liberators and that paves the way towards new opportunities that lie ahead for him. He becomes aware of his chances when other Germans single him out, because of his skin color and the little English he knows, to negotiate with advancing allied troops (255-56). All of a sudden, Massaquoi is supposed to speak aloud and is even exploited to be the spokesperson for his white fellow countrymen. However, he is not supposed to speak about the cruelest time of his life, but rather to use his skin color and language skills to the advantage of all the other white German residents of the shelter (255-57). Thus, even though this incident is not a real breaking of the oppressive silence, it is the first step for Massaquoi to find a means to overcome it although others are using him here. He sees that learning the language of the liberators, namely English, will help him to articulate his ordeal and fight for his rights. In the end, his autobiography is indeed written in English, the language that becomes Massaquoi's tool for redemption.[89]

Massaquoi befriends African-American G.I.s and Werner, a young German fellow with an American father. Werner enlightens him on the fact that many African-Americans might not like to be reminded of their links to Africa. Massaquoi's romanticized vision of an America for everyone gets a scratch when Werner advises him to tell the African-American troops that he has an

---

[89] Massaquoi exchanges English for his German mother tongue when he moves to the USA in 1950.

African-American instead of a Liberian father. Accordingly, Massaquoi tells the soldiers the story that

> [his] father was an American instead of a Liberian. This "little white lie," [he] had discovered, could make the difference between cordial acceptance as a brother and cold rejection as an unwelcome stranger. It hadn't taken [him] long to find out that most black Americans [he] met in the years immediately following World War II considered Africans and Africa backward and thus a personal embarrassment. With slavery just a few generations behind them, they preferred not to be reminded of that aspect of their past. (316)

Underlying this predicament is the long historical dilemma of a shameful slave past versus the achievements of African-Americans, who do not want to be reminded of the humiliation of preceding generations or the "squalor" in which many of their African contemporaries still live.[90] As a result, Massaquoi complies, once again, in keeping his mouth shut and he constructs another background in order to fit in, or, as in this case, to ameliorate his situation.

After World War II, his Jewish friends Ralph and Egon Giordano have already figured out their future plans as journalists. "I realized that, although we had much in common, we were miles apart in our agendas. Or, more correctly, they had an agenda and I didn't" (260). Whereas the Giordanos are already politically active and want to ensure justice vis-à-vis Nazi atrocities, Massaquoi is still very much preoccupied with himself in this new situation after the end of the Nazi era. He only becomes politically active much later when living in the USA, as a fervent supporter of the Civil Rights Movement. While in Germany, Massaquoi has no connection to African-Germans. Consequently, Massaquoi's agency to support contemporary African-Germans in Germany does not surface until the end of his autobiography; and it is there that he again picks up the crucial function of silence versus speaking up. For him, mainstream German society, though not totally silent, is too quiet nonetheless when it comes to the subject of racism. In his chapter called "Reflections" he also warns "if it happened once, it could happen again; [. . .]—it could happen anywhere" (436). He continues,

> Initially, the purveyors of racism need no more than the silent acquiescence of the public. In the case of Nazi Germany, first Germans and then the entire world turned a deaf ear to the flagrant human rights abuses until it was too late to prevent the architects of racial madness from carrying out their evil schemes. That sad

---

[90] Massaquoi's findings do not stand in opposition to what Hartman experiences. Of course, many African-Americans were still ashamed of being the descendents of slaves; however, later they wanted to reconnect to Africa and its past, glorious stories. This African heritage tourism was only sparked decades later.

chapter in history suggests that it is never too soon to confront bigotry and racism whenever, wherever, and in whatever form it raises its ugly head. It is incumbent upon all people to confront even the slightest hint of racist thought or action with zero tolerance. (437)

Massaquoi's motivation for writing the book is manifold. First, he is a professional writer interested in the African diaspora and its struggle for equal rights. Second, his life's story is indeed exceptional and the encouragement of his author friends Giordano and Haley to write an autobiography seems not at all far-fetched. Third, by the autobiographical act of writing this book, Massaquoi also tries to overcome his former ambiguous role as victim *and* wrongdoer, for many times in the book he confesses his (childish) enthusiasm for the military and the Nazis and his initial disgust with Jews due to Nazi propaganda. He breaks the silence about his past Nazi sympathies and shows his coming of age, namely his change of mind about the Nazis. A fourth aspect only comes into play at the very end, which clearly distinguishes Massaquoi's work from the other African-German ones discussed here. Only at the very end of the book, while reflecting on his life and work and discussing the present-day situation of African-Germans with the founder and president of the organization for Colored and Parentless Children in Germany, Al Hooseman (433-34), does Massaquoi become aware of his role model status. He then realizes that he is somehow also responsible and must support African-Germans in Germany, and so he participates in a meeting of the *ISD* (*Initiative Schwarzer Deutscher*), an initiative for and of black Germans, in 1997. The members

> convinced [him] that much work still needs to be done—by the German federal government and the private sector, as well as individual citizens—to assure the absolute equality and complete economic and social integration into German mainstream society of Germans of African descent and other racial minorities. (436)

At the end of *Destined to Witness*, the mentioning and brief discussion of African-Germans, their situation, and their institutions already provides them with a bigger audience, and Massaquoi, by drawing attention to their cause, becomes a sort of international political agent for them.

Massaquoi's political motivation is hidden behind his impressive story and only comes to life by his refreshed memory and encounter with other African-Germans. He suffered from isolation and also from Nazi terror, which forced him to give in to the prescribed mode of silence. "As long as I could remember, I had always had to face the Nazi menace alone," and he continues to explain that he did not really have anyone besides his mother to share his inner thoughts and fears with (239). He breaks this silence, though with a great time and geographical lag, by writing about the atrocities and thus rewriting history.

Coming of age within the African-American community, however, as an active member of the Civil Rights Movement and an American citizen, Massaquoi only came to support the cause of African-Germans after his return to Germany in 1966 and especially in 1997. It was only by meeting with and hearing about the experiences of African-Germans that he became aware of his enduring connection to them. Unlike many African-Germans in Germany, Massaquoi has overcome questions of his identity within the mainly white society of the USA since the 1950s. In addition, Massaquoi wrote his autobiography in English and it was published in both German-speaking and English-speaking countries, which has given the African-German cause a much wider audience than works published only in German. In comparison, Usleber's autobiography reaches not as extensive an audience as Massaquoi's does, because Usleber did not make the bestselling lists and the book was published in German only. Usleber, nevertheless, achieves in addressing the target audience: German society.

When considering the motif of silence in Usleber's *Die Farben unter meiner Haut*, it is not as prominent an aspect as it is in the other works. Silence is overcome rather in a more figurative sense insofar as the entire life writing is meant to make plain the persistence of racism and discrimination in Germany. Whereas Massaquoi speaks of his support for African-Germans only at the very end of his work, Usleber clearly defines his motivation right from the start:

> In Deutschland leben viele von Geburt an Deutsche mit einer dunklen Hautfarbe, ich möchte nicht für sie sprechen, denn sie haben ihr eigenes Leben und ihre eigenen Erfahrungen. Aber ich möchte auf sie aufmerksam machen und wenn möglich, ein wenig Mitfühlen mit ihnen wecken. Ein wenig Bewusstsein dafür wecken, wie schmerzhaft es manchmal sein kann, im eigenen Land nicht als gleichwertig akzeptiert zu werden. (9)

Usleber's disclosing of his hurtful past is most likely indicative of the lives of many other African-Germans, and he wants to galvanize German society. Here, Usleber's outward political activism becomes visible, which is the result of long-term isolation and racism.

The reclusiveness in which Usleber lives is partly extrinsically effectuated and partly self-inflicted. In his very first chapter, entitled "Keine Heimat" (11-14), Usleber talks about his feeling of not belonging, i.e., of not having had a sense of home. He describes the town he was born in, Idar-Oberstein, as a place located in the middle of nowhere in Germany. Also, "man trifft häufig auf einen sehr eingeschränkten Horizont, auf kleine Welten" in Idar-Oberstein (13). The extrinsic factors that force him into what he dubs the "'Out-Group'" are his dark complexion, living without a father, but even more so, he claims, being poor (13). During the years of growing up in Idar-Oberstein, he meets many Germans who treat him worse than they treat other white Germans. His experiences certainly are one reason why he later on isolates himself, but it is foremost his mother's mistrust of Germans in general that influences him and even encourages him to wall himself in. "Ich begann, eine Mauer um mich zu bauen" (30). He uses a telling metaphor to underline the complicity of society in his isolation: "Die Umwelt schleppte mir die Steine in Form ihrer Vorurteile und ihres Hasses an, und ich fügte sie zusammen und zementierte mich zu" (30). Thus, society and his mother are responsible for the wall which surrounds all three (mother, brother, and himself) so their "selbstgewählte Isolation wurde immer perfekter" (31). Consequently, from then on "fand eine wirkliche Kommunikation nur noch unter [den Familienmitgliedern] statt" (30). Society discriminates against Usleber and his family publicly, thereby supporting their self-chosen isolation, which for them is, above all, a security measure against discrimination. No communication or in other words silence, is the peace pact between both parties.

During his problematic youth in Idar-Oberstein, Usleber not only lacks a community, but friends as well. There is no one to defend him during racist attacks like the one at school, when others bully him due to his skin color. When writing this book, Usleber is still deeply hurt and his experiences were so painful that they render him speechless. He says he can still not express the racial slurs "weder mündlich noch schriftlich" (16). However, during his youth he finds two ways of coping with the racism on the one hand and expressing himself on the other. The world of music is one means that offers Usleber a secure place of listening and of expressing himself. He quotes the lyrics of Pink Floyd (13), Herbert Grönemeyer (21), and of several American songs (e.g., 93). Strikingly, he also quotes Bob Marley twice. The first quotation is from Marley's "Get Up Stand Up," which calls for defending one's rights (45). The second is from "Zimbabwe:" "*Every man gotta right to decide his own destiny*" (55; italics in original). Both references underline Usleber's political agenda, which is to fight for your own right individually against an oftentimes hostile environment (external political activism). Moreover, he compares his situation with African-Americans, or rather other Africans from the diaspora, and their music. "[S]o halfen mir die Lieder von Bob Marley und Stevie Wonder, die von der Unterdrückung der Afroamerikaner in den USA erzählten, meine Situation in Deutschland zu identifizieren" (44-45). Clearly, after having visited his father and family in Chicago, his affinity for the USA becomes visible here.

Books constitute another way for him to break the silence. Like all other authors, he finds the world of books a safe haven. One reason for this is that Usleber can lose himself in the fantasy worlds created by Karl May and others. "Geschichten von erdachten Personen, die an fernen Orten und in anderen Zeiten spielten, wurden meine Welt" and replaced the real interaction, including communication, with the outer world (31). Moreover, he quotes from Brecht, Kant, Proust and others, and again he refers to America when mentioning *Tom Sawyer* (20). By quoting from lyrics and literary texts, he makes great use of intertextuality, which is one of the trademarks of African-American writing. Usleber uses texts within a different context, thus extracting new meanings from them and in this case they become important agents for and are applied to African-German issues. Usleber's writing resembles Hügel-Marshall's work, for he also enumerates his experiences and his gradually gripping of his developing identity. It is not surprising that he read *Daheim unterwegs* and even quotes from Hügel-Marshall's work, which shows how she inspired him and portrays the similarities they share (22; 26). Reading proceeds to the hobby of writing, which is Usleber's new outlet for his feelings. He quotes from his own writings: "'Ich glaube, ich lese so viel, weil ich niemanden habe, dem ich zuhören kann, und ich glaube, ich schreibe so viel, weil ich niemanden habe, dem ich etwas sagen könnte'" (41). This quotation reveals and depicts Usleber's loneliness, his lack of friends or communal backing, and it also underlines the speechlessness, the loss of topics and of words to communicate. In summary, music and the written word are his only connections to the outer world as a child. Even as an adult author he must borrow phrases from lyrics and texts whenever he lacks the words. His autobiographical act is a direct way to overcome his silence, but his writing uses indirect paths.

There are many instances in the book that hint at the fact that Usleber is still not fully coping with his past and present experiences, and that his identity is still suffering from discrimination. Evidence for his internal quandaries is his vicissitude, which becomes apparent in different realms, for example his faith. He quotes from the Bible throughout the book; however, even though he claims to believe in God and to be a good Christian, he, at times, deviates considerably from his Christian, altruistic path.

> Obwohl ich an das Neue Testament und die Worte von Jesus Christus glaube, belehrt mich die Erfahrung, dass es oft genug nichts nützt, auch die andere Wange hinzuhalten. Im Gegenteil: der andere wird dadurch noch bestärkt und wird nicht von seinen Handlungen ablassen. [. . .] Ein Freund sagte mir dieser Tage: "Wenn dich einer auf eine Wange schlägt, dann schlage viermal zurück!" (36)

This quotation allows the assumption that Usleber is demoralized and has established his own code of conduct from experience.

Another example of his vicissitude is his political activism. Throughout his work, Usleber proclaims individuality, i.e., that everyone has to fight for his own right. This belief goes hand in hand with his statements that nothing can be changed by words or on a larger scale. Several sentences underline this belief:
- "Aber man verändert nichts durch Diskussionen und ruft lediglich Gegenreaktionen hervor" (25);
- "Es gibt nur eine Möglichkeit, [Ungleichheit] zu überwinden: indem man daran arbeitet, sich seinen Platz im Leben zu erobern" (51);
- "Die Vorstellungen in den Köpfen der Menschen kann man nicht durch Kampagnen jedweder Art ändern, und Massendemonstrationen gegen

Ausländerfeindlichkeit sind nutzlos. [. . .] Ich denke nicht, dass man mit Forderungen etwas erreicht. Ich kann nur als Einzelner in einzelne Menschen ein Samenkorn setzen" (60);
- "Manche Menschen sind nicht zu erreichen, die breite Masse schon gar nicht" (61);
- "Jeder Mensch braucht eine ganz persönliche Identität, und dementsprechend muss auch jeder Mensch seinen ganz eigenen Weg beschreiten" (77).

Taking the last statement, it is obvious that Usleber believes that each person creates his or her own destiny and identity. However, a person is never completely isolated from everyone else; and in addition to a personal identity, an individual has other identities and roles, such as cultural/communal identities and a national one as well. Usleber sways back and forth between an outward political attack against what he perceives as white racist Germans and an inwardly targeted motivation for African-Germans and other minorities to not wait for help but to help themselves. Although the external political motivation outweighs the internal one, this circumstance comes closest to African-American political activism of both, directed at the members of the African diaspora and its communities as well as at the respective white societies surrounding them.

His strategy is inconsistent, though, for on the one hand he proclaims that discussions and demonstrations or events on a larger scale do nothing. On the other hand, he does not really practice what he preaches for he writes an autobiography, which is published, and with it he tries to reach as large an audience as possible. He claims that he does not demand anything, but he actually does when he asks for attention and compassion for African-Germans (9), or when he says he campaigned for "Chancengleichheit" (120). His everyday job is also evidence for his underlying agenda of helping others individually, but due to the high volume of people being served in a German *Amt* (civil agency) where he works, he also helps on a larger scale. "In meinem Beruf ist es unter anderem meine Aufgabe, Ausländern, die Probleme in der deutschen Gesellschaft haben, zu helfen" (25). Thus, Usleber does indeed speak up for a sort of community in his personal and vocational life, namely for foreigners and for African-Germans through his work and by his autobiographical act. Even though he claims that words cannot change anything, he actually does use them to ameliorate his own life and those of others. He seems to believe in keeping silent on a larger scale and only fight a one-on-one battle, but he overcomes this silence and speaks up later on as a member of a political party (120) and as an author. In the end, Usleber's work is one of speaking up and out with a foremost externally targeted political agenda but also with traces of an inward political motivation.

4.3.2 Writing Oneself into Being to Overcome Racism, Sexism, and Exoticism

Until recently, African-Germans have only had a low public profile and have not figured in the German consciousness and conscience. A part of German society continues to believe that it still is a white Western homogenous society, ignoring the new demographic realities and attempts on the part of the German government to recognize ethnic Germans (Janson 63). These new initiatives have also provided a forum for African-Germans to come out and claim recognition in German society. One prominent way African-Germans express their existence are various forms of life writing, just like the three authors at hand do. It is their way of overcoming the racism, sexism, and exoticism which deprive(d) them of having a normal life, as they claim. The autobiographical acts of Hügel-Marshall, Massaquoi, and Usleber are their coming to life and into existence as African-Germans within German consciousness, culture, and history. By this act, they begin to take control of and make public their oppressed past lives. All three authors, by writing down their lives, contribute to the creation of a black world in Germany, and Hügel-Marshall even joins and actively shapes the African-German movement. As a result, she and others create a black world within a white German one.

Hügel-Marshall starts out her work by enumerating the answers to the one question of her life; she begins each paragraph with the following: "Was hätte ich meinem Vater sagen sollen, wenn ich ihm begegnet wäre?" (12-13). The various answers to this question constitute her identity quarrels, which she is now able to voice. She uses anaphoras to stress the importance of the question, or rather the answers to it, in her life. The answers, which she gives herself, reveal or even put in a nutshell the story of her life that is about to unfold in the autobiography. Even though Hügel-Marshall is not a professional writer, she has learned from and has been influenced by Audre Lorde and her teachings of the African-American literary tradition. Thus, Hügel-Marshall attempts to write a book that does not only have a story to tell but whose words have a deeper meaning as well. Hügel-Marshall poses herself a question ("Was hätte ich meinem Vater sagen sollen") and answers it directly as if the addressee were also in the room. This technique is reminiscent of the African-American oral tradition that Gates dubs the speakerly text. It is a device to create the illusion of a speaker telling a story, which authenticates black writing in America (*Signifying* 181). Moreover, like African-Americans, Hügel-Marshall makes use of white literature but speaks with a black voice, which is the ur-trope of African-American writing, i.e., the double-voiced text called the talking book. Hügel-Marshall, just as in Alice Walker's *The Color Purple*, becomes the "protagonist creating her self by finding her voice, but finding this voice in the act of writing" first, instead of or before speaking out loud (Gates, *Signifying* 131).

For Hügel-Marshall, her non-person status and the discriminatory treatment resulting from it are the most painful side effects of her exotic looks. Throughout the book she gives numerous examples when she is ignored or simply overlooked. Until the age of approximately five years she lives a rather uneventful and peaceful life. "Die ersten fünf Jahre wuchsen wir relativ unbeschwert auf, so wie die meisten anderen Kinder" (17). Before entering an institution like school, African-German children like Hügel-Marshall and Massaquoi benefit from a sort of exotic "cuteness bonus." However, hatred was already seething under this surface, which can be seen in the following pages, where Hügel-Marshall provides quotations from *Das Parlament* (18-19). Then it dawns on her that the first years were only harmless on the surface: "Ich war fünf Jahre alt und ahnte nicht, dass [. . .]" (18-19). She alternates the quotations with the anaphoric statements that foreshadow the racism she will soon encounter. When Hügel-Marshall is forcefully torn away from her family and put into a children's home, she finds out that she is not only different from other children because she lives in a *Heim* but more so because she is a black "Bastard" (24). This double burden renders her "anders 'anders'" (31). Thus, even in the children's home, where, presumably, they are all in the same boat of being excluded from society, Hügel-Marshall is furthermore *othered from the others*. She is the exotic other in çomparison to the white orphans and problem children in the *Heim*, who are perceived as more "normal" and "better." Her skin color, above all else, separates her very starkly from the other kids, since she is "das einzige Schwarze Kind im Heim" (45).

Hügel-Marshall struggles to survive the inhumane treatment in the home, which literally strikes her twice as hard as the other kids because of the shade of her skin. She is beaten several times; she is told that her blood "ist nicht rein" (35), which still stems from the Nazi obsession of a pure Aryan blood line; she is forced to eat what she has thrown up (26); she has no real toys or books other than the Bible to distract herself with (25-26); and she is excluded from higher education (48). Her way of enduring all this is by writing down her thoughts and emotions.

> [Ich] zeichne oder schreibe kleine Verse auf. Nur auf Papier gelingt es mir, Dinge auszudrücken, die ich nicht auszusprechen wage. Meine Gedichte und Zeichnungen lege ich immer säuberlich gefaltet unter meine Matratze. Dort werden sie eines Tages entdeckt. (35)

The *Schwester* who finds Hügel-Marshall's notes tears them apart and Hügel-Marshall is forced to throw away the pieces of paper representing her soul. Hügel-Marshall is not allowed to have a life of her own, secrets or a safe place to which she can withdraw. Even her hobby of writing, which is even more than a hobby for it seems to have saved her sanity, is taken from her.

In the following years, Hügel-Marshall uses writing merely as a cry for help. Throughout the book she claims that she feels very lonely and this feeling already starts when she is ten and a half years old (31). Being treated as inferior and stupid due to her skin color makes her become depressed. "Völlig verwirrt laufe ich in den Waschraum, schaue verzweifelt in den Spiegel und wünsche mir so sehr, nicht so zu sein, wie ich bin. Wenigstens für einen einzigen Tag will ich weiß sein, ganz besonders dann, wenn es Zeugnisse gibt" (29). Her following development towards self-hatred, self-negation, and even suicidal tendencies are similar to the feelings described by Massaquoi and Usleber, and thus those feelings and doubts seem indicative of the African-German experience. "Ich beginne meine Hautfarbe zu hassen. Fortan gibt es für mich keinen sehnlicheren Wunsch, als weiß zu sein" (38-39). Furthermore, "ist es kein Wunder, daß ich mit allen Mitteln versuche, mein Schwarzsein zu ignorieren, und daß mein Bedürfnis, nicht aufzufallen, immer stärker wird" (46). This situation is comparable to Massaquoi's wish not to be the center of attention, and that he does not like to be seen with his aunt Fatima, who wears her Afro proudly. Nothing, however, helps because African-Germans are "immer sichtbar" (46) and thus can fall prey to racism. Hügel-Marshall's feelings of self-hatred culminate when she claims: "Ich fühle mich tot" (47). All positive emotions are drained and she begins to have suicidal thoughts; in fact, she already feels as if dead. As a last lifeline she chooses to write again, but this time she writes a letter to the management at the boarding school where she lives at that point in her life. In her letter she articulates her problems and tries to make herself heard. It is her last hope of being accepted and seen as a human being. In addition, she writes down her suicidal thoughts but, unfortunately, her intention for receiving help backfires, for no word of consolation or support reaches her. Instead, the management forwards the letter to the *Jugendamt* (youth welfare office), where a cruel officer summons Hügel-Marshall to reprimand her and to literally hand her a rope so that she can hang herself (57). This has a reverse effect on Hügel-Marshall and she resolves to fight instead. Accordingly, Hügel-Marshall undertakes another attempt at writing. Her wish to get to know her father, to whom she owes her skin color—which she perceives as the source of her troubles—becomes ever stronger so that she decides to write a letter to him (60). She mails the letter but after some weeks she receives her letter back with the note: "Retour/Return to Writer/Address Insufficient" (61). Thus, all of her writing efforts, either for help, personal use, or for the means of communication, result in disappointment and isolation. This is a paramount reason for her later activism in and for the African-German community. Moreover, Hügel-Marshall's successful autobiographical writing for a larger audience functions as a form of redemption for her former disappointments.

Her sufferings, however, continue. The *Heim* and society "versuchen [. . .] systematisch, meine Persönlichkeit zu zerstören, und ich helfe ihnen dabei, indem ich mich selbst verachte, um akzeptabler für sie zu werden" (52). Throughout the book, Hügel-Marshall exemplifies the psychological terror and underlying oppression by intermittently weaving in statements by others, mostly general and anonymous ones: "'Das arme Kind, eigentlich trifft es keine Schuld, daß es so ist, wie es ist. [. . .] Die Kleine wird mal genauso unmoralisch und labil wie die Mutter'" (31); or: "'Heiraten, du? Für die Männer biste doch nur Freiwild'" (74). Another example is: "'Wie, du willst mal nach Amiland, wo mehr Schwarze sind, das sind doch alles Verbrecher'" (92). Oftentimes, Hügel-Marshall's flow of writing is interrupted by a new paragraph providing these statements by friends and people on the street. The numerous interjected statements become annoying to the reader after a while, which might be the effect Hügel-Marshall wants to achieve, for she has had to listen to these prophecies and judgments all her life. She also does not only underline the frequency of the statements but also their generality. By having interrupted what she is doing, thus what she is writing down, and by afterwards trying to proceed from where she has left off before, Hügel-Marshall draws a dialectic picture of her everyday life: The opposing and negative statements or even prophecies by others are put in contrast with her fight for a normal life and are proven wrong. At this point, a comparison with African-American rappers' technique of "doin' the dozens"[91] is possible. In this case it is not black man versus black man, but a hostile white community against a single black person. Thus, Hügel-Marshall creates a new form of writing within African-German literature, which I earlier called a dialectic racist discussion. This dialectic racist discussion is reminiscent of the concepts of "doin' the dozens" and the speakerly text. By reliving the instances, she tries to overcome the inherent racism and continue with her life without having others destroy her personality. The autobiographical act is a form of coping with her past and it constitutes the development of her African-German identity in order to shape her present, and possibly future life.

    Hügel-Marshall has come a long way from the beginning of her life up until the present, from the first chapters in her book up to the epilogue. Even though at times she still feels ignored, she has overcome her non-person status by finding two important communities, namely the feminist movement and the newly forming African-German community. Her autobiographical act is meant to finally reach a wide German public and make them, the German people, see that she, Hügel-Marshall, is indeed African *and* German. "[I]ch ging in den Kindergarten, zur Schule, ich habe studiert, und ich arbeite, doch im Bewußtsein der meisten weißen Deutschen existiere ich noch immer nicht" (12). Hügel-Marshall herself had to take the path to expose this fact and to fight exoticism, racism, and sexism. By giving the account of her life, she also wants others to acknowledge her equal status as an African-German. She joined the (white) feminist movement, where she fought for gender justice, but her special status as a black woman was still being ignored. "Einzeln und gemeinsam kämpfen wir für Gleichberechtigung und gegen Unterdrückung. Nicht jedoch gegen Rassismus" (82). In the following, she takes Taekwondo classes and finally

---

[91] See chapter 3.3.1.

decides to meet other African-Germans and even joins their newly founded community. "Es gibt eine Gruppe, der ich angehöre und die mich braucht. [. . .] Überleben [ist] für mich nicht länger eine Frage von Mut oder Stolz, sondern eine Entscheidung" (91) and this decision leads to her renaming herself. She wants to leave her old, humiliated self behind, including the name Erika that her mother gave her at birth.

> Solange ich nicht weiß, was ich will, wissen es grundsätzlich die anderen. Solange ich mich nicht selbst definiere, nicht selbst weiß, wer ich bin, werden mich die anderen definieren; sie wollen bestimmen, was und wer ich bin und was ich zu wollen habe. Der Name Erika war für meine Mutter der schönste Name, den sie mir geben konnte, ein Name den ich bis zu diesem Zeitpunkt mochte und auch immer noch mag. Doch heute nenne ich mich Ika, und die meisten anderen nennen mich auch so. (93)

This act symbolizes that she now has the support of an African-German community. She takes charge of her life and wants to create a new identity, a new life for the present and future. Even though she partly breaks with her past, she makes sure she does not break with her mother. Renaming is a common issue among Africans and Africans in the diaspora. Lorde did it, Hartmann did it, Obama liked to be called Barry[92] and Massaquoi preferred being called Mickey during and right after the war. Thus, renaming becomes a pattern that can be traced in the African, African-American and also African-German traditions; it is supposed to help create a self-chosen identity by shedding one's scarred black skin in order to cultivate a new skin without the scars of racism and deprivation.

Hügel-Marshall, by getting to know and being influenced and motivated by Lorde, turns to letters again and her writing incorporates poetry. She is introduced to the African-German gatherings and in her work she includes a poem of how she felt then. She also exclaims: "'Ich brauche Hände, eure braunen Hände'" (90). At this point in her life she is able to embrace other black Germans, something she has not been able to do before. Speaking about what she feels in verse form seems to make her stronger and more self-confident. Lorde teaches Hügel-Marshall to claim her voice, to articulate and pronounce her feelings, and she gives her the tools to do so, one of which is poetry. Poetry provides Hügel-Marshall with a forum in which to speak out. She even dedicates a poem to her father, after she meets him in the USA (126-27). The last stanza is:

> Ich strecke meine Hand aus
> meiner Schwarzen Familie entgegen

---

[92] Obama later changes his name back to the original again.

> mein Vater, meine Familie
> hier ist meine Reise zu Ende
> hier fließt die ganze Welt zusammen (127)

Her life's path, her writing, and her autobiographical act have finally helped her overcome discrimination. By the end of the book, Hügel-Marshall claims that she lives a fulfilled and happy life because she, finally, has the means and tools to do so. Strikingly, after having found her roots, her father and her American family, she does not seem to yearn for emigration. It appears as if finding one's roots help to calm down the inner restlessness and any sort of wishes that life could be better somewhere else. The last lines of her book underline the notion that Hügel-Marshall has found her inner peace.

> Ich hole mir heute die Welt zurück: mein Leben, meine Sehnsüchte, meine unbeschwerte Fröhlichkeit, Humor, meine Liebe, meine Achtung und den Stolz auf mich selbst. Jeden Morgen wache ich auf, freue mich auf den anbrechenden Tag und erlebe die Welt neu. Ich schaue in den Spiegel und freue mich, denn ich möchte um nichts in der Welt anders sein, als ich bin. (140)

It is a feeling that other African-Germans share, just like Usleber who also claims that he would have been a different person without his skin color and that he is very happy nowadays to be who he is and would not want to change it anymore (Usleber 52; 139-41). Through the act of autobiographical writing Hügel-Marshall recounts her past and actively shapes her present while writing herself into the contemporary minds of many Germans; and thus she tentatively begins to influence her prospective life. Her activism in the formation of the African-German movement and her writing help propel an acknowledged African-German community.

Hügel-Marshall's writing herself into being follows a chronological order. Thus, her work is, just like most autobiographies, a chronological account of past events. Massaquoi's *Destined to Witness* is no exception. He writes about where he was and when, what he did then and there, and which "kinds of identities and social relations [were] possible within those chronotopes" (Bergland 136). The three major chronotopes are:
1. Massaquoi in Germany from 1926 until 1948;
2. Massaquoi in Liberia from 1948 until 1950;
3. Massaquoi in the United States of America from 1950 until today.

He breaks the larger chronotopes up into many small episodes. There is no table of contents in *Destined to Witness* to give an overview over the numerous chapters. Just as in Hügel-Marshall's work, the lack of a table of contents is analogous to the author's path in life, since he never had any guidance and never knew what the next day would bring and, accordingly, only thought from one situation to the next. The reader is thus put into a similar position as the author was in and has to find his or her way through the book. Nevertheless, the chapters do have headings. In effect, there are one hundred and five chapters in *Destined to Witness*; this high number underscores the countless disruptions and reorientations in Massaquoi's life. Hence, the reader has to take one step at a time to follow the author on his difficult and dangerous path, and the short chapters ensure that the disquieting content is digestible for the reader. The relatively brief chapters with an average length of three pages and their headings without numbers, stem from Massaquoi's professional background as a journalist and support the notion of his established personality as an African-American journalist. In *Destined* headings such as "The New Kid on the Block" (17), "Hitler Strikes Home" (54), "Quest for Converts" (97), and "The War Comes to Hamburg" (140) resemble newspaper or magazine articles[93] because Massaquoi is used to a journalistic style of writing deriving from his background as an editor. This style helped him to cope with the volume of material he had in his mind, enabling him to write down one episode of his life at a time. Haley had advised him to start writing as if he were to write an article for *Ebony*, and Massaquoi successfully acted on Haley's advice and shaped his autobiography in this fashion (Massaquoi, *Hänschen klein* 127). Massaquoi emphasizes his time in Germany, as already suggested in the title, for he dedicates eighty-three chapters to it. The preoccupation with his time in Germany under Hitler is an "autobiographical act [which is] [. . .] a re-enactment [. . .] of earlier phases of identity formation" (Eakin, *Fictions* 226). Going through the early stages of the development of his identity helps Massaquoi to reappraise his arduous past with 20/20 vision and with a stable identity.

Massaquoi's life writing is an existential part of his transatlantic identity formation. "An autobiography, after all, is but an extended reply to one of the simplest and profoundest of questions: who are you and how did you come to be that way?" (Stone 115). By the time he writes his first autobiography,[94] Massaquoi is an American citizen and has resumed his contacts to Europe and Africa. With his life writing he tries to answer how he came to be what he is. However, writing an autobiography is not only an explanation but a process of reconciliation and identity formation as well. Massaquoi had not quite reconciled all of his former and present selves. After his departure from Europe and Africa, he had sought and found a stable national and ethnic identity in America and had abandoned his horrible memories of the past. The act of exploring his past and of writing it down serves "as a form of psychotherapy or as an instrument in the process of self-discovery" (Hornung, "Autobiography" 222). As Eakin points out,

---

[93] Massaquoi also included a number of photographs in *Destined*. The first section of photographs appears after approximately one third of the book and the next one after two thirds. Using photographs to illustrate what he writes about also reminds one of a magazine or newspaper article that uses pictures for support.

[94] *Destined to Witness* is his first life writing, followed by *Hänschen klein*.

> [T]he act of composition may be conceived as a mediating term in the autobiographical enterprise, reaching back into the past not merely to recapture but to repeat the psychological rhythms of identity formation, and reaching forward into the future to fix the structure of this identity in a permanent self-made existence as literary text. This is to understand the writing of autobiography [. . .] as an integral and often decisive phase of the drama of self-definition. (*Fictions* 226)

Massaquoi, by writing down his life's story, repeats the phases of his identity formation as an African-German and relives the rejection of his African-German identity by many Germans and Liberians, and arguably also (African-) Americans. However, by writing down this special life and reliving it, he (re-) establishes his African-German identity.

Massaquoi is the only African-German writer in this analysis whose book is a retrospect of a long life. Hügel-Marshall and Usleber are too young to claim a full-length life writing. Massaquoi, however, began to write down his story as a summation of his achievements in a transatlantic career. He wrote this book not just as another life story about human existence. Instead, his intention is to recapture and recreate his former African-German identity in order to come into existence as a human being in Germany and to make sure the world gets to know the story of other minorities during the Nazi era. By the time of writing, his USA citizenship is clearly established, his embracement of an African-American identity confirmed by his participation in the Civil Rights Movement, and his career as a successful journalist acknowledged. His African-Americanness was

> the solution to the conflict which so many biracial people experience regarding their racial identity. I could not be a living witness to the ongoing heroic struggle for black survival and equality in racist America, document in article after article the countless achievements of blacks in the face of staggering odds, and not feel black and proud myself. (xv)

Thus, he becomes a proud black person in America, who, as a journalist for the black magazines *Jet* and *Ebony*, has written himself and has contributed to write the African-American community into American society and consciousness. Today, with this book, his motivation is to claim his original African-German identity through his autobiographical act. By writing down his life and publishing *HIS*tory in Germany and elsewhere, he reclaims and affirms the transatlantic connection of his person and now feels as an African-American who has German ethnic roots (Massaquoi, Hans J. Letter to the author 2). Thus, his work differs from Hügel-Marshall's and Usleber's insofar as Massaquoi has achieved acceptance as a human being elsewhere, in the USA, and can look back on a long and succesful life; however, he also wants to write himself into German consciousness and world historiography. He does this by writing about his special exotic status, the racism he encountered, and the stereotypes he himself once believed in. By doing so, he takes control of the shaping of his past, present, and future selves.

In *Destined to Witness* the apparent frankness with which Massaquoi tries to recapture his past self is striking. The racism he encounters definitely weighs heavily, and the Nazi terror determines his everyday life. However, Massaquoi's own prejudices and stereotypes are also displayed, which render parts of the book a mild form of self-criticism. Through the act of writing it down as a document of confession the work also redeems his past self. As a writer he wants to stress the fact of how easily people were influenced then. Moreover, Massaquoi tries to take charge of his former African-German identity by painting an honest picture of himself while giving the best possible picture of his mother as well as other family members and close friends. For instance, Massaquoi becomes "an unabashed proponent of the Nazis" and when he "had gotten [his] hands on an embroidered swastika emblem, [he] had Tante Möller—who didn't know any better—sew it on a sweater of [his]" (41). Here, Massaquoi portrays *Tante Möller* as not knowing any better, which means that she did not want to do any harm but just wanted to fulfill Massaquoi's wish. This simplistic way of protecting close friends must be regarded as critical in light of many Germans' ignorance toward Nazi tyranny.

Furthermore, Massaquoi occasionally gives examples of his enthusiasm for Hitler and the Nazis, but he mitigates his guilt and thus confession by ensuring to tell the reader that he was still a young boy and enthralled by the Nazis' "best shows and best-looking uniforms, best-sounding marching bands, and best-drilled marching columns" (41). He exposes how much the Nazi propaganda manipulated his thinking when, after having watched films at school aimed at portraying Jews as filthy, he also regards Jews as "*Ungeziefer*" and despises them (54). At this time, Massaquoi himself has not yet understood that he, as a black person, is also the target of Nazi scorn. Massaquoi tries to give as honest a picture of himself as is possible in his situation, while simultaneously putting forth the most glorifying picture of his brave mother. "Unlike me, she had paid little attention to the election activities in the neighborhood," and she protects him like a "tigress protecting her cub" (45). Whereas he can take part in the blame, for he is not only wrongdoer but also and foremost victim, his mother and his family and friends are protected in his text and put in the right light. Through the autobiographical act, Massaquoi overcomes the racism of the Nazi past directed at him and his own racial attitudes against Jews and thus takes control of shaping his self-representation as well as the image of his mother and others.

Most of the work is preoccupied with the fact of Massaquoi's non-person status and how, by diverse acts and fates, he in the end becomes a human being. Massaquoi's autobiography is characterized by what I defined earlier as performative constructedness. He starts out his odyssey as a non-Aryan nobody in Nazi Germany and actively transforms his voided identity in Germany to an African-American self via the detour of a Liberian identity. Of course it is the story of his life, but the way he retraces his life's steps, picks out and recreates exemplary instances, Massaquoi drafts his coming of age. The blackboard incident is one of the crucial moments of Massaquoi's life. It is exemplary not only for his individual non-person status, but it also stands for the status of all African-Germans. Massaquoi's class participates in its school's competition in which the class that first reaches a one hundred percent Hitler Youth membership of students wins a day off. Massaquoi's teacher, *Herr Schürmann*, draws a chart and every day fills in the names of those students in his class who join the Hitler Youth one by one. On account of his non-Aryan background, Massaquoi is not allowed to join the Hitler Youth and thus not considered to be a full member of the class. Therefore, he is not counted in the one hundred percent class membership when all but him have become members so that his class wins the competition. All of Massaquoi's classmates get a day off, except for him. The teacher's act of erasing the last empty square spot on the black board chart—a void space that represents Massaquoi—exemplifies German thinking of that time about African-Germans, namely that there was no room for African-Germans (102).

At this point in the text, Massaquoi is not simply the other who is ostracized and discriminated against. He is basically non-existent due to his hybrid genetic background. Not only has his person, and consequently his identity, been previously challenged and thrown into crisis by a number of racist attacks, but his name is erased and eliminated by the teacher's action with the chalk brush. This scene symbolizes prevalent German thinking of the time, namley that "the Afro-German identity is not the *antithesis* in the dialectic of (white) German subjectivity: *it is simply non-existent*" (Wright, "Others-from-Within" 298). The actions and reactions of the white people in Germany at that time bring to light the "inability on the part of many white Germans to understand so simple a concept as one being both Black *and* German [. . .]. [W]hite Germans insistently and consistently misrecognize Afro-Germans as *Africans*" (Wright, "Others-from-Within" 298). Thereby, Massaquoi and all "African-Germans are definitionally excluded from the idea of German" (Asante 1) because in the eyes of many Germans it was a "contradiction [. . .] being *both* African and German" (Opitz 142). This is one reason for the isolation of African-Germans, which subsequently led to their efforts to establish an African-German community.

The precarious status of Massaquoi and most African-Germans, which Wright defines as "others-from-within," becomes apparent in Massaquoi's autobiographical craft as a writer who recreates the stages of a dynamic and metaphoric identity development. Massaquoi performs his identity in his narrative and uses such examples as the blackboard incident to reveal and eventually overcome the apparent racism in the autobiographical act for the formation of his self. His authenticity and the fact that he is the "other-from-within" is allowed for by the stylistic device of showing off his German vocabulary, even his Hamburgian brogue, such as "'*Kloppe!*'" (physical fight of street gangs) or "*Schako*" (street talk for policemen) (78). Massaquoi clearly has also been influenced by the African-American tradition of the black vernacular and the spoken word, which he substitutes in his autobiography with German terms and special Hamburgian brogue vocabulary. On the one hand, this stylistic means underlines Massaquoi's and other African-Germans' status as "others-from-within," while on the other hand it provides for authenticity and agency. At the same time, by the spoken word and German terms, Massaquoi performs his identity dynamically. After the emptiness of his identity has been established in real life (the blackboard incident) and in literary terms (the autobiographical act of writing this incident down), Massaquoi can now follow his life's steps and plot his narrative towards writing himself into existence within German society and thinking.

One indicator of Massaquoi's exoticism and encounter with racism is the recurring motif of hair. Massaquoi's hair serves as a symbol for his link to his African roots, and it reoccurs throughout *Destined to Witness*. As a young boy Massaquoi detests his hair as a visible sign of his African heritage, which entails social exclusion and discrimination (92-93). By elaborating on his attempt to straighten his hair as a young teenager and by showing how much he hated himself at that time, Massaquoi appeals to the readers' visual senses and lets them partake in his early identity crisis. At school, one of the boys approaches Massaquoi and makes fun of his hair, touching it and asking, "'Why do Negroes grow sheep wool instead of hair on their heads?'" (37). His mother's and his own fear concerning the probable reactions to Massaquoi's hair suddenly materialize in this form of mockery. This is only one of many incidents he describes in his life writing that contributes to the loss of his self-esteem. He describes how he internalizes the racism:

> "[I]nstead of putting the blame for my problems with racists where it belonged, I blamed myself. More than anything, I blamed my appearance—especially my African hair, which I had come to loathe. [. . .] [M]y self-esteem had plunged to a frightening low" (92).

As a result, Massaquoi cuts his "kinky" hair short and tries to straighten it, but to no avail. He reaches the point where he uncompromisingly transfers white racial ideology and white Western aesthetics to his person (see Cross 100-01). In the following, Massaquoi tries to shape his mirror image according to the racist ideology the Nazis had put in his mind. "Convinced that if [his] hair were straight, half of [his] problems would be solved" (92), he does not give up and makes every endeavor to straighten his hair in order to come closer to the Aryan ideal.[95]

Massaquoi's identity is being constructed performatively and develops proportionately to the growth and acceptance of his hair. Later, when he is a swingboy,[96] hair becomes an issue again. At that point, Massaquoi does not hate his hair anymore because he is not ostracized due to his racial traits. On the contrary, he now tries to grow his hair, as it has become a requirement of an authentic swingboy (159-60). "This meant wearing [their] hair long and with sideburns in contrast to the short, military-style haircuts and clean-cut look prescribed by the Hitler Youth leadership" (159-60). Massaquoi is not ashamed of and does not need to hide his hair anymore. He even grows his hair longer, which is a sign of swingboy membership (159-60).[97] The fact that Massaquoi, due to his feelings of not being isolated anymore, accepts his African heritage, especially in form of his hair, underpins his growing self-esteem and black identity formation. In an interview, Massaquoi himself stated that not being allowed to participate in anything was the worst experience for him during his time in Germany ("Growing Up" 27). Consequently, when he becomes part of the swingboy movement, he enjoys all the benefits of group membership,[98] and his black identity is allowed to surface again. Massaquoi takes up this hair symbolism again in *Hänschen klein* when he describes that he is a proud African-American with an Afro (48). Unfortunately, Massaquoi later starts losing his hair, which he has since come to appreciate (Massaquoi, *Hänschen klein* 200). Massaquoi uses the symbol of hair as the thread and parallel reference of his identity formation throughout the book. He skillfully interweaves the motif of his hair with bits and pieces of how he overcomes self-denial, exotic otherness, racist attacks and discrimination in order to come into being as an African-American by accepting his African roots, i.e., his African physical traits. His narrative and identity are performed and developed simultaneously in the autobiographical act so that he is now able to come into

---

[95] Emde, an African-German woman, experienced the same. She states the following: "[w]hen I was about thirteen I started to straighten my 'horse hair' so that it would be like white people's hair that I admired so much. I was convinced that with straight hair I would be less conspicuous" (103).

[96] The swingboys were "an unchartered, unorganized, and leaderless, yet highly visible fraternity." They listened and danced to "jazz music, which [they] had adopted as [their] favorite music because it was banned by the Nazis as Negermusik" (Massaquoi, *Destined* 159).

[97] A common punishment by the Hitler Youth was to cut the long hair of the swingboys. Once, when Massaquoi was singled out to get a haircut, the Hitler Youth withdrew from cutting his hair because they did not care about *his* hair. Massaquoi felt humiliated because the swingboys who had their hair cut "were regarded [. . .] as the martyrs of the movement" (Massaquoi, *Destined* 162). The Nazis, again, excluded Massaquoi from achieving respect.

[98] The advantage of being a member of a group is the support of a network of friends, who provide help and protection. Moreover, a strong sense of mutual interests and respect supports the positive development of one's own identity.

being as an African-German. He shapes his past and present selves and sets the direction for his future life.

Through the writing and the success of his autobiography, Massaquoi defines himself and stakes a claim for his African-Germanness. After its publication, *Destined to Witness* appeared "auf der Bestsellerliste verschiedener Magazine, so vor allem auf der des *Spiegel*" (Massaquoi, *Hänschen klein* 257). Massaquoi undertook a promotion tour throughout Germany and gave many interviews. Moreover, a documentary film about him and his friend Ralph Giordano was produced (Massaquoi, *Hänschen klein* 257). A difference between Massaquoi on the one side and Hügel-Marshall and Usleber—and most certainly the majority of contemporary African-Germans—on the other, is that the temporal and geographical lag between Massaquoi's experiences in Germany and his contemporary stable identity allow for a number of moments of reconciliation on Massaquoi's part. Even though he still sees some problems in contemporary German society, he disagrees that under the Nazi regime "all Germans were tainted and thus culpable" (xv). He also tries to place former German youths in a better light: "I suspect that despite the massive, and much publicized, presence of Hitler Youth at Nazi rallies, the percentage of German boys and girls who were active participants in Hitler Youth activities on a regular basis was relatively small" (104). He reaches out to Germans in order to make peace and find closure, which is certainly part of his achievement. Through his success, Massaquoi, as an African-German, has finally entered German history, German historiography, and has found his way into German consciousness and memory. He has filled in the gap between the "official" history Germans got to know and the one he experienced, which is the one that never entered historiography, namely the story of African-Germans under Hitler (Campt, *Other Germans* 1). Finally, Massaquoi has come into existence as an African-German and has undone the symbolic "non-person status" established by his former teacher, *Herr Schürmann* among others (102). He has reconciled himself with his biological roots and has "persuade[d] the world to view [his] self through [his] own eyes" (Shapiro qtd. in Adams 11). The success of *Destined to Witness* proves Massaquoi's achievement in reclaiming his African-German identity and insisting upon his acceptance among the German population.[99] Massaquoi has written himself into (German) history and thereby has gained the African-German identity formerly denied to him.

In general, Massaquoi draws a more differentiated picture of Germans than do Usleber and Hügel-Marshall. This is due to the time and space that distances Massaquoi from his bad experiences in Germany. Usleber's work resembles Hügel-Marshall's insofar as both authors boldly admonish white German society and its racist attitudes towards African-Germans right from the start. The two authors' opinions are forcefully stated and directed to the readers

---

[99] *Destined to Witness* was published in Germany and in the United States of America but was and is widely read throughout Europe (for example Great Britain and Austria), as evident in the letters to Massaquoi in *Hänschen klein* (263-80).

from the beginning, unlike Massaquoi, who takes on the topic of contemporary racism at the very end of his autobiography. Usleber does not postpone the issue, but jumps to the core of his life's problem: having been an ostracized black man among white racist Germans.

> Ich selbst habe mich nicht immer als einen Deutschen wahrgenommen, aber auch für meine Mitmenschen war mein Deutschsein alles andere als selbstverständlich: Die meisten Menschen haben mich nicht—jedenfalls nicht von vornherein—als einen Deutschen gesehen. (9)

He claims that Germans always see his skin color and his outer, exotic appearance first, which makes them jump to conclusions, or rather to exclusions. Thus, his intention of sharing his life's story is to point to the problems of African-Germans, and, if possible, "ein wenig Mitfühlen mit ihnen wecken. Ein wenig Bewusstsein dafür wecken, wie schmerzhaft es manchmal sein kann, im eigenen Land nicht als gleichwertig akzeptiert zu werden" (9).

Like Hügel-Marshall later on in her life and work, Usleber supports the notion of a union of African-Germans even before he starts the first chapter of his autobiography. The proclamation of his intention and of the severity of African-German issues at the very beginning of his book show that his work follows in Hügel-Marshall's and others' footsteps. The book itself becomes a blueprint for the African-German experience, and the content reflects the lonesome struggle of becoming a human being while fighting against one's exotic status in what they portray as a racist society. Usleber's techniques to overcome racism range from musical lyrics to literary texts. His life and writing can be characterized by his need for and use of idols in order to strive for the best. These idols he finds in music, for instance in music of the African diaspora, like Bob Marley's or Stevie Wonder's songs; in American literature, as in John Steinbeck's novels; or in African-American history, especially in the stories about slavery. Above all, what is striking is that he quotes from Hügel-Marshall and that his writing style is influenced by her. Interestingly, she in turn has been influenced by African-American writers, especially by her friend and teacher Audre Lorde. There are patterns in both life writings, however, that stem from typical African-German experience and become characteristic of African-German writing: The authors write themselves into being in order to leave behind the racism and discrimination that have marked their lives in Germany.

Like many others, Usleber suffers from his visibly "exotic" appearance, most obviously displayed by his darker complexion. "Ich war dunkelhäutig und vaterlos, eigentlich schon allein Grund genug, von der Idar-Obersteiner Bevölkerung abgelehnt zu werden" (13). He claims that he had his first real negative experiences while going to school (16). Hügel-Marshall and Massaquoi similarly enjoy a relatively carefree and normal life up until the age of five or six. The younger the biracial child, it seems, the more he or she is accepted and characterized as cute; however, "[je] älter ich wurde, desto mehr nahm die anfängliche Zuneigung meiner Umgebung ab" (19). In a racist society, children of mixed genealogical background seem to be vulnerable to this phenomenon. Massaquoi and Hügel-Marshall illustrate similar observations. Underlying this phenomenon, apparently, is that some people believe that no harm or imminent "danger," such as a "contamination" of pure Aryan blood, is to be expected from a young, cute child. When the child grows up and becomes an adult, however, the attitude towards him or her changes due to the possibility of miscegenation. Racial inequality entailing discrimination becomes an issue at school, which, through the descriptions of the authors, seems to be an institution that tolerates or even perpetuates racism. When entering the school system, the child is on his or her way to adulthood and is supposed to conform to the status quo and to the rules. However, if one is different already from the outset, namely one's appearance, it is difficult, if not impossible, to assimilate into a white Western, supposedly homogeneous, society like Germany's.

African-Germans, just like Usleber, are bullied because they do not fit in and they do not have anyone to defend them. At school, older boys make it a habit to single out Usleber in the schoolyard. "Schließlich hatte ich keine einzige Pause mehr, in der ich unbehelligt war. Die Folge war, dass ich Angst hatte, in den Pausenhof zu gehen" (16). Moreover, for the first time in his life, "wurde [er] nun auch mit den bekannten Schimpfwörtern für Menschen mit dunkler Hautfarbe bedacht" (16), and those degrading terms still ring in his ears years later. As a result, he does not belong to any group or clique—he becomes the other, the outsider. Usleber uses English terms to describe this fact when he hints at the reality of groups like friends, clubs, and jobs. "Alle diese Kreise erzeugen ein Verhalten, das man 'In-Group—Out-Group'nennt," and he "war natürlich 'Out-Group' und zwar fast überall, wo [er] hinkam" (13). According to Usleber, blacks in Germany are thus doubly excluded, for not only are they an out-group, but even within a white out-group they are also exotic due to their "visibility." Using English terms within a German book might have the effect of sounding sophisticated, as if this phenomenon were true elsewhere and scientifically proven. Also, it underlines the influence of American literature or the English language and his own American genealogy.

> Meine größte "Schwachstelle" war jedoch im wahrsten Sinne des Wortes offensichtlich. So wie Kinder mit roten Haaren, mit Sommersprossen, mit einem Sprachfehler oder auch nur mit einer Brille bei Streitigkeiten immer mit einer beleidigenden Benennung ihres äußeren Merkmals beschimpft wurden, so war es bei mir die Hautfarbe. (21)

The difference, though, is that he does not have a community, no "Leidensgenossen" and Usleber claims that from all the above-named groups, he stands at the very bottom of the hierarchy, and all by himself (22).

The racist attacks against Usleber have the same effect as they do on other African-Germans because they adhere to the categorization put forth by others, which culminates in self-loathing. Usleber, accordingly, turns against himself and his appearance.

> Warum konnte ich nicht so aussehen wie die anderen? Warum gehörte ich nicht dazu? Ich fühlte mich "nicht normal" und legte damit gleichzeitig für mich fest, was "Normalität" überhaupt bedeutete: hell zu sein. (23)

Usleber, just like other African-Germans, has reached the point of a very low self-esteem. He hates his skin color and other African traits, which make him visible and hence vulnerable.[100] As a result, he internalizes white Western beauty standards and the codes by which a racist society defines its norms. Usleber turns against himself rather than the bigotry that surrounds him. It becomes apparent that even after many years of claiming that he has come to terms with his skin color and life, he still very much adheres to white Western beauty standards.

> Im nächsten Jahr kam meine Tochter zur Welt, ein gesundes und hübsches Mädchen. Ich glaube, dass sie in der multikulturellen Stadt Dietzenbach wenig Probleme haben wird, und infolge ihres Namens und ihrer nur leicht getönten Haut wird sie auch anderswo kaum auffallen. (126)

Thus, he has not freed himself of the chains of preconceived opinions and has indeed made them his own as well when he projects them onto his daughter. Even though he claims he does not want to change his own skin color anymore (139), he emphasizes his happiness that his daughter turned out to have a light skin; she, having a Western name, will blend in. It is one of the instances mentioned earlier, when Usleber's inconsistency surfaces. Although he declares acceptance of his skin color, even his happiness about it (52), and that he has benefited from it, he vindicates the light shade of his daughter's skin and values it as favorable and helpful. Thus, he assigns white Western values to skin color while at the same time critiquing Germans for doing the same (9). More inconsistency becomes visible when he condemns any sort of categorization of people (9); he says that all people are individuals and that someone "kommt nicht weit, wenn man sie in Kategorien einteilt und Gruppenzugehörigkeiten zu

---

[100] To blend in is a wish that most African-Germans share and so they move into bigger cities; both Hügel-Marshall and Usleber move to Frankfurt, which is characterized by a higher level of multiculturalism than other, especially smaller, cities. Massaquoi moves from Hamburg (via Liberia) to New York, where he blends in when he walks on 125th Street in Harlem. As a result, many African-Germans either want to pass as white or at least blend in, so that they do not become the center of attention, or worse, ridiculed.

definieren versucht" (90). However, throughout the book he himself draws clear lines between Germans and himself, between racists who do mean no harm ("nicht böse gemeint") and racists who propagate their "Fremdenfeindlichkeit" publicly (85). In this way, he distinguishes between "'gute' Rassisten" and bad ones (82).

Making public his identity quarrels and the mutability of his opinions and thoughts becomes a tool for Usleber to write himself into being and to accelerate the process of coming to terms with his past. Being black and white, African and German at the same time, is still a contradiction for some Germans, and so his writing mirrors the at times incoherent identity formation and life's ruptures. By his autobiographical act and publication, Usleber is successful, like the other African-German authors, to write himself into being. However, he does not fully overcome the racism he encountered or still encounters, for the tone of his work and the inconsistencies stem from a person still very much deeply hurt and not yet forgiving. Nevertheless, he is on the path to finding peace of mind in his writing acts. When he first started out writing, as a hobby, the content is preoccupied with accusations, but after a while, "waren meine Inhalte keine Anklagen mehr, sondern versuchten auf erzählerische Weise Stimmungen, Gefühle oder Situationen zu beschreiben" (50). This process is intertwined with the development of his identity. He soon learns to accept himself, which he sees as crucial several times throughout the book. "Man muss sich selbst akzeptieren, um von anderen akzeptiert zu werden. Sich selbst akzeptieren aber heißt, seine eigene Identität zu finden. Diese Identität besaß ich in meiner Jugend noch nicht" (77).This acceptance took a long time to come through. Usleber, just like Hügel-Marshall, shows how difficult it has been to fight against the prejudices and judgmental statements of others. He uses the technique introduced by Hügel-Marshall, which I earlier called a dialectic racist discussion, and which seems to become more and more characteristic for a developing African-German literary tradition. Throughout the work he provides statements by his mother and other people on the street to give the reader an inside view. He interjects several statements, such as, "*Afrikaner sind auch Menschen wie wir!*" (83) or, "*Sie sind ja gar nicht so dunkel!*" (84; italics in original), and analyzes them in their succeeding paragraphs as a kind of answer on his part. By his individual struggle, Usleber has accepted himself and written himself into being. However, he has not overcome racism yet, which shines through when he claims, "dass es diese Gleichheit [which every minority is longing for] nie gegeben hat, nicht gibt und auch nie geben wird" (51). It is questionable whether this statement is realistic or rather just displays a moment of pessimism, or whether this statement can help him in overcoming racism or if racism will be prolonged. Most likely the statement gives both, a realistic and pessimistic picture; however, it does not support Usleber and others at achieving an ideal and at leaving behind a hurtful past. Usleber's strategy is to make it anyway—the word he oftentimes uses is *trotz* (in spite of, despite). He will make it *trotzdem* (anyways, in spite of anything) and by himself. Usleber's strategy is comparable to that of the American self-made man. "Überall gibt es Menschen, die sich nicht wohlfühlen, überall besteht aber auch die Chance, selbst etwas zu tun, damit man sich wohlfühlt" (101); therefore, he is in favor of doing it yourself because you are responsible for your own life. In the end, he is successful in reaching out to the German consciousness by achieving an esteemed status in Germany, that of a civil servant, a *Beamter* (105).

Massaquoi, the only author looking back on a long life, has overcome racism—as much as is possible if one belongs to a minority—through his African-American Civil Rights struggle and the support of the African-American community. Hügel-Marshall is still very much hurt, but through her active participation in the feminist and African-German community she finds the strength and devices to more and more defeat discrimination. Usleber, however, illustrates that many African-Germans still fight a lonely battle and have not joined the African-German community. Consequently, African-Germans find themselves, naturally, several steps behind the African-American struggle. The writers at hand, though, have been able to overcome racism to some degree. The foundation has been laid. Nevertheless, to effectively defeat discrimination, African-Germans need to be accepted as "real" Germans by everyone. In addition, Usleber and others who are fighting a lonely battle must get organized in order to successfully and sustainably, actively and positively shape their future. Racism, as displayed in all these books, is still an existing phenomenon in Germany and African-Germans are just beginning to get organized. At this point, it needs to be emphasized that the dichotomous view of the works is the one of the authors and which stems from their negative experiences in Germany. However, German society is not *per se* a racist society even though it is undeniable that racism still exists and that the authors endured deprivation and discrimination on account of the color of their skin.

Chapter Five: Autobiography As Healing – A Comparative Analysis of African-American and African-German Life Writing

It does not matter how slowly you go so long as you do not stop.

Confucius

After having scrutinized each work individually, this chapter comprises a comparative analysis of the mentioned African-German and African-American life writings with the main focus on autobiography as a form of self-therapy and identity formation. First, I research the importance of white Western individualism in contrast to African-American communities and African kinship for Africans in the diaspora. Then, I pair and juxtapose African-German and African-American works which share certain common issues before taking a closer look at how far kinship, identity, autobiographical writing, and wholeness are intertwined and how far the authors achieve what they have been searching for.

5.1 Individualism versus Community versus Kinship

The order of the terms in the above title—individualism, community, and kinship—is made on purpose. The usual order here would be from a small unit to a larger concept, so that the typical sequence would start with the individual person, followed secondly by his or her kin, and then thirdly by the community surrounding him or her. In the case of Africans[101] in the diaspora, there was a rupture between the individual and his or her kin. Therefore, many Africans in the diaspora have been disoriented by the two larger concepts that determine their very being, namely by that of a white, Western individualist society that stands for mature achievement and a society that is built upon family ties and tribalism in Africa. Consequently, they have to find or form their own communities, which have taken the second place, i.e., the one of family relations. Thus, the term individualism has two almost opposing meanings in this context: one, it depicts the individualist, successful societies in the West, and two, it stands for the sometimes lonely battle of Africans in the diaspora.

The preceding analysis illustrates that the issue of either having to fight the battle against discrimination alone or together with others plays a crucial role for the stability of hyphenated identities like African-Americans and African-Germans. Resulting from this observation, I claim that a form of togetherness, of community, is paramount for Africans everywhere in order to survive. The need for a community lies not only in the African tradition of communalism, but also in the fact that Africans in the diaspora constitute

---

[101] One should keep in mind that the term "Africans" is one that can hardly represent, least of all unite all the different nations and tribes from which Africans in the diaspora stem. It is an umbrella term for the many different backgrounds of Africans which might also cause problems in the formation of a community of different African people elsewhere.

minorities in larger Western societies, and so they have to congregate in order to achieve something. Africans in the diaspora are not always successful in establishing a functioning community, or as in the case of African-Americans, a community that is, in the end, satisfying their hunger for kinship. Thus, many Africans in the diaspora are searching for something that is missing in their lives, i.e., for a concept that connects them to Africa, to others, and even to themselves.

There is an artificial, a man-made connection between Africans of the diaspora and the white societies in which they live and in which they were born and socialized. Africans in the diaspora do not unrestrictedly fit into the categories described by Sollors's *descent* or *consent* culture, for it is neither a hereditary "(by blood or nature)" (Sollors 6) nor "contractual" (Sollors 5) situation that Africans in the diaspora find themselves in; hence, the link to white society in this case is what I call *dissonant* culture. I derive the term not only from the differences between Western societies and African ones, not only from reasons for racism, but from one important aspect mentioned earlier, namely the contrast of Western individualism and African kinship. On the one hand, the result for African-Americans is that slavery has erased the memory of their genealogical African cultures where they originate. Also, most Africans do not want to be reminded of that time and deny a kinship with the descendants of slaves. On the other hand, a number of African-Americans still do not fully feel at home in white America and so America has not really become their consent culture, but rather their dissonant "home." As a consequence, African-Americans find themselves in a middle position between the Western individualism of America,[102] a society that they are part of, and African communalism in the form of a mythical kinship, which is something they are longing for. Thus, African-Americans are searching not only for their descent culture in Africa, but hope to find their consent culture there, too, even though they do have a community in the USA rather than with other Africans in the diaspora. A dilemma arises, however, because Africans of the continent do not consider them kin (anymore).[103]

In comparison, African-Germans have just started to build up a community within the society they live in, which is a dissonant white, individualist culture as well. Moreover, German culture is still more exclusive than American because Americans have learned, over centuries, to integrate others into their society. Thus, African-Germans are beginning to form a

---

[102] An example of American individualism is the preeminence of the American Dream of the self-made man in a capitalist society.

[103] Sollors's terms were used to describe a different context. Although both terms can never fully account for reality and are rather schematic reductions, they can serve to analyze a situation. It is also important to mention that African-Americans and African-Germans do not think in those terms. They simply act on their feelings and longings. One of those longings is the relation to Africa, a kinship, which, however, has been cut off a long time ago and can only exist as a mythical vision.

community, their consent culture, and they are, just like African-Americans, searching for their hereditary culture, their bloodline, which lies outside of the boundaries of Germany. African-Germans are, indeed, looking towards the African diaspora, more precisely to their African counterparts in the USA, rather than to Africa and Africans. This is partly due to the fact that many African-Germans have direct familial bonds to African-Americans. They look to and up to African-Americans as well because of the status African-Americans enjoy in the world, which stems both from the hurtful past and their achievements.[104]

Most African-Americans have fought to be accepted as self-determining subjects over the centuries. They seem to be ahead of African-Germans (or any other group of Africans in the diaspora) when it comes to community-building and a literary tradition. They are on the level with African-Germans, however, when it comes to searching for their roots, although African-Americans have a stronger support system behind them. The search for one's roots is the inevitable fate of dislocated people and/or people who have genealogically mixed backgrounds. African-Americans have (or had) to learn the hard way that the direct connection to Africa was irreversibly cut during slavery. Thus, a kinship that African-Americans might wish for cannot be reestablished. The genealogical descent culture of Africa and Africans themselves are very much in denial about a relation that formerly existed. Although African-Americans respect and have come to function within their dissonant white culture of America, they are in search of their origins, whose contemporary offspring, however, reject them. Apparently, African-Americans have ignored this problem and have turned to superficial relations with Africa and its traditions as well as to romanticizing Africa. The African-American authors at hand, though, additionally underline a more recent development, namely the de-romanticizing of Africa and the acknowledgement of a hybrid African-American identity that moves back and forth between individualism, black community, and a disenchanted notion of a lost African kinship.

African-Germans, first and foremost, step out of their isolation as scattered black individuals in Germany by writing about their lives. This act helps them to come together, to begin to form a community and raise awareness, just as their slave author counterparts did centuries ago. As a second step, which does not take a predominant role as of yet, many African-Germans are also looking for their genealogical background, which is often times, and simply by the fact of direct bonds to America, the African-American community.

At this point, the aspect that is missing becomes clear. Africans in the diaspora share the same fate, namely their dispersal and dislocation as well as their common experience of suffering (Gates, *Signifying* 128). Mostly, African-Americans are descendants of African slaves and most African-Germans are

---

[104] Consequently, African-Americans have earned a special status among Africans in the diaspora due to their background, thus the term "exceptionalism" as promoted by Garvey. However, African-Germans try to not blindly follow their African-American brothers and sisters but to go their own path as well.

descendants of members of the US Army (who in turn mostly stem from descendants of African slaves); however, they all share the same origin: Their forefathers were uprooted and their ancestors (and themselves) endure(d) many wrongdoings within a white, individualist world. Thus, the combination of what Sollors (whose model refers to immigrants in general) calls a consent and a descent culture for all Africans in the world (living in a dissonant society) lies not only in their small, hometown communities, but in the larger African diaspora, which Gilroy depicts as the Black Atlantic. The Black Atlantic, however, is a rather cultural symbol than a mere biological and contractual form of belonging.[105] The slave trade triangle of Africa, Europe, and America acquires a new dimension, namely that of individualism promoted by the West (Europe and America), kinship represented by Africa, and the missing link of an inclusive home, a community, for Africans in the diaspora. Africans in the diaspora are still searching for a solution to their identity difficulties; however, it seems that they are moving closer towards a solution simply by setting in motion the process of finding their roots and clearing their misty-eyed view of their origins (Africa in the case of African-Americans, and the USA for African-Germans).

Continents—fixed stretches of land like fixed identities or paradigms of thinking—cannot be applied to Africans of the diaspora because the continent(s) prove(s) to be foreign and hostile territory. It is the Atlantic, the Black Atlantic, a floating and constantly moving body of water, that has given birth to a folk that does neither belong here nor there. This concept of the Atlantic as a reference for their kinship and the connection between all Africans in the diaspora is true for African-Americans and African-Germans alike. It does not matter whether one's ancestors were of direct African descent and were turned into commodities hundreds of years ago, or whether they were troops during times of war, or if they were other migrants that traveled the Atlantic and made their contribution to the birth of a new folk somewhere else. The difference between contemporary African-Americans and African-Germans is their sense of background and community. African-Germans are still in the process of recovering or creating a background and a community for themselves, whereas African-Americans have already done so due to their long history in America. Now, African-Americans dig deeper in history; they must acknowledge that the diaspora is their home and the place of their kin, not Africa. For African-Germans, it is easier to grasp direct kin in America, but nowadays migrations and the mixing of cultures makes it also difficult to establish strong ties with one's relatives across the sea. In addition, not all former African-American soldiers who have fathered children in occupied Germany want to have much to do with them. Ultimately, African-Germans also have to recognize and accept the fact that the diaspora and the Black Atlantic are their frames of reference, and that although one's genealogical background is important to explore, one

---

[105] See Gilroy's *The Black Atlantic*.

can hardly build up one's life from a cut-off relationship. It is the consent community, rather than family, that makes up for a solid basis. In the following analysis, I want to illuminate the concepts of individual, community, and (mythical) kinship within the pattern of thought introduced above. In order to find differences and similarities between African-American and African-German life writings, I have paired the works for analysis. The decision of how to form the pairs is grounded in patterns that occur in the paired writings and which make their juxtaposition not only fruitful but even necessary. Therefore, *Destined to Witness* by Massaquoi and Obama's *Dreams from My Father* are compared because of their authors' nature as bonding agents between them and their unusual families, communities, and friends. In the works of Usleber and Golden, the authors represent themselves as those Africans in the diaspora who are torn between idolizing the countries of their kin and acknowledging reality. The last pair, Hartman's *Lose Your Mother* and Hügel-Marshall's *Daheim unterwegs*, represents a new era of Africans in the diaspora. They pave the way to overcome old doubts and woes in order to become self-determined individuals within their communities.

5.1.1 Massaquoi and Obama as Bonding Agents

When looking at the works at hand, the comparison of Massaquoi to Obama is not at all obvious. However, there are remarkable similarities and differences that make a comparison plausible. First of all, in their early years, they were in very different yet at the same time very similar situations. Both have white mothers from the majority society they live in. Both lack a father figure, or at least they do not have contact with their biological father, who is in both cases from Africa. Whereas Obama grows up in sheltered environments in Hawaii and Indonesia in the sixties, Massaquoi, after having moved out of the consulate, lives in life-threatening danger in Nazi Germany. Obama's white family in Hawaii and the multicultural environment on the island do not really challenge Obama's life, or rather his life style. When his mother remarries an Indonesian man, they move to Jakarta, where Obama does not face racial problems in the beginning and his stepfather supports him in general. Soon, however, as a young boy in Indonesia, he becomes aware of the fact of the absence of his African father and of racial differences. Both Massaquoi and Obama, even though facing different outlooks, live a more or less secluded life. They do not have many friends or a community to back them up; in Obama's early life he is not in need of a strong support system, whereas Massaquoi lives in constant danger and would benefit from such a system.

Both learn to defend and protect themselves as individuals, because both have an exotic status wherever they live. Massaquoi lives as a "shame" to the Aryan race, as a *Neger* and *Mischling* in Nazi Germany, and barely survives. He does not know any other African-Germans and in order to guard himself he joins a boxing club. At the "Bramfeld Boxing Club" (139) racial views still dominate, yet in a positive sense because his teammates and his coach see Massaquoi's boxing talent as his "'natural ability'" as a person of African descent (137). Massaquoi feels safer as a trained boxer and everyone around him sees him as the new Joe Louis, so his "prestige soared to an all-time high" (137). Also, he is a member of the boxing team and no one has a problem with his skin color. Massaquoi is not only tolerated, but even respected and wanted in the club. First, it is striking that his life at the boxing club "was strangely detached from the Nazi politics that seemed to pervade everything else. It was an apolitical island in a sea of rabid Hitlerism" (139). Second, his race and the absence of his biological father make it necessary for Massaquoi to join the boxing club; however, Massaquoi agrees with the views of the others and is proud that he most apparently inherited the physical strength and talent from his absent African father (139). At this point, an African-American boxer becomes an idol for an African-German boy, and it becomes clear that their African heritage lies at the core of it. Massaquoi claims that "[he] hadn't enjoyed that feeling of pride in [his] African ancestry since [his] grandfather left Germany six years earlier" (116). When Obama is a young boy living in Indonesia, an older boy from down the road bullies him and they have a fight. After this incident, his stepfather Lolo decides to teach Obama how to box, and "when he came home from work the next day, he had with him two pairs of boxing gloves" (36). Whereas Massaquoi does not have any father figure who teaches him, Obama does not have to fend for himself. Without big families to support them and while living on foreign or hostile ground, both Massaquoi and Obama learn to fight for themselves, even though one of them fights for his life while the other one fights bullying.

The idol status of African-Americans becomes a tool of survival for a lonely African-German in Nazi Germany. What is striking is that Massaquoi feels a much greater connection to the USA than to Africa, where both his father and beloved grandfather originate from. During the Olympic Games, Massaquoi knows exactly who he favors:

> I never was torn by conflicting loyalties between the black Olympic athletes and the athletes of my motherland. From the very beginning of the games it was clear to me that the black athletes' victories were my victories, that their defeats were my defeats. I immediately felt a surge of pride over the very special kinship that linked me with these men from America [. . .]. (122)

Although Massaquoi has no direct ties to African-Americans, he feels very early on in his life the special bond of Africans in the diaspora, and to stress this importance he uses the term *kinship*. Whether this connection was as clear to him at that time, as he portrays in his book, is left open for discussion; however, the fact that he depicts the situation as such paves the way for his identity formation towards becoming an African-American, i.e., he performs the construction of his membership in the African-American community. After the war, African-Americans are among the liberators, the people who ended the war and Massaquoi's sufferings. They have become (his) heroes. Whereas before, Massaquoi never saw one other black person, now he sees his heroes everywhere. He envisions his future in the USA rather than in Africa for two reasons: one, there are many African-Americans living in America and two, they live in a Western society, which is what Massaquoi is used to.

It is Obama's mother who decides for him that he has to move back to America, that "the life chances of an American" are better than those of an Indonesian, that Obama is indeed American, "and that his true life lay elsewhere" (Obama 47). By contrast, Massaquoi *chooses* to become an American because he thinks that the USA, with its large African-American community, is where he belongs. Both Obama and Massaquoi do not belong to this community *per definitionem* due to their "other" backgrounds of direct ties to Africa and their upbringing.[106] For the first decades of their lives they have had to fend for themselves. They now see that it is paramount to establish one's place in the world by finding a community of like-looking and like-minded people, because they are unable to claim a descent culture of kinship to their African branch of family. They acknowledge that this community of hybrid persons and hyphenated identities is where they can find some solace. However, both still have to pay their dues in order to become members in the African-American community. Before, during their adolescent years, both try to find groups to become a member of. For Obama it was still easier than for Massaquoi, who was the only African-German near and far.

Nevertheless, Massaquoi, after having been excluded from the Hitler Youth and expelled from the boxing club, becomes a member of the Hamburg swing movement. Again, a clear link to the African-American community becomes visible, for the swing-boys listen to jazz music, which the Nazis banned as *Negermusik* (159). The precursors of jazz music among African slaves in the colonial period "became a tactic for survival, a vent for frustration, and a reclamation of the body" (Lemke 60). Jazz music as a cultural heritage of Massaquoi's African roots, and of the African diaspora, comes to his aid at a difficult time in his life. The hybridity of jazz due to its African and Western components, and its ever-changing character, render the music and its swing-boy community a place where Massaquoi can be himself and belong, just as the precursors of jazz were for African slaves a long time ago. In addition, it is a tool of resistance against the Nazis for all group members. More and more, it becomes clear that Massaquoi, even though he is the offspring of a German mother and a Liberian father, sees his kinship in the African-American community rather than in his direct relation to Germans or Liberians/Africans.Massaquoi juxtaposes terms such as "countrymen" (253) for fellow Germans, and "brother" (239) or "kinship" (122; 240) for African-

---

[106] Massaquoi was brought up in Germany and Obama was brought up in Hawaii (which is part of the USA although not continental America) and Indonesia.

Americans or Jews with whom he either wants to connect, or with whom he inevitably sits in the same boat.[107] As a consequence, even though his fellow German citizens are part of his own genealogy, his descent culture on his mother's side, he actively chooses to become part of another community in which he sees more similarities and affinities. Hence, he wants to be part of collective groups such as the Jews. In the long run, he hopes to be "adopted" by African-Americans. When the Allies arrive in Hamburg, Massaquoi is "struck by the sentimental notion to leave Germany and to get to know '[his] people' in the United States" (271). He is fed up being the center of attention and being isolated as a black drop within a sea of whites. His American Dream is born when he decides that one day he will join his consent culture of the African-Americans in America. He even invents a story of having direct family bonds with African-Americans whenever he meets others. Donald, an African-American soldier he meets, does Massaquoi a favor by always introducing himself as Massaquoi's "cousin from Chicago" (317). In addition, Massaquoi calls himself "Mickey," which sounds more American. The relationship to African-Americans, if only in parts imaginary and tentative, has been established.

When Obama's mother sends him back to Hawaii after four years (1967-71) in Indonesia, she hopes that Obama will grow up a self-confident American. She thinks he will not have to face any difficulties there because "the legend was made of Hawaii as the one true melting pot, an experiment in racial history" (24). Reality is different when Obama's teacher articulates his name in front of the class and everyone starts to laugh (59-60). Later on that first day, a girl even wants to touch Obama's hair (60), which starkly resembles the experience of Massaquoi at school (Massaquoi 37). Obama feels that he "didn't belong" (60), and this feeling continues to grow and complicate his life.[108] The story makes a leap in time to his high school years, when Ray becomes his friend and introduces Obama to black life on the island (72-91). Also, the language of the story changes to black vernacular, which underlines the beginning of Obama's transformation into an African-American teenager (73). Obama has found a community, however small, of African-Americans on the island. As a teenager, it is normal to struggle with issues of identity. As a black person in a society dominated by whites, the issues become bigger and so Obama sees that "things had gotten complicated" (74) and soon he "was engaged in a fitful interior

---

[107] In addition, Massaquoi finds true friends in the Jewish brothers Ralph and Egon Giordano:
> As long as I could remember, I had always had to face the Nazi menace alone. [. . .] Now, for the first time in my life, I had found a true brother, someone who knew from his own experience the terror of being regarded as a subhuman enemy [. . .]. All of a sudden I felt a strong kinship with Egon [. . .]. (239-40)

[108] When his father visits over Christmas that year, Obama is entirely confused (64-71).

struggle. [He] was trying to raise [himself] to be a black man in America" (76). One important aspect to mention is that Obama, here and elsewhere, often prefers the denomination *black* American instead of African-American. In the introduction, he claims that the book turned out "a record of a personal, interior journey—a boy's search for his father, and through that search a workable meaning for his life as a black American" (xvi). This observation of his in-betweenness, meaning his status as the offspring of a white American mother and a black African father, and the way he defines himself as a black person emphasize his idea of identity and belonging. Obama is the bonding agent between black and white, America and Africa. Due to his background that has, at least directly, not much in common with other African-Americans and their slave past, he consciously utilizes the more inclusive term *black*. This term also includes other people of a mixed background, namely all the descendants of the Black Atlantic, but it is not restricted to the Middle Passage.

The school's basketball team becomes Obama's new community, just as the swingboy movement and later the African-American troops in Germany become a haven for Massaquoi. "At least on the basketball court could I find a community of sorts, with an inner life all its own. [. . .] [There] blackness couldn't be a disadvantage" (80). In comparison, for Massaquoi being a black person was certainly an advantage to participate in the swingboy movement. However, Obama describes how badly he is torn between the love for and loyalty to his white mother and relatives, and the hatred towards whites in general that he has learned from his black friends (80). It is a tension which arises from his *consent* community culture, his *descent* origin from a white mother, and living in a *dissonant* white society. As a consequence, Obama

> learn[s] to slip back and forth between [his] black and white worlds, understanding that each possessed its own language and customs and structures of meaning, convinced that with a bit of translation on [his] part the two worlds would eventually cohere. (82)

The process of harmoniously synthesizing his identities and worlds would take some time and effort, for instance his search for his African roots in Kenya. The African-American community that he has found is a must-have basis, a support system that provides a feeling of belonging in order to go out and explore one's opposing genealogies. However, Obama first has to prove himself a worthy member of the African-American community. The first step he takes is at college, when he becomes "hungry for words" (105) and gets involved in the so-called divestment campaign that organizes a rally. The circumstances are reminiscent of former slaves beginning to speak up, but even more clearly of contemporary African-Germans who also find their voices and form a community. Obama later takes the second step of becoming a full member in the African-American community when he chooses to be a community organizer in Chicago.

Massaquoi, after his initial attempts at an identity transformation, from being an African-German and becoming an African-American, enters American society at the time of the Civil Rights Movement. Hence, he becomes an active member thereof, personally and professionally as a journalist, and fights for the rights of African-Americans—and himself. This, obviously, earns him the respect of African-Americans and the membership to their community. By comparison, Obama faces a difficult challenge as a community organizer in an urban, still visibly segregated, Chicago but his efforts are welcome and so he enters the community while fighting for and with them. Obama acknowledges in hindsight that his past, background, and experiences influenced his decision of becoming a community organizer: "I can see that my choices were never truly mine alone" (134). The community he wants to work for first had to be built up, for "communities have never been a given in this country, at least not for blacks. Communities had to be created, fought for, tended like gardens," and Obama wants to make the garden flourish (134). Both authors went through early "apprenticeships" in order to foster the African-American collective. Massaquoi found true "kin" in Egon and Ralph Giordano, in his African-American soldier friends who taught him how to behave, talk, and eat like an African-American, in the swingboys, in Werner, and so forth. It is, of course, an elected form of kinship—not a biological one. Obama joined the small African-American community in Hawaii, the basketball team, and later on went to college in L.A. and became an orator and activist for the black cause. The two authors started out as "atypical" African-Americans. They went through a process from a lonely, individual battle against an individualistic but majority society to communal belonging. They fought and still fight for black rights together with their chosen, i.e., consent community, which is responsible for part of their healing process, namely the connecting of the seemingly opposing components of their identities. The success of their professional lives as well as the literary achievements render them, on the one hand, idols for their community, but on the other hand, they are also the result of a Western world: they have become self-made men.

One cannot neglect Obama's and Massaquoi's ties with and travels to their fathers' countries in Africa when considering the success of settling their identity dilemma. Many African-Americans who start to think about their ancestors and maybe even travel to the African continent imagine a noble history of their family lineage. As Hartman and others disclose, this romantic notion of Africa, this longing for a dignified rather than a shameful past is, in most cases, mere wishful thinking and does not contribute to the resolution of identity crises. The ancestors of the first African-Americans were for the most part commoners and socially low-ranking tribe members, sold by their own kin and by whites. It is not surprising then that Obama's grandfather shares Obama's hope of a noble ancestry on his father's side when he informs tourists that Obama is the "great-grandson of King Kamehameha, Hawaii's first monarch" (25). When thinking about his father, Obama becomes interested in his own past and tells his classmates the lie that his "father was a prince" and his grandfather a chief (63). He makes up an interesting story and "a part of [him] really began to believe the story" (63). Obama tries to find out more about his father and "had visions of ancient Egypt, the great kingdoms [he] had read about, pyramids and pharaohs, Nefertiti and Cleopatra" (64). When he discovers that his father's tribe consists of nomads raising cattle, his disappointment runs deep. Massaquoi, on the other hand, actually has an African family consisting of nobles. His grandfather, Momolu Massaquoi, was the "hereditary ruler of the indigenous Vai nation" in Liberia and had been King Momolu IV for ten years prior to his departure to Germany as Consul General (3). Obama's and Massaquoi's backgrounds differ from the "typical" African-American one insofar as their fathers were from Africa and did not have direct links to slavery, and even Massaquoi's father was the offspring of a real African king. The shared experience of racism and suffering in the New World from the slave past is not part of their experience because, even though a rupture also exists between them and their African parent, they at least get to know parts of their African history and family. However, Obama and Massaquoi go to great lengths to prove that black people in general need a community, so they earn their membership to the African-American community.

After World War II Massaquoi is actually in the position to choose whether he wants to make Africa his home. He lives in Liberia for two years and gets to appreciate living in a country where his skin color is like everyone else's. "In addition to the many exotic sights that helped convince me that I had finally succeeded in getting out of Germany, a pervasive sweet smell of tropical vegetation heightened my sense of being a long way from what used to be home" (341). In addition to viewing Africa as an exotic country, due to his German and Western upbringing, he has to face the fact that this country and its people do not feel a real kinship to him either. After tasting very spicy food at his father's house and almost suffocating from it, his own father says, "For a moment I had forgotten that my son is a European and not an African" (347), an issue which will remain the core problem during Massaquoi's stay in Liberia. There, Massaquoi is not fully accepted in society, just as in Germany, because of his mixed racial background. In Germany he was the black man and in Africa he is viewed as the white man (389), just as Obama gets the "white man's price" in a market in Kenya (Obama 310). Even though Massaquoi himself overcomes his prejudices vis-à-vis Africans when visiting *his* Vai tribe (358) and comes to appreciate African life-style and tradition, there are too many reasons that force him to follow up on his American Dream. One reason is the prevailing stereotypes, such as those that Hartman describes and experiences, (e.g., 215). Massaquoi tells the reader that his father has a very low opinion of "'American Negroes'" (358) because his father thinks that African-Americans look down on Africans. But what is behind this hatred is that the existence of African-Americans reminds Africans of the dark chapter of slavery in their own history. What is all the more disturbing to Africans is that they believe that African-

Americans now lead a much better life than Africans themselves. Another important reason for Massaquoi to opt against staying in Africa is that he encounters African-style racism and becomes disillusioned with finding a stable African identity in Africa. Massaquoi was born in Germany but was never considered German. He gained a Liberian passport and lived in Liberia, but still did not belong there either. Thus, he retraces the former slave route to Africa and then to the New World, the USA, in order to make a life at a place of his own choosing, and he is successful. He has to cross the Atlantic (in direction of America) that his forefather crossed in the past (in direction of Europe), and his crossing had a great effect, namely Massaquoi's birth. Massaquoi's appreciation for Africa and his heritage is one component of his success in America, for he has tried to live in the country of his father and has made peace with his mixed identity. Through his travels to Africa and later on to Germany, he comes full circle with his life and identity struggles, and moreover, is successful in establishing a link between Africans in the diaspora, birthed but also separated by the Black Atlantic.

Obama was born in Hawaii, lived in Indonesia, Hawaii, and the continental USA and only later on in his life travels to Africa, to get to know his family there. His job as an organizer sparks his deeper interest and so he actually undertakes the journey with an "uneasy status: a Westerner not entirely at home in the West, an African on his way to a land full of strangers" (301). What he finds in Africa is a huge family embracing his arrival. His former notion of family and belonging implodes. "For family seemed to be everywhere" (328). "It conformed to my idea of Africa and Africans, an obvious contrast to the growing isolation of American life, a contrast I understood, not in racial, but in cultural terms" (328-29). Obama at this point juxtaposes Western individualism and isolation to African communalism, tribalism, and kinship. The difference between Africans in Africa and in the diaspora is that the latter do not have a natural circle of kin. Africans in the diaspora have built their communities on shared experiences, whereas in Africa, a community is based on strong family ties.

Obama and Massaquoi, though, by acknowledging this fact, and by their backgrounds and consent communities, become bonding agents between lost families and newfound homes, between left-behind identities and newly created ones. After having explored both sides of their genealogies, and due to their absent direct connection to slavery, they can put aside the question of the color of their skin and their kinship to Africa, and instead, focus on their chosen community. Their development trajectory of getting to know their roots shows, however, that this process of searching and of acknowledging the importance of the Black Atlantic, even if only unconsciously, is existential. It is the process to find one's inner home within a consent culture like the African-American community. Their achievements can be seen as a paradigm, as hope for a happy end to unsettled hybrid identities, for they both find a balance between their opposing genealogies, individualism, tribalism, and communalism. It is impossible to choose one's family, but one can choose friends, and friends can substitute family. Obama and Massaquoi show that it is important to know one's heritage, one's kin; but it is all the more important to define one's consent relations and for Africans in the diaspora this relation is grounded in their shared dislocation. Thus, they have to build their own form of kinship on the basis of the abstract concept of the Black Atlantic. For Obama and Massaquoi, the African-American community provides this kinship, but they have defined themselves by their search for roots via the African diaspora as come forth by the Black Atlantic.

5.1.2 Idolization and Realism in Usleber and Golden

Golden's autobiography can easily be compared to Massaquoi's because the storylines share many similar incidents. For instance, when the authors travel to and live in Africa, they each try out African food and have similar reactions; they each describe Africa as exotic when they arrive; they each have domestic servants; and they each begin to weave in more and more African terms into their writing. Golden and Massaquoi stay longer in Africa than the other authors and try to make it work before finally leaving. Golden and Hartman also have similar issues that they discuss,[109] but while Golden goes through a number of stages of idolizing Africa and gradually grows out of this romantic vision in favor of a more realistic picture, Hartman begins her journey and investigation from a more advanced level of realism. However, the aspect most prominent and worth analyzing is Golden's view of Africa as the place of a kinship she always longed for and as the only place where she believes she can become whole. Her idolization of Africa mirrors a general perception held by her African-American contemporaries. After Golden has passed that stage of a blurred vision of Africa, she comes to understand that others have not yet made this progress: "But very few blacks were interested in my tales of Africa. They had all taken two-week trips to Ghana or Senegal and preferred their surface impressions to my intimate knowledge" (223). Golden publishes her autobiography in 1983, which is after the decade that many African-Americans took advantage of heritage trips to Africa in order to be redeemed. Apparently, African-Americans want to keep and cherish both this romantic version of their experience and their wishful thinking of a glorious past, believing that Africans do embrace them as their lost brothers and sisters.

The decision to compare Golden to Usleber originates from their determination to go out and find their *Heimat*, to even cut their relationships with their families in order to find new "families." Both authors have a very strong will to be successful and happy any way, *trotzdem*, and after passing through the stage of romanticizing their dreams and the countries of their dreams, they arrive at a point of being able to accept themselves as who they

---

[109] One example of issues both authors deal with are the screams of former slaves they are hearing and not hearing in the dungeons (Golden 74 and Hartman 116).

are. Their journeys of looking for a community and being torn between individual struggles and kinships are reflected in both tables of contents. In Usleber, a recurring motif is that of *Heimat*. The first chapter is called "Keine Heimat," where he describes that he does not belong to Germany, where he was born. One of the chapters in the middle has the title "Aufbau einer Heimat," which begins to chronicle how Usleber builds up a life, a home, and a community of friends for himself. The second to last chapter, "Die Menschen, die meine Heimat sind," is an acknowledgement of the people in his life who have become his home, his community, and his chosen kin. Golden depicts the process of finding her home by splitting up her life writing into three main parts: "I. Beginnings," "II. Journeys," and "III. Coming Home," which already hints at a sort of closure, since the magical number of three (chapters)—a beginning, a middle, and an end—is symbolic for coming full circle. Golden and Usleber come to similar conclusions, namely that home, the chosen community, is not a place like Africa or the USA, nor is it one's kin, i.e., one's genealogy; instead, it is something that you have to form and find yourself. Usleber claims at the very beginning, "Ich hatte keine Heimat" and that the term *Heimat* itself is "inhaltsleer" (11). This statement suggests that you have to go out and fill this term with meaning, your own meaning as an African in the diaspora. "Wenn ich mich jetzt auf den Weg mache, die wirkliche Heimat zu suchen, so muss ich an Menschen denken, nicht an Orte" (14). Golden's answer to the question of home is connected to the one of identity, i.e., it is always changing. "I had wandered. Will wander still . . . and will take home with me wherever I go" (234). Apart from people, her home is an inner point of reference, the "bedrock inside [herself]" (234). Due to the different circumstances of African-Americans and African-Germans, it is not surprising that African-Americans seem to have reached a step further, namely to have found a community that supports them. For African-Germans, it is still the premier goal to find *people*, a community, which then provides for a comfortable path to becoming self-confident. African-Americans are born into a community of African-Americans, even though this community had to be built up a long time ago and always needs refashioning. To be born into an existing community is an advantage, and a great difference between these two groups of the diaspora. The process of how to get to some sort of satisfaction, calmness, and acceptance is similar for Golden and Usleber. They are looking for idols and blueprints throughout their lives, for some form of guidance that will navigate them through their identity dilemmas and search for a community of consent and descent kin. What they learn from following their itineraries is that a home lies in a more stable self among friends within one's community.

Whereas Golden is born into the African-American community, a larger group of like-looking and like-minded people that already exists, Usleber is born into a mainly white and in his experience hostile society; he has to fend for himself. Even though in Germany there live "viele von Geburt an Deutsche mit einer dunklen Hautfarbe," they are not accepted as "gleichwertig" in their own country (9). Thus, African-Germans are scattered about the country and are, by birth, Germans with a German passport, yet they still feel they do not fully belong. They experience an unequal treatment in what they perceive as a racist, individualist society.[110] Usleber's description of African-German life stresses the importance for African-Germans to come together and fight for their equality. As Usleber states, even possessing a German passport does not amount to anything in daily life.

> Ein deutscher Pass hat zwar einen großen rechtlichen Stellenwert, im Alltagsleben jedoch überhaupt keine Bedeutung. Viel zu viele Deutsche machen die Akzeptanz eines Deutscher [sic] an vier Merkmalen fest: Aussehen, Sprache, Name, Stellung. (32)

Usleber seems to have a clear and realistic view of racism in Germany. At times this view is also pessimistic. "Wir alle müssen jedoch damit leben, dass es diese Gleichheit nie gegeben hat, nicht gibt und auch nie geben wird" (51). More than once in his book does he proclaim an individual fight; however, he sees later on that he is looking for more justice and equality and even though he tries to convince himself that it does not exist, he nevertheless searches and fights for it (115; 120).

For Golden as well as for Usleber there are certain impulses that trigger their wish for a better future by way of finding a community *of kin*. Usleber has been in the "'Out-Group'" all his life and what he lacks are other "Leidensgenossen" (22), whatever the social hierarchy or whatever fights he has to outlast. Soon, he no longer considers himself German (29). As a result, he is isolated on both sides, from his German family and countrymen and from his African-American family. He has created a vision of finding his place in the USA, and after having met his father shortly, his wish of immigrating to the USA is born[111] (31). There are two experiences that initiate Golden's wish to go to Africa and explore her forefathers' homeland. Her fantasy and interest are sparked by the stories of Cleopatra, Hannibal, and the Sphinx that her father tells her when she is a young girl (4). It is these glorious stories that many African-Americans are hoping to trace when going to Africa, namely the search for a noble past in order to make up for the horrible history of enslavement and oppression. The other event is the assassination of Martin Luther King, Jr. (13-14). After this incident, adolescent Golden begins to embrace Black Power and the notion of Africa as the solution to her problems. It seems as if the African-American community itself no longer suffices as the backdrop to her identity

---

[110] This view is the African-German authors' perspective, which is subjective and dichotomous for the generalization that all Germans are racists cannot be maintained; it is rather a minority of Germans who discriminate against foreign-looking people.

[111] However, he later claims that leaving Germany would amount to a failure in achieving his goals and that he believes that God placed him in Germany for a reason (101); thus he stays.

formation. The communal breakdown caused by the assassination pushes Golden to more radical measures to shape not only herself, but the African-American and mainstream American community as well. But stable history, tradition, and descent cultures are still hidden away on the other side of the ocean, not only for Golden but also for Usleber.

Hartman depicts slavery times as to *lose your mother*, as literally and figuratively having to leave the African continent. In addition, for contemporary Africans in the diaspora, identity issues are also evoked most often by the fact of lacking a father figure, i.e., *to lose your father*. As with all three African-German life writings and Obama's as well, Golden and Usleber lack a reliable father figure for the most part of their lives. Both authors take similar paths in order to come closer to their fathers (or forefathers) and to form a stronger identity. They look for idols and blueprints. Usleber, before getting to know his father, fills his absence with musical lyrics, especially from singers from the African diaspora such as Stevie Wonder and Bob Marley. He idolizes them and uses many quotations throughout the book to make sense of his own life and to follow their example, for his absent father cannot function as a model. He relates that this specific "Musik half mir, eine Identität zu finden" (44), and music becomes his implicit and notional ersatz for a community. He continues,

> Und so wie die Afrikaner, die vor Hunderten von Jahren gewaltsam aus ihrer Heimat entführt wurden und nach Amerika gebracht wurden, dort die Spirituals und Gospels erfanden—Lieder, die von der Unterdrückung des Volkes Israel in Ägypten handelten, aber ihre eigene Unterdrückung in der Sklaverei meinten—,so halfen mir die Lieder von Bob Marley und Stevie Wonder, die von der Unterdrückung der Afroamerikaner in den USA erzählten, meine Situation in Deutschland zu identifizieren. (44-45)

Usleber looks across the ocean to the achievements and struggles of African-Americans and is fascinated by their strength and accomplishments. He longs for what they have built up, a community and a subculture that African-Germans can only dream of. Thus, Usleber makes up for a nonexistent father figure by supplementing his individual struggle by learning from his contemporary (music) idols in the USA, who have evolved a tradition of music over the centuries. The antebellum African-American music tradition relied on an allegorical interpretation of the Old Testament to deal with oppression under slavery, and similarly, Usleber interprets twentieth-century civil strife in America allegorically as his own situation in Germany. Thus, Usleber takes on a blueprint of a blueprint.

The relationship between Golden and her father deteriorates after her parents separate; not too long afterwards, her father dies. Throughout her work, Golden never portrays her father as a very strong character, unlike her mother, who dies middle-aged. Golden grows up in turbulent times in America and due to the lack of a father (and later a mother) she first finds some guidance in the Black Power movement. As a student, the New York Nigerian community offers her even greater solace and hope, and she falls in love with a Nigerian man. He is very strong-willed and Golden subdues herself in deference to him more and more. He becomes her lover and husband and fills the gap of two major yearnings: a strong male presence in her life, as well as a longing for her African roots in order to find out who she is and to reconnect with her African kin. From the very beginning she is drawn to his exoticism and strength and idolizes him. "'Tell me everything about Nigeria. Then tell me everything about you'" (50). Her love life becomes entangled with her search for her kin in Africa, and she states that she "read about [her] past and now it sat across from [her]" (51); soon, she would live in Nigeria in search of her connection to Africa and her future self. Thus, while musical lyrics and the culture of African-Americans open up a new path for Usleber, it is this African man, Femi Ajayi, who paves the way for Golden's romanticism of Africa and her painful coming of age. Golden and Usleber exemplify how Africans in the diaspora oftentimes idolize Africans or African-Americans, and how they dream of the homeland and culture of their fathers and forefathers. Usleber and Golden, among others, believe that by going to Africa or America and becoming part of those cultures and communities, the wounds that their African (-American) heritage and the white dissonant culture have caused can be healed.

The progression from sentimentalism to realism is a long and painful but necessary course of growth for Usleber and Golden. It supports their coming of age as individual Africans in the diaspora, and by trial and error, shows them who their kin are. Golden follows Femi Ajayi to Nigeria, where they live.

> Among theses Nigerians I had found a haven. The turbulent waters of my recent past had washed me ashore. Here I would find peace. Here I would find love. [. . .] Eagerly I strained to understand and meld into a community grounded in a sense of family and connectedness—the ethic that would heal my wounds. (58)

Though written in hindsight, Golden hopes to find salvation in the future while living in Nigeria, which is depicted by the term "would;" however, at the point of writing she knows that she will fail in reconnecting with "Mother Africa," her descent kin. Even though she experiences many backlashes and difficult, almost insurmountable problems, she does hold fast to her dream of belonging to one extended African family, her kin, and in that sense of belonging finding true love and happiness. The metaphor of the turbulent waters associates her journey with that of the former slave trade on the Atlantic. This metaphor supports my notion that Africans of the diaspora can only find peace and their "true" kin by turning towards the community which they are part of now and to the place that gave birth to them: the Black Atlantic. Their consent *and* descent kin are all the other Africans in the diaspora, not Africans from the continent or African-

Americans from the USA. Kinship then becomes a more cultural, a symbolic rather than a biological manifestation. Nevertheless, Africans of the diaspora are traveling to the shores that frame the Atlantic in order to have a firm ground under their feet. They want to stay steady after a life of instability and not to keep floating adrift on the sea, as would be the case if their destination were the Atlantic itself. What they oftentimes find is not what they are looking for, which is a stable self in a stable, homogenous community of family ties. Golden, unconsciously feels that her journey will not provide her with what she wishes for when looking out to the Atlantic, namely full African kinship. "The sea smashed against the shoreline, tortured and angry, matching the emotions I felt inside" (75). Thus, the sea, represents all the uprooted Africans of the diaspora, who have been traveling from one shore to the other and have not found a place of belonging on either continent. They "smash against" the African shoreline because Africa is unwilling to accept them as "real" kin, as family; African-Americans like Golden are tortured and become angry, which is how she feels then.

Regardless of her disappointments and subliminal emotions, Golden unflinchingly works at making her dream of love and a life in Nigeria as part of this African family come true. She even fools herself into believing in this illusion she has built up for herself. She continues to draw an idealized picture of Africa. "The black faces I had seen became a reflection. [. . .] And each face echoed my father's stories. Told me they were real" (73). This quotation emphasizes the notion of Africa as one big family of blacks, especially of blacks with a noble history, neglecting the fact of tribal wars and the truth about the slave past. And so Golden, just like many other African-Americans, "psychologically leapt past cotton fields and auction blocks back to the empires of Timbuktu and Mali, village life, Swahili, noble kings and tribal tongues" (65). However, Golden finds out that life in Nigeria has very little to do with this picture but nevertheless wants to keep up appearances. To become part of this community, she has to give up her Western ideas of individual rights and love. She must love not only Femi but his entire family and also share everything with them; individual love and achievement are subordinated to the supreme law of communal or familial love and well-being (53; 142). Although Golden embraces this overarching sense of community and togetherness, she sees that there are things that are difficult to accept for a modern Western woman like herself.

There are several incidents that initiate a realization process in Golden. When she is pregnant for the first time and sees the happiness on Femi's face, she realizes that "if she could not give him a child he could never imagine a way to love her" (151). However, she still is a woman and an individual and wants to be loved for her own sake. Soon afterwards, she loses the baby and Femi blames her. As a consequence, family ties cut deeply when Femi tells Golden he has to pay more to the family because they do not have a baby (177). Further, women are not considered as autonomous individuals and are expected instead to cater to the needs of the family and the greater community (176). In addition to sexism, she also encounters the negative side of tribalism and sees the downside of Nigeria. Early on, she has a conversation with an American who tells her that tribalism is "as bad as racism at home. And it's in everything they do, think, feel" (76). In fact, later on, Femi is denied a job due to his tribal background (116), and thus Golden experiences tribalism directly. Femi's vocational failures contribute to the strained financial situation that surely aggravates their marital problems. Consequently, life in Nigeria more and more turns into a nightmare for Golden, who sees that sexism and racism are as present in Africa as in the USA and that life can become unbearable if the cultural circumstances straightjacket a modern woman like her. She has to admit to herself that even though she has given her best to adapt and fit in, she has failed. There are irreconcilable differences between her socialization and concepts of love and respect and those of a Nigerian man. The romantic vision of Africa has come crumbling down and when Femi beats her for the first time, she knows it is time to go back to the USA. Despite her disappointments, she does achieve one of her goals, which had been to no longer be the "Negro girl;" she comes back to America as a black woman (20). She has searched for a home, a deeper form of community, represented as such by African kinship, and has found out that neither a specific place nor her African ancestors or their offspring can provide her with a feeling of belonging. She finally comes to the conclusion that home is an inner point of reference; she has found home in herself (234).

In Usleber, there is a non-linear movement rather than a clear progression from sentimental notions of the USA to a realistic picture. Usleber's written performance provides for a seesaw impression, which is rooted in his still unruly personality. In addition, Usleber finds himself still very close to the bad experiences of the past. "All das Erzählte liegt noch nicht weit zurück, und ich bin immer noch damit beschäftigt, es zu realisieren und einzuordnen" (134). One of those things recounted ("All das Erzählte") is his trip to America and meeting the American part of his family. Traveling to the USA as a heritage tourist, but as a tourist nonetheless, does not uncover all of the unwelcome details of a country that Usleber had begun to glorify from an early age onwards.[112] As a child, he listens to African-American music and reads African-American literature and is enthralled by these stories and accomplishments. When visiting his family in the USA, he learns about the African-American culture and is awestruck.

> Mir schien, als ob sich die Schwarzen in den USA wie eine große Familie fühlen. Sie hören "ihre" Musik, also die Soul-, Jazz- oder HipHop-Songs der schwarzen Künstler und schwärmen von ihren Sportlern, den Williams-Schwestern oder Michael Jordan, lesen

---

[112] Here, Usleber's trip resembles that of many African-Americans who travel to Africa in search of their roots. Unwelcome facts seem to be easily ignored by heritage tourists.

gerne Literatur von schwarzen Autoren oder sehen sich "Oprah Winfrey" im Fernsehen an. (132)

Strikingly, African-Americans, as has been shown, do look for their former, even more extensive, family in Africa because, even though African-Americans have come together as one big family and community in America, they feel the urge to find their roots.[113] Usleber's first-degree roots lie in America, so he considers the African-American community, with its established and comparably large subculture, as his kin. Just like African-Americans traveling to Africa, Usleber is enthralled by their sense of togetherness and cultural heritage. His romantic hopes for a home and a feeling of equality and belonging seem to come true.

A common prejudice that other peoples have towards American, and consequently African-American, friendliness is that Americans do not mean it and that they are superficial (131-32). Usleber's very subjective experience with his own American family prompts him to generalize their forthright kindness and hospitality, and he hopes to falsify the European assumption of American superficiality. "Das amerikanische Verständnis von Freundschaft wird in Deutschland oft als 'oberflächlich' bezeichnet. Ich kann dem nicht beipflichten" (131). He adds, "wird von vielen Deutschen behauptet, die Amerikaner würden ihre Worte nicht so ernst nehmen, sie wären oft nur so dahingesagt. [. . .] Die Menschen aus meiner Familie haben sich als alles andere als oberflächlich erwiesen" (132). His new feeling of belonging and the view of looking into so many black faces in America give Usleber a new sense of confidence. He cannot but romanticize the USA and his African-American family and community.

However, there are specific points in the work where he does not see things through rose-colored glasses but is aware of the fact that the USA is not a country without problems. Through his reading and studies, Usleber knows that racism is still a big issue in America. He says, "man sehe nur auf die Diskriminierungen, die Schwarze in den Vereinigten Staaten ertragen, einem Land, das keiner der dort Lebenden (mit Ausnahme vielleicht der Ureinwohner) als 'sein Land' bezeichnen kann" (61). Even though Usleber enjoys his new experiences in America, he is aware of still existing problems. The trip to the USA itself, however, supports his identity development since he gets to know that part of his genealogical background that was obscure to him before. More than once in the work he claims that you have to accept yourself before accepting others but in order to accept yourself you have to know who you are and where you stand (46). Therefore, the "pilgrimage" to the place of one's kin and roots, even if it does not heal the wounds completely, is a necessary step towards a realistic picture of oneself and an acceptance of one's identity and place in society. As has become apparent, this is true for Usleber as well as for

---

[113] Certainly, there is a vast array of backgrounds among African-Americans, some of which are not all directly linked to Africa but rather to the Caribbean, Middle and South America, and other places.

Golden. Consequently, even though Usleber sees many advantages in the African-American community, he realizes that no matter where you go and what communities you belong to you have to accept yourself and live your own life:

> Ich glaube inzwischen, dass ich hierhin gehöre und hier meine Aufgabe zu erfüllen habe. Deutschland zu verlassen, würde für mich im Moment bedeuten, dass ich einige meiner Ziele, die ich mir gesteckt habe, nicht erreichen könnte. Dafür bin ich jedoch zu hartnäckig; ich möchte es hier schaffen! (101)

Usleber and Golden go through similar but very different odysseys, yet they arrive at a very analogous finish line: racism exists wherever you go and you cannot choose any kin as you like but have to find peace within yourself. A community of sorts is important for the stability of one's identity, especially in the case of African-Germans, but accepting oneself and establishing one's own safety net, one's own *Heimat* in the form of friends for instance, is paramount for Africans in the diaspora.

5.1.3 Courageous Women: Hügel-Marshall and Hartman

> It is only when you are stranded in a hostile country that you need a romance of origins; it is only when you *lose your mother* that she becomes a myth; it is only when you fear the dislocation of the new that the old ways become precious, imperiled [. . .]. (Hartman 98)

There is an elementary difference between the works of Hügel-Marshall and Hartman. On the one hand, Hügel-Marshall wrote an autobiography, which is characterized by a very personal tone. On the other hand, Hartman's work is a scholarly investigation into the retracing of African-American roots and identity issues back to Africa. Hartman's personal story only emerges tentatively here and there. The decision to compare Hügel-Marshall's work with that of Hartman is justified by their pioneer train of thought as well as their progressive personal developments and viewpoints. Hügel-Marshall is one of the first African-German women to challenge forms of German discrimination, and she actively campaigned (and still campaigns) against it by way of the feminist movement and the African-German movement. In addition, she makes her life and struggle public in the form of her autobiography. Hügel-Marshall is special in this sense because she shows a tremendous personal development, from an oppressed and depressed black girl to a proud and forgiving African-German woman.[114] In comparison, Hartman, as an African-American scholar, ventures into a new and uneasy terrain, which is the one of a realistic view of Africa and what Africa can

---

[114] This differs from Usleber, who wrote his autobiography after having read Hügel-Marshall's and who presents himself as still resentful and unsettled. Hügel-Marshall seems to have left behind her embitterment caused by the discrimination she has encountered.

and, above all, can*not* be for African-Americans. From her research and her field investigations in Africa, Hartman is able not only to advance her own romanticized vision of "Mother Africa" to a more realistic picture of the past and present, but moreover that of her fellow African-Americans. They, too, for a long time, have rather wanted to believe that traveling to or living in Africa will provide a cure for their identity problems. The audacity of both women to open up new paths and follow them makes room for new possibilities. Hügel-Marshall can be seen as an idol for African-German women because her identity development is extraordinary and her struggle progressive. Reading her story makes it clear that if only more African-Germans were to come out of their isolation, the African-German community could become stronger and develop into an accepted part of German society and consciousness. In comparison, Hartman's work is able to precipitate a new chapter within African-American thought, namely to look for alternative solutions for African-American identity problems. Her implied suggestion is that even though African-Americans need to look for their roots, they should not do so with rose-colored glasses. Once they have explored Africa, they should accept the fact that the past cannot be revived and that Africa is no longer their home even if it is still part of their lives. African-Americans need to realign themselves with their own African-American community and must accept the fact that although their forefathers were indeed "reborn" as slaves during the Middle Passage on the Black Atlantic, that this is not shameful. Hügel-Marshall and Hartman are also courageous because they take on new *individual* paths in order to overcome questions of genealogical *kinship* and reach a new livable and veritable sense of *community*. Hügel-Marshall becomes politically active, while Hartman endorses the black cause with her scholarly expertise and publications.

The search of who they are and where they stem from is what drives both women to venture into new territory psychologically and also geographically and temporally. On this journey, they hope to find kinship as a form of belonging grounded in consensus *as well as* descent. For Hügel-Marshall, there exists "keine andere Heimat, keine Sprache, die [sie ihrem] Vater näherbringen könnte," but she also says that she wants to know who she is (11). Thus, long after having found stability within the feminist and African-German movements, she goes to a foreign country with a foreign language at the age of forty-six (123-24), namely to the USA to finally meet her father. Hartman undertakes a similar yet very different journey, when she sets out to Africa to reconnect to her ancestry. When she arrives in Ghana, African children greet her by calling her *obruni*, stranger (3). Just like Hügel-Marshall, Hartman also takes the journey "to cross the boundary that separated kin from stranger" (Hartman 17). This boundary is not only a geographical border, but a temporal one as well, especially in the case of African-Americans. "Being a stranger concerns not only matters of familiarity, belonging, and exclusion but as well involves a particular relation to the past. If the past is another country, then I am its citizen" (Hartman 17). Hartman and others set out to trace their roots in Africa. It is where, in the past, their ancestors lost their connection to their ancestry, most importantly to their mothers.

To "lose one's mother" seems to be a rupture that is worse than losing one's father, for the mother gives birth to and nourishes the child. Earth is also often referred to as "Mother Earth," the cradle of all beings, whereas Africa is regarded as the cradle of humankind. Thus, "to lose one's mother" in Africa, as Hartman also includes in her title, is a cataclysm that seems not only to have originated slaves but even has the means to put an end to humankind and humanity. Hartman stresses the severity of the events that happened a long time ago but still have today seemingly irremovable repercussions. Interestingly, the notion of losing a parent as the link to at least one part of one's genealogical background is paramount for many Africans in the diaspora. Most of the African-Germans "lost" their fathers (who in many cases are/were African-Americans) and consequently, like Hügel-Marshall, they fly to the USA to the land of their fathers[115] (99). The main idea and core problem behind this is that to lose one's parent is equivalent to losing one's identity and one's kin, no matter how long ago it happened or how far away the ancestors might have lived; Africans in the diaspora bear this same sense of severance.

Long before Hügel-Marshall finds the strength to travel to her father's country, she is an abandoned and very insecure black girl in a children's home. She relates that there exists "keine Gemeinschaft, zu der ich gehöre, auch wenn alle davon reden" (31). She is the only black child in the home (45), so not only is she different from other children who do not live in a home, but she is doubly othered, she is "anders 'anders'" (differently different) as a black child among white children in a children's home (31). In what follows, she undergoes a personal transformation from feeling dead and even having suicidal thoughts after having endured so many wrongdoings (47; 56) to becoming a politically active woman. Hügel-Marshall becomes more and more outspoken and courageous, especially when she joins the feminist movement, where she finally finds a community after a life of deprivation and isolation (81). Within the feminist movement, the women fight "[e]inzeln und gemeinsam" for the women's cause, but not against racism (82). Therefore, Hügel-Marshall then joins the African-German movement (89-90). She immerses herself into this community and, just like her African-American idols, begins to call the other members of her community "Schwestern und Brüder[ ]" (92). In contrast, an African-American living in Ghana cautions Hartman against thinking of every black person in Africa as her brother and sister (28), and his wife even says, "'You know they hate us'" (29). Later on, Hartman experiences the distinction between kin and others first-hand, when her colleagues refer to her as the "friend from the diaspora" while categorizing the rest of the group as "brothers and sisters from the continent" (215). Africans in Africa feel connected to each

---

[115] One's home, one's mother country is called *Vaterland* in German. Hügel-Marshall leaves the country where she was born and socialized in, her actual *Vaterland, Deutschland*, to find her father in the USA, the real land of her *Vater*.

other but not necessarily to the Africans from the diaspora. The term *Africa* in African-American usage has no link to the notion that Hartman's colleagues have of Africa and of them: "Africa ended at the borders of the continent" (215). African-Americans and African-Germans, however, call others sisters and brothers to indicate that the community they have formed has substituted the family, or rather the missing part of their heritage. African-Germans, just like African-Americans, have formed a *consent* community, which is also based on a *descent* culture of suffering and mixed genealogy, a *kinship* of sorts of Africans from the diaspora. Thus, when both women, Hügel-Marshall and Hartman, have a community behind them, they go out and have the strength to search for the forefathers (in the form of Hügel-Marshall's biological father as well as those enslaved hundreds of years ago as the ancestors of African-Americans). Whereas Hügel-Marshall can reconnect to her origins directly, Hartman cannot because of the time lag and because she is excluded from the category of being a relative. She nevertheless tries to settle her quandaries of being a descendant of slaves (Hartman 8-17).

Many Africans from the diaspora want to go someplace where there are more blacks, so that they can blend in and so that they are no longer the visual antithesis to a white mainstream.[116] Hügel-Marshall feels comfortable when in Columbus, Ohio (99), and even more so when in St. Croix. "Überall Schwarze Menschen, und zum ersten Mal zähle ich in umgekehrter Reihenfolge: wie viele weiße Menschen im Gegensatz zu den vielen Schwarzen Menschen? Glück überkommt mich" (100-01). While African-Germans travel to America and feel more comfortable there than in Germany due to the greater African-American community, African-Americans travel to Africa with the wish to disappear into this black continent. When the children in Ghana call Hartman a stranger, even the children draw a clear line between Africans from the continent and Africans from the diaspora. It soon dawns on Hartman that "a black face didn't make [her] kin" (4), especially her face, which is "a blend of peoples and nations and masters and slaves long forgotten. In the jumble of [her] features, no certain line of origin could be traced" (3-4). As a result, it is a utopia to believe that Africa will embrace and welcome all black people; this fact dashes "whatever hopes [Hartman] had of losing [herself] in a sea of black faces and experiencing the intimacy and anonymity of the crowd" (57). After this disappointment, instead of falling prey to the romanticized vision of Africa, Hartman continues her endeavor to find a way to unlock the mysteries of the past in order to live a candid future. In comparison, for African-Germans there at least exists a viable connection to their roots, mostly in America, where there are also more black people than in Germany, which makes them feel more comfortable. Some wish to immigrate to the USA. Even though Hügel-Marshall actually receives USA citizenship, she remains in Germany.

---

[116] Massaquoi, for example, had the same experience when arriving in New York (*Destined* 413).

Hartman is courageous when she dismantles the romantic longings of African-Americans, which she herself has shared.

> They left the States hoping to leave slavery behind too. America had made them, but Ghana would remake them. They had faith that the breach of the Middle Passage could be mended and orphaned children returned to their rightful homes. [. . .] The dreams that defined their horizon no longer defined mine. (39)

Hartman also has (had) expectations and views that have been influenced, even corrupted, by her Western upbringing (49; 55). She herself had once dreamed about living in Ghana (56). Her investigation in Ghana, however, excavates an "unbridgeable gulf between stranger and kin" (56), and she is unable to harbor sentimental views or longings any longer. On the contrary, African-American heritage tourists "preferred romance to tragedy" and looked to great civilizations (40). Hartman, however, does not want to build her future on false dreams. For her own sake and future, she wants to overcome these romantic visions by bringing to light a realistic view of Africa. Her main question is, therefore, "What was the future of the ex-slave?" (45). "I, too, live in the time of slavery, by which I mean I am living in the future created by it" (133). Hartman wants to settle the inner turmoil she feels when thinking about her past and her slave ancestors so that she can lead an honest and peaceful life as an African-American woman.

In order to live a life that is satisfying, both Hartman and Hügel-Marshall refuse to accept either the status quo or the past as presented by others. They seize the moment to shape their future by rewriting, by transliterating history. Hügel-Marshall does so not only by investigating black life in Germany, but also by publishing an account of her own life.

> Nur wir können eine Schwarze Geschichte in Deutschland schaffen, die so notwendig und wichtig ist für alle, die nach uns kommen. Es ist schwer, tagtäglich ums Überleben zu kämpfen und gleichzeitig Schwarze Geschichte sichtbar zu machen. (103-04)

Hügel-Marshall provides examples of distinguished African-Germans who have been overlooked by German society in general. She not only wants to dig in history's forgotten drawers, but she wants to write herself and other African-Germans into Germany's historiography and thus its consciousness. While African-Germans are fighting a contemporary battle to become acknowledged and part of society, African-Americans fight on a similar front; but this battle takes place, to a great extent however, on a different continent and in the past. Hartman claims,

> History is a battle royal, a contest between the powerful and the powerless in "what happened" as well as in the stories we tell about what has happened—a fight to the death over the meaning of the past. The narrative of the defeated never triumphs [. . .]. (192)

Hartman tries to take on the challenge of this battle royal and wants to turn the story of slavery from one of defeat into one of victory so that she can make sense of her past, resolve her identity problems, and redeem the lost souls of the Middle Passage. Consequently, both writers undertake a very difficult task in fighting against oblivion, indifference, and powerful societies.

An African-American living in Ghana pleads to Hartman, "Don't lie when you go back home. Everyone goes home and tells lies" (33). He continues, "We have to stop bullshitting about Africa. The naïveté that allows folks to believe they are returning home or entering paradise when they come here has to be destroyed" (33). Hartman does not promise him to do that because she knows that telling "the truth risked savaging the dreams of those who might never travel to Africa [. . .] [and] risked sullying the love of romantics who kissed the ground as soon as they landed in mother Africa" (33). However, her intention is exactly that, namely not to promote further lies but to tell the truth, even if it hurts and cuts the umbilical cord to an imaginary kinship. Moreover, part of this act of rewriting history, and through this shaping of one's future, is to rename oneself. Renaming is a symbolic act of taking charge of one's identity and destiny. Hügel-Marshall shortens her name Erika to Ika (93), and Hartman chooses an African name, dropping Valerie in favor of Saidiya (8). At some point, these women take control of their lives and symbolically change their given names so that the outer world can see that they have become self-determined subjects. In what follows, they then take into their hands the task of writing and publishing the "real" story of Africans in the diaspora. They tell it as it is and as they experience it, instead of how whites portray history or how African-Americans recount more digestible stories of Africa.

In the end, for both women of the diaspora it comes down to losing one's parents and building one's own communities (of chosen "kinship"). Some African-Germans still have the possibility of finding their African-American fathers and reconnecting with them. "I found you and I will never lose you again," is what Hügel-Marshall writes in a letter to her father (134). However, she does not leave Germany for America. Instead, with the knowledge of her roots she has the energy to keep on fighting at home, in Germany, and to support her own African-German community. In another letter to her father she claims, "I am proud to be black, but it was a long way feeling that way" (117), and at the end of the work her message is that she has accepted herself no matter the circumstances. In contrast, African-Americans have to face the fact that they have (symbolically) lost their mothers and cannot bring them back. "To lose your mother was to be denied your kin, country, and identity. To lose your mother was to forget your past" (Hartman 85). Even though Hartman tries to "connect the dots between then and now and to chart the trajectory between the Gold Coast and Curaçao and Montgomery and Brooklyn" (129), she knows that the events of the past cannot be reversed, and neither can her personal experiences. A connection to one's former kin in Africa is no longer possible, for Africans do not share a "unanimity of sentiment in the black world" (75), and thus the solution is in the understanding "that the experience of slavery had made *us* an *us*, that is, it had created the conditions under which we had fashioned an identity. Dispossession was our history" (74; italics in original). For Hartman, and hence for African-Americans, there exists no possibility to reconnect with long-lost kin. Hartman's courageous message is to accept the fact that "the breach of the Atlantic could not be remedied by a name and that the routes traveled by strangers were as close to a mother country as [anyone] would get" (9). In addition, Hartman "knew there wasn't a remedy for [her] homelessness. [She] was an orphan and the breach between [her] and [her] origins was irreparable. Being a stranger was an inveterate condition that a journey across the Atlantic could not cure" (199).

As a result, the aspect that bonds Africans in the diaspora, from Germany and from the USA, is that they form their own communities, their *consent* culture, within these countries in which they were born and socialized, no matter how hostile, their *dissonant* homes. Thus, the connection of Africans in the diaspora lies not necessarily in reestablishing the biological link to their ancestral homelands (*descent cultures*), but in accepting the routes traveled across the Atlantic as the missing aspect, the point of reference. The Black Atlantic as the common chord of suffering for Africans in the diaspora is an elusive paradigm, yet the only viable one. Therefore, I claim that the Black Atlantic becomes the symbolic and literal *descent culture* for Africans in the diaspora, not necessarily the continents of their relatives or former kin (America and Africa). Welsch, in his article "Transculturality," makes it clear that "[p]eople can make their own choice with respect to their affiliation" in today's world, hence their *consent culture*. "Their actual homelands can be far away from their original homeland" (Welsch 211). Moreover, I state that for Africans in the diaspora nowadays it is not the soil, the place, the territory as well as former African kin from the continent that solely distinguish their belonging or their cultural identity for that matter. It is rather the concept of the Black Atlantic, its diffuse texture, which supports the connection of Africans in the diaspora. Here, Hügel-Marshall and Hartman are pioneers in accepting their seemingly contradictory identities and their difficult pasts. By being or becoming a member of communities and by being strong individuals in a *dissonant culture*, they acknowledge unwelcome details of their genealogy and thereby establish an implicit connection between Africans in the diaspora, via the Black Atlantic, instead of to their direct and indirect kin.

5.2 Identity, Catharsis, and Wholeness

A whole is that which has beginning, middle and end. We are what we repeatedly do.

Aristotle

The analysis and comparison of the African-German and African-American works at hand underline the importance of community and a form of connectedness for reasons of survival and establishing a *Heimat*. The togetherness of Africans in the diaspora lies in the sharing of sentiments of dispersion and discrimination, and they find themselves in a middle position between the white Western individualism of their surrounding society and the African or African-American heritage of their ancestors. Despite communal backing, being a person of mixed genealogy or of black folks living in a white, sometimes racist society, one will most likely develop identity problems due to discrimination and deprivation that go beyond the psychic quarrels that everyone can have. Establishing communities, fighting against everyday racism, searching for one's roots, and the like contribute to the wish of many Africans in the diaspora to find happiness by "fixing" their identities, by becoming "whole."[117] I adhere to the above-mentioned notion of wholeness by Aristotle, who describes wholeness as having a beginning, a middle part, and an end. Thus, becoming whole, in this sense, takes on a tripartite structure which represents a form of completeness. I claim that the authors from the USA as well as from Germany share a sort of transatlantic odyssey and the autobiographical acts of writing down their lives' stories represent their quest for reconciliation with their genealogical origins, their past experiences, as well as their hybrid identities; they do all this in order to become whole. The authors' accounts, moreover, even transliterate history by filling in the gaps in the story. Massaquoi even complicates Germany's fragmentary historical "digestion" by literally adding color to its Nazi past.

All authors, in the end, claim in some way to have accepted who they are and have come to be whole. Some authors even use the term "whole" or "catharsis." At first sight, the reconciliation of the diasporic selves of the authors with their genealogies, their pasts, and their identities seems fruitful. Does this mean they fully reconcile(d) their hyphenated identities into whole ones? What does it mean to be whole? Achieving a kind of unity with oneself and the world seems to be a natural human goal. Therefore, when an identity is in crisis, to achieve wholeness can be seen as a means for reconciliation with oneself and the world, however ideal or unrealistic this wholeness might be. When it comes to autobiographic writing, Chandler views wholeness as "a fundamental principle in organic medicine and a ruling metaphor in psychotherapy" and that it "is a formative notion in the construction of personal narratives" (19). In this

---

[117] Nietzsche also claimed that hybrid individuals seek to stop the inner war of the inherent cultures and identities within them (see Nietzsche's *Beyond Good and Evil*).

context, the debate on "What is identity?" is not an invention of recent postcolonial or autobiography studies; it dates back to ancient times. In past decades, philosophers and scholars of many fields have contributed to the debate surrounding identity and the self. The main argument raised is the tension between the *essence/substance* and the *process* dimensions of identity, i.e., what is fixed and what is changing in our identity (Brockmeier, "Identity"). I agree with most postcolonial and other contemporary scholars who acknowledge that "the traditional concept of identity as an unchangeable and substantial self lost ground in favour of a concept of a life-long process of construction and reconstruction, a continuous writing and rewriting of one's self" (Brockmeier, "Identity"). Autobiographical writing does just that.

In this context, the notion of identity and *hybridity*, as introduced by Homi K. Bhaba, comes into focus. Postcolonial subjects as Africans in the diaspora often carry multiple selves determined by their particular backgrounds and by the cultural clashes brought forth by colonialism and the dispersal of folks, influencing the identity development of the subjects. Therefore, hybridity is defined as "*the interdependent construction of postcolonial identities, which combines and intersects binary oppositions in complex and ambiguous ways*" (Meyer 151; italics in original). I suggest to view identity neither totally fixed nor totally changing but rather as an already very diversified, i.e., hybrid set of genealogical backgrounds and life experiences; identity is continually in transition to revision and never fully completed until the human being dies, which includes that a terminal wholeness of character can never be achieved. Connecting this idea to life writings, Smith and Watson bring forward a performative view of life writings and say that "identities are not fixed or essentialized autobiographical subjects; rather they are produced and reiterated through cultural norms, and thus remain provisional and unstable" (*Reading* 143). This supports the aspect of autobiographies as sites for performative constructedness, as described earlier, namely that the autobiographer performs his or her life on paper and thereby constructs not only a story but his identity as well (see chapter 2). In addition, the quotation strengthens my thesis above that the authors at hand cannot claim to have formed or found a fixed self but that they are still in a state of flux and becoming, although the autobiographical act can provide a temporal or rather literary form of wholeness through the repetition of his or her life's experiences. Olney, in agreement with this view and Chandler's view, argues that "autobiography, if one places it in relation to the life from which it comes[,]" is "a monument of the self as it is becoming, a metaphor of the self at the summary moment of composition" (*Metaphors* 35).

To make my thesis complete, I claim that although a form of wholeness of the human being is not possible in terms of a constant psychological or mental state, the authors at hand find an ersatz wholeness by imagination and narration, by creation and performance through the autobiographical act, and arrive at a *textual wholeness*, which seemingly provides them with comfort and ease. This wholeness is only achieved by the reiteration of one's life's stories. A text has a beginning, a middle, and an end. It can be created to come full circle and to resolve any kinds of problems. Thus, the autobiographies at hand create a textual wholeness—even if to differing extents—that replaces a personal, mental wholeness which can never last forever (if it exists at all). It is not a wholeness of character, which is impossible to gain, but a literary ersatz wholeness. This ersatz wholeness supports the author to cleanse himself or herself of the past and of identity quandaries (*catharsis*, see below) after which the author is free again to progress in/with life. Chandler observes,

> Narration has always been involved with healing. The Greeks believed that the expressive arts drew healing energy from the gods, as do traditional societies that still enact healing storytelling rituals. [. . .] Autobiography might be regarded as an evolutionary development of these other forms of healing. (5-6)

Strikingly, the African-American literary tradition, which partly relies on the concept of the talking book, can be regarded as an expressive art by its means such as the speakerly text (see chapter 2). This tradition stems from African storytelling, i.e., from *griots*. In the analysis, aspects of this African-American literary concept as well as others, such as performative constructedness, intertextuality, etc., could be detected. Thus, the link between the Greeks' notion of narration as a form of healing in the sense of a textual wholeness and the diversified literary means within the African diaspora is immanent.

In this context, the Greeks introduced a concept called catharsis. Aristotle used the term to describe the phenomenon that tragic literature evokes particular emotions in the audience, namely pity and fear. The emotions, as can be seen in the following quotation, result in a pleasant and even healthy state of what Aristotle depicted as *katharsis*, and what is translated in different ways as purgation, purification, and catharsis (Aristotle, *Politics* 1342a4-15; Waugh 44). "Tragedy is an imitation of an action that is admirable, complete and possesses magnitude; in language made pleasurable, each of its species separated in different parts; [. . .]; effecting through pity and fear the purification [*katharsis*] of such emotions" (Aristotle, *Poetics* 10). Catharsis in dictionary entries means purgation and purification. Aristotle, however, because he never really defined the term, left it open for interpretation. In some scholars' view, catharsis

> is an intellectual 'clarification': the audience learns something about humanity, and learning produces pleasure. According to this view, catharsis is a fundamentally cognitive experience: we gain a clearer and better sense of the world, and thus end up feeling better and wiser when the tragedy draws to a close. (Waugh 45)

There are others who claim that the meaning of catharsis lies in "a 'purgation' of the emotions, a release of strong feelings that leaves us [as the audience] feeling drained but also relieved" (Waugh 45). Why should one favor one interpretation over the other when Aristotle was not keen on finding a strict definition himself, and when the differing concepts of catharsis actually seem to complement each other? The term itself has found its way into psychoanalysis and other fields and, therefore, becomes useful in the context of autobiography criticism as well. I use the term catharsis to characterize the process of releasing one's traumatic experience(s) and the accompanying emotions—whether the person releasing them is aware of them or not—in order to cleanse oneself from negative associations. As a result, one arrives at a state of mental health, well-being, integrity of one's identity/self, and to a certain extent even a clearer view of the world, even if only for a short time or in a narrative form. Aristotle targeted foremost the emotions of the audience. However, I want to include and stress the significance of this purifying process for the autobiographer. Thus, the process for the autobiographer to reconcile his identities and experiences in order to find a form of being or becoming whole—namely a textual wholeness—is oftentimes via the route of catharsis. This means that the author has to cleanse and free himself or herself of past mistreatments, misconceptions, and ill feelings by way of writing about, i.e., literarily repeating, them and thereby leaving them behind. In the following, I examine the African-American works in terms of identity, catharsis, and wholeness before comparing the results to the contents of the African-German works.

Barack Obama's background differs from the typical African-American line of heritage, for his father was a Kenyan student in Hawaii and his mother a white woman from Kentucky with traces of Indian blood. As a teenager he becomes well aware of racial differences and discrimination in Hawaii and in the continental USA as the preceding chapters scrutinize. Notwithstanding his different background, or rather because of it, Obama wants to belong to this great African-American community, but he knows he has to "earn" his membership, to suffer as they suffer(ed), and to feel their pain as well. Thus, his identity transformation from being the exotic black boy from Hawaii and Indonesia to becoming a full member of the African-American community lies in his cathartic route as a community organizer in Chicago. He states:

> The continuing struggle to align word and action, our heartfelt desires with a workable plan—didn't self-esteem finally depend on just this? It was the belief which had led me into organizing, and it was that belief which would lead me to conclude, perhaps for the final time, that notions of purity—of race or of culture—could no more serve as the basis for the typical black American's self-esteem than it could for mine. Our sense of wholeness would have to arise from something more fine than the bloodlines we'd inherited. It would have to find root in Mrs. Crenshaw's story and Mr. Marshall's story, in Ruby's story and Rafiq's; in all the messy, contradictory details of our experience. (204)

Clearly, in this quotation Obama proclaims that he is not the "typical" African-American but that he longs to be part of the larger concept of Africans in America (or elsewhere). He states that bloodline is no longer the deciding factor of who belongs and who does not. This finding supports my thesis, namely that Africans in the diaspora do not find a fixed self and thus salvation by trying to reclaim long-lost kin in Africa. Instead, they can find another form of kinship within the African diaspora, one that is built upon shared sufferings and dispersion, i.e., the symbolic kinship of the Black Atlantic, of Africans in the diaspora. It is the shared stories of suffering and experience, just like Gates claims, that hold the community together. For Obama, those experiences provide for the entrance ticket into the African-American family, no matter how different they are. By claiming this, Obama is also included in this community despite his genealogy being different from the "typical" African-American one and his life's story being uncommon. The sense of wholeness, he claims, lies in the *stories* and not in bloodlines, which already exemplifies that he is talking about a narrative, a textual form of wholeness rather than a wholeness founded upon a physical and mental form.

Nevertheless, everyone longs for a stable self and thus Obama attempts to mend his hybrid and somewhat scattered identity into a whole one by "organizing, through shared sacrifice" in order to earn his African-American membership and so that "the uniqueness of [his] own life" is accepted (135). As an organizer, he "didn't make any money; [his] poverty was proof of [his] integrity" (135). Thus, he tries to suffer as many other African-Americans in Chicago suffer. By writing about one's life and trying to ameliorate it, a cleansing of sorts takes place. It is a narrative evocation of emotions, and Obama not only writes about them in retrospect, but as an organizer he tries to align word and action to make a better life. He earns his way into the community and also feels better when dedicating a part of his life and his energy to African-American issues. He hopes not only to make their lives better, but he also wants to become whole himself. However, organizing cannot fill the hole of the missing African part of his background and his African half-sister "Auma's voice simply served to remind [him] that [he] still had wounds to heal, and could not heal [himself]" by way of organizing (138). He must reconcile his hybrid identities also through different means.

Therefore, Obama feels the urge to talk to his dead father. "I needed to search for him, I thought to myself, and talk with him again" (129). The strained and more or less non-existent relationship to his father and therewith his African family across the ocean is like a heavy burden on Obama and his identity quarrels. After having become an organizer and through this having become part of a community, which stands strong behind him, something is still missing. In all of the works at hand, it becomes apparent that an actual transatlantic journey only becomes possible if the person has found a strong community. After having become a member of the African-American community in continental America, Obama himself claims that his history is incomplete (301) and he asks himself whether a "trip to Kenya [would] finally fill that emptiness" (302). During a service at church, Obama reflects on his own life and experiences as an organizer, and the passage seems like a form of conversion, a coming to belief, and a release of emotions.[118] Suddenly, he seems to see clearer as to what he needs to do in the following. His catharsis does not end there. Instead, this experience is the initiation to go to Kenya, a trip as part of Obama's continuing cathartic route to fill in the gaps of his own story (293-95). Obama finally travels to Kenya, to his roots in order to understand himself and to settle his inner quandaries.

The clear aim of Obama for traveling to Kenya is to "somehow force [his] many worlds into a single, harmonious whole" (347). What he finds, however, is a huge family with complicated relations and at odds with one another. Thus, finding a fixed sense of self, a stable whole one, suddenly seems unattainable. Notwithstanding, when Obama learns about the history of his family by his Granny and other relatives, he at least fills the blank spaces of his own history and background, making it complete by the *griot*-like tales from his family (394-424). Obama, here, uses the technique of the talking book when he provides Granny's story in the form of a speakerly text page for page. The reader feels like sitting in the midst of the family, listening to the stories for hours.

> I heard all our voices begin to run together, the sound of three generations tumbling over each other like the currents of a slow-moving stream, my questions like rocks roiling the water, the breaks in memory separating the currents, but always the voices returning to that single course, a single story . . . . (394)

Even though there are still bits and pieces of the story missing or faulty, the family and the story become one again by simply plugging the holes and continuing with their versions of the story, rendering the story into a whole, a narrative wholeness instead of an actual one. In addition, Obama includes himself in the storytelling when he talks about "my questions" and "our voices" running together. As a result, by becoming part of this experience *and* by filling the last pages of his autobiography with the story of his African background, he underlines the fact that his life and their lives are inevitably interwoven. Moreover, he makes his own life's story and history complete, whole, by writing about his experience and actual background.

Obama travels to Kenya to find out about his family's background and thus his own. The stories of past events and people help him to come to terms with his own identity. When he visits his father's and his grandfather's graves, after having learned many details about their lives, he finally understands it all:

---

[118] The passage about the sermon and Obama's thoughts and feelings remind the reader of former white Western spiritual conversion literature and underline the influence of Western traditions on Obama's life and writing.

their lives, their sufferings, their behavior, his own identity and life choices. He recalls the scene in the following way:

> For a long time I sat between the two graves and wept. When my tears were finally spent, I felt a calmness wash over me. I felt the circle finally close. I realized that who I was, what I cared about, was no longer just a matter of intellect or obligation, no longer a construct of words. (429-30)

Telling the stories of his father and grandfather and how it was all an unfortunate combination of circumstances and outdated traditions, Obama forgives them and finds "calmness." He can finally leave old calamities behind and by weeping over their graves he cleanses himself. Through the "release of strong feelings" Obama feels "drained but also relieved" (Waugh 45); it is his personal catharsis, and at that point in his life he feels whole for his "circle finally close[s]" (430). "It wasn't simply joy I felt in each of these moments. Rather, it was a sense that everything I was doing, every touch and breath and word, carried the full weight of my life; that a circle was beginning to close, so that I might finally recognize myself as I was, here, now, in one place" (376-77). Obama is clear-minded enough to know that although this experience in Africa helps him to acknowledge himself and his background, he knows "then that at some point the joy [he] was feeling would pass and that that, too, was part of the circle: the fact that [his] life was neither tidy nor static, and that even after this trip hard choices would always remain" (377). This conclusion is very important and Obama stresses the elusive, the flexible nature of identities, namely that they are never fixed or as he calls it "tidy" or "static." Identities are always in flux and always need to accommodate to new findings and situations. Earlier, I claim that identity is never complete. Identity is "a product in process" and the narration, the autobiography, is the consistency, the textual wholeness, underlying identity developments (chapter 2, p. 30). Thus, Obama sees that the wholeness he feels is also only temporary. The detection of the temporal nature is an effective way of resolving one's identity crisis instead of always aiming at finding a utopian set and whole self. By writing down his autobiography in a detailed manner, i.e., by providing all aspects of his diversified genealogy, and by splitting his writing up into three parts—Part One: Origins, Part Two: Chicago, Part Three: Kenya—Obama adheres to the concept of coming full circle through a beginning, a middle and an end, thus a textual wholeness. It is a wholeness that can last whereas a wholeness of identity or the like can only be temporary if at all. In addition, the cathartic journey and the narrative wholeness help Obama (and others) to not stand still or run around in circles, but to proceed with life.

Migrations of the Heart is also divided into three parts: I. Beginnings, II. Journeys, and III. Coming Home. This is the same trichotomy that can be found in Obama's work, but Golden gives the chapters very telling titles: *beginning* for beginning, *journey* for the middle part, and *coming home* for the end. Even though Golden is not old, she emphasizes that she has come full circle, at least for the subject of the story she tells in this work: becoming a happy, satisfied African-American woman who can accept herself as who she is. Therefore, one can see right from the start that Golden aims at a narrative form of completion, i.e., wholeness. The reason for her quest to become whole lies in her childhood. Her mother was subservient to her father although she was a successful boarding house owner up until her father lost it all to gambling. They separate and her mother dies early. In addition to personal issues resulting from her family background, Golden grows up in Washington, D.C., during the time of the assassination of Dr. Martin Luther King, Jr., and she becomes a disenchanted young woman who engages in African-American activism. Her young black female identity is restless and she looks for love and happiness. For her, identity issues, matters of race and inheritance, and of love are intertwined and so she looks for men who can make her whole. "I closed my eyes and remembered all the men I had loved, too busy, too afraid to take me, incomplete, and make me whole" (53). But at that point in her life Golden finds "a haven" among a Nigerian community she is introduced to (58). "The turbulent waters of [her] recent past had washed [her] ashore" (58). Her Black Atlantic identity that has been drifting aimlessly on the ocean now finds a shore to land on. She thinks she will find "peace" and "love" and "hope" among her new friends from Nigeria (58). Golden tries to "understand and meld into a community grounded in a sense of family and connectedness—the ethic that would heal [her] wounds" (58).

Soon she immigrates to Nigeria, to join Femi Ajayi, her newly-wed husband. By marrying an African man and moving to Nigeria, Golden hopes to find her inner peace, to accept herself as a black woman, and to resolve her identity problems. Her identity is in development and she shares the steps she has taken thus far with the reader.

> In my parents' house I was Marita Golden, molded like clay by the touch and warm breath of their legacy. In college I reached for a torch and added the postscript "black woman." Now, I wondered, in the house that one day would be Femi's and that would also be mine, who would I be? This quest, spurred by love, was just beginning. I had become an Ajayi. (113)

The reader can trace the different roles she has played. Her identity development does not seem to be linear if the goal is independence, though, because as soon as she becomes the wife of a Nigerian man and a new member of an African family with a new last name she subdues herself to old customs and duties, which she is about to find out. Golden still believes that someone else, not herself, can make her whole and happy and she holds fast to this dream.

Life in Nigeria as a woman is not as easy as Golden thinks. She becomes pregnant, but all she wants to do is write. "The fetus was gobbling me whole. [. . .] Writing was the only child I wanted then, and I was racked by a sense of guilt because of my inability to nurture it" (160). Note that her feeling of guilt refers to her inability to nurture her writing; the baby inside her causes this inability. As a professional writer Golden had started to write a novel "inspired by all the people and experiences [she] had known. Distilling, selecting from remembrance and dream, [she] conjured up characters that [she] prayed were real enough to meet on a street corner, to care for and love" (131). While living in Nigeria, Golden continues "to give life to the people on those pages. They were never to claim an existence between hard covers, but they performed the tasks of all good friends—they kept me sane. They made me whole" (131). Golden struggles to deal with life in Nigeria. By writing a piece that is part autobiography and part fiction, she hopes to stay sane, just like psychologists use journal writing to heal the wounds of their patients. By making up stories that are missing from her life and by twisting others, she fills in the gaps of her own life and molds her own story in order to become whole, which is her outspoken goal. She is the only author of all six authors discussed here who talks about becoming whole and finding her identity this openly. Obviously, her husband and her life in Nigeria cannot fulfill her wish of making her whole as she had hoped.

As soon as Golden loses the unwanted child, she starts to be herself again and resumes writing. Still, she tries to reconcile her two contrasting roles. She struggles to be an obedient wife like other Nigerian women around her while simultaneously nurturing her independent American character. Golden, when returning home after the miscarriage, immediately

> began to write furiously, with the fervor of a long-awaited eruption. [She] filled page after page with an outpouring the loss of [her] child released. The writing affirmed [her], anointed [her] with a sense of purpose. Most of all, it slowly began to dissipate the sense of failure that squatted, a mannerless intruder, inside [her] spirit. The writing redeemed [her] talent for creation and, as the days passed, made [her] whole once again. (170)

Golden cannot yet "create" a new life, i.e., a child; writing, however, is something she is able and above all willing to do and thus she can create something that keeps her sane, something that creates a form of wholeness. In addition, this quotation shows that Golden, like Obama, has come to learn that wholeness is a temporary feeling ("made me whole once again" [Golden 170]). Only by writing about her experiences and feelings can she create something that stays, even though it is not the same for it is a textual wholeness and not the real feeling of being complete as she experiences in this moment of time.

The final pages of her autobiography reveal that the very act of writing down her life before and in Nigeria, and by this displaying her coming of age, functions as a form of healing, of creating a wholeness that can stay, even if only on page; once she puts it in writing, she can proceed with her life. She flees Nigeria to rebuild her life in America. Two days before Golden's thirtieth birthday she tells her therapist: "'I am a writer,' I began. 'And I've been unable to write for several months.' [. . .] 'I can't write because what I'm trying to write about is too painful to remember'" (225). This statement clearly underscores that writing means reflecting and thus healing, not only for professional writers like Golden but everyone else as well. Remembering and processing past events help finding closure and the act of writing also supports her identity construction and development. In the end, Golden is able to resume writing and she publishes her autobiography. Obviously, writing helps her (and others) to initiate a self-therapeutic process (see Kaminer 481-86; Holm-Hadulla 360-64; Hornung, "Autobiography" 222). Just like Obama, Golden becomes aware of the fact that she can never become whole as a person and stay that way. Instead, she knows that everything needs to progress and develop: "I had wandered. Will wander still . . . and take home with me wherever I go" (234). This, her last sentence, stresses that Golden can accept who she is and this is home, an inner point of reference and not another person or place. She accepts herself and can continue life's journey.

Hartman's work is not an autobiography in a narrow sense like Golden's and Obama's. In the foreground, Hartman, as the scholar and researcher, claims to want "to bring the past closer" and to understand it in order "to tell the story of the commoners" so that the names and lives of the lost souls are redeemed and the gaps of historiography filled (17). In the blurb on the back cover of Hartman's work, Gates states that Hartman is able to combine "'the depth and breadth of a scholar of slavery with the imagination and linguistic facility of a novelist'" and that her work "is a memoir about loss, alienation, and estrangement'." This is certainly true, for Hartman's work is extraordinary and a genre in itself; Gates continues that the book "speak[s] to a new generation of readers," namely those who do not deny the truth about Africa and slavery anymore, and who want to leave romantic notions behind in order to progress in their lives. The reason for Hartman to write this book, apart from being interested in this topic because of her scholarly background, can be found in the work itself. Her own family's historical mysteries, inconsistencies, and secrecies lead her to begin to close the gaps and knit a full story. She hopes that by researching on a grander scale, for the entire African-American community, she will not only serve to assemble the community's heritage fragments but also her personal ones. To lose one's mother means to lose one's identity and past. Filling in the gaps for the sake of the lost souls of slavery and her own incoherent inheritance is the means to not only complete the history of all African-Americans but to make the community *and* herself whole again. Thus, in a broader sense, *Lose Your Mother* is a form of autobiography as well; it is about her own identity and finding closure in order to continue with her life.

Hartman claims that there is a stark difference between her trip to Africa and that of the émigrés in the 1950s and 60s or any other heritage tourist, namely that she is attracted to ruins while they were hoping for "rebirth" (40). "They went to be healed. I went to excavate a wound" (40). Even though Hartman has a different idea of Africa and does not put it on a pedestal anymore, she also wants to be healed and heal history's open wounds. Her approach is what is different. She does not want to cure the symptoms only, as many others do, but she actually wants to find a diagnosis and treat the injury. In addition, instead of adhering to romantic dreams and instead of attempting to heal her individual identity problems, she prioritizes a more complete solution for African-Americans while moving her own issues to second place. Hartman excavates the past and faces its ferocities and thereby also tackles her individual predicament. She states that her research "was personal too" (130). Hartman does not use the term autobiography except once, when she is "[h]overing in an empty room" in her "attempt to figure out how this underground had created and marked [her]" (130). "Why else begin an autobiography in a graveyard?" (130). Hartman goes back in time, to a graveyard where the enslaved who did not make it are "buried" so that she lives, as the descendant of slaves who survived the ordeal. At any rate, Hartman discovers there is no opportunity to guide history into a more fortunate direction; instead, she has to cope with her findings and feelings.

There is nothing to be found in Africa that can actually make her and African-Americans whole. Hartman finds out that they cannot find a cure "because it was not the kind of hole that could be filled and then would go away. Coming here was simply a way to acknowledge it. There was no turning back the clock" (199). However, by making this revolutionary discovery, that there is no African remedy for African-American identity problems, Hartman and African-Americans can be relieved of the burden of finding salvation. It is like a liberation and it can evoke feelings of happiness and satisfaction as well. Hartman and African-Americans can now concentrate on the neglected hard truths so that they at least can supplement history and research. To achieve an historical and thus a textual wholeness, Hartman investigates all sides of the story black and white, master and slave, royal and commoner. She investigates how history took the wrong turn with the arrival of the Portuguese at the coast of Africa. She never misses providing the reader with original terms (e.g., 61) and to look into the archives for factual data. She includes the background of the Dutch slave trade and explains Dutch terms such as "*Bastaard,*" "*kop,*" and so forth (78-80). The research is sound and wherever there is a personal story missing Hartman uses her own imagination so that the story comes alive as she does in the case of the young girl who was murdered on a slave ship (136-53). She skillfully weaves together the facts from the trial transcript and other sources with the imagined different viewpoints of the people involved.

Consequently, Hartman creates a piece of art, an amalgamation of fact and fiction, that forms a complete unit; and although the book cannot provide for healing in terms of coming home—to Africa, to inner peace—for African-Americans, it becomes a manifest for a textual wholeness in twelve chapters. The book's chapters can be divided so that a trichotomy, as in Obama's and Golden's writings, can be detected which provides for coming full circle. Foremost, Hartman's work tends to the catharsis that Aristotle described, namely a catharsis for the audience. Hartman's African-American audience comes to a lucid and candid knowing of their past by retracing the ordeal and coping with the truth. This process is able to cleanse her readers but also herself of false romantic notions; by digging up the dirt and writing it down, a cathartic process is initiated that can help African-Americans to feel better and see clearer.

All three African-American authors experienced some sort of identity issue in their early lives which motivated them to come to terms with their lives and selves. Obama, Golden, and Hartman each undertake a journey to Africa for they believe the key to succeeding in life and coping with their identity issues is hidden there. It is a cathartic route because the trip to Africa enlightens and liberates them; however, although it is well worth the trip to visit the place of relatives and ancestors, Africa itself and its inhabitants cannot mend their hybrid identities into a whole one. Going there, though, makes them realize that they can only themselves deal with their personal quandaries and that a unified, fixed sense of self is a self-delusion. Thus, all three write about their experiences and thus substitute the utopian wholeness of self by a textual wholeness of the autobiography.

For African-Germans questions of identity, catharsis, and wholeness demand similar yet at the same time disparate answers. German society does not accept African-Germans as fully Germans, and the fact that the African-German community is still relatively marginal makes up for a considerable contrast to the situation for African-Americans. As the preceding chapter exhibits, African-Germans' first concern is to form a community and to script themselves into existence and into white Germans' apperception. Therefore, resistance to and establishment of an African-German culture are not as far progressed as they are within the African-American community. African-Americans, due to their slavery past, are in search of answers and salvation in Africa and history; they have a much clearer focus, namely they want to be whole and redeem the slave past. African-Germans, to begin with, simply want to exist and be accepted. African-Germans are coming into existence and this process is part of the acknowledgement of their identity and genealogy within German society. The works at hand show that African-Germans have also begun the procedure of healing by way of writing and speaking out. Thus, they have begun their route of catharsis as well, but due to the different starting positions and circumstances, they are not dealing with and therefore not talking about catharsis and wholeness as the African-American authors do. While initial African-Germans' healing lies in the present (mostly), African-Americans' healing has progressed to the acceptance of the past.

Although both parties, African-Germans and African-Americans, have identity dilemmas due to their mixed backgrounds, a literal existential difference between the African-German and African-American authors of this study is that the African-Germans' existence is/was actually challenged in German society. Massaquoi, for instance, simply did not exist, i.e., he had no right of existence, in the Nazis' worldview. The incident at school underscores this discrimination: "[His teacher] then took a wet sponge and carefully erased the last remaining empty square, the one that represented [Massaquoi], thereby graphically emphasizing [his] non-person status" (102). Hügel-Marshall experienced similar humiliations; she explains that she was born and raised in Germany among white people, "doch im Bewußtsein der meisten Deutschen existier[t] [sie] noch immer nicht" (12). The same is true for Usleber, who also describes the same phenomenon right at the beginning of his life writing.

> Ich bin ein Deutscher. Bin ich es? [. . .] Ich selbst habe mich nicht immer als einen Deutschen wahrgenommen, aber auch für meine Mitmenschen war mein Deutschsein alles andere als selbstverständlich: Die meisten Menschen, denen ich begegnet bin, haben mich nicht—jedenfalls nicht von vornherein als einen Deutschen gesehen. (9)

Some white Germans do not accept African-Germans, which is exemplified by the experiences of the three authors. For some white Germans it seems to be even impossible to view someone with a darker skin shade as German (Wright, "Others-from-Within" 298; Janson 63). Hence, the authors do not feel integrated into German society and therefore do not feel at home themselves. Questions like the ones that Hügel-Marshall hears (How long have you lived in Germany? or: When are you going back?) are what all African-Germans experience, and those questions aggravate the feeling of not fitting in and not being welcome (67).[119]

Understandably, the African-German autobiographers describe instances in their young lives when they wish to be or appear as whites so that they are accepted and loved. Massaquoi even actively attempts to transform his "racial traits." He, for instance, blames his appearance for his problems and he is "[c]onvinced that if [his] hair were straight, half of [his] problems would be solved" (92). On that account, Massaquoi tries to straighten his hair but fails. Everything Hügel-Marshall does wrongly is considered to be the "Resultat [ihrer] Hautfarbe" by the whites surrounding her (47), and therefore she wishes "nicht so zu sein, wie [sie ist]. Wenigstens für einen einzigen Tag will [sie] weiss sein, ganz besonders dann, wenn es Zeugnisse gibt" (29). Also for

---

[119] Wright also gives examples of similar questions ("Others-from-Within" 298).

Usleber, being white would solve many problems because whiteness is seen as "normal." "Warum konnte ich nicht so aussehen wie die anderen? Warum gehörte ich nicht dazu? Ich fühlte mich 'nicht normal' und legte damit gleichzeitig für mich fest, was 'Normalität' bedeutete: hell zu sein" (23). All these quotations display a phenomenon that African-Americans also experienced; however, it is not so much an issue for African-Americans anymore. Mainly in the past, African-Americans also had the wish to be white or at least to *pass* for white. For example, Obama remembers to have read an article in an American magazine when he was a little boy that dealt with blacks who tried to bleach their skin with chemicals (29-30). Michael Jackson had often been suspected of having whitened his skin, and Nella Larsen's *Passing* is a famous novel with regard to the topic of blacks pretending to be white and thus blending in and moving up in society. The analysis shows that most African-Americans are past this stage of self-doubt in relation to their looks while African-Germans still have to struggle through this dark chapter of their identity development.

Usleber, Massaquoi, and Hügel-Marshall, after having confessed their pejorative adolescent identity frictions, all three continue to outline their metamorphosis from the "ugly" and marginalized black child with an almost non-existent self-esteem to an autonomous, reinvented and strong black adult. Retracing the steps they took to reach a happier, more fulfilled level in life, and sharing these steps in written form, is a way to treat themselves. Writing about the issues and the developments becomes a form of self-therapy, a site for healing and understanding the complexities of their existence. Massaquoi, after many different steps, begins to model his American identity earnestly when the war ends; his friend Werner tells him, "'You really look like an Ami now. If I didn't know you, you could have fooled me'" (302). Later on, Massaquoi does not have to pretend anymore because by joining the Civil Rights Movement in America, and by becoming an American citizen he has reached his goal of an American identity. Hügel-Marshall's personal development takes shape when she starts to take taekwondo classes (78-88), and this development is accelerated when she becomes part of the African-German movement and friends with her later mentor Audre Lorde (95). The sport, the movement, and the friendship to Audre Lorde all contribute to Hügel-Marshall's self-acceptance and also self-revelation through her autobiography. For Usleber, education and music become the catalysts for his successful self-approval. Above all, it is his hobby of reading and writing that turn into an "Ersatz für eine wirkliche Unterhaltung," which he does not have anymore (42). Although Usleber realizes that he needs real conversations and friends, for the time being during his adolescence he shapes his identity by continuing school, listening to—almost analyzing—the songs of Bob Marley and others, and by reading and writing. All this helps him to dissect and then put together again his identity so that he is finally able to accept himself as he is.

All three African-German authors lack the clear-cut chapter outline of a beginning, a middle, and an end that the three African-American works display. This shows again that African-Germans are cognitively much less preoccupied with issues of coming full circle, hence wholeness, which is merely part of their journey and their focus on retracing the steps of their lives in order to leave unwelcome incidents behind. Thus, they want to construct a strong identity, which is why they have to heal their wounds. Their route to healing is by traveling to the USA to get to know their fathers and their roots.[120] In addition, the self-therapeutic scripting is helpful in their identity development as well, but they do it without the clear or conscious aim in mind of finding a form of wholeness; they simply want to heal. Hügel-Marshall recites a situation when she meets her father and feels coming full circle:

> Tränen für einen Augenblick
> Tränen, die mich nach Hause bringen
> [. . .]
> Ich strecke meine Hand aus
> meiner Schwarzen Familie entgegen
> mein Vater, meine Familie
> hier ist meine Reise zu Ende
> hier fließt die ganze Welt zusammen (126-27)

She is the only African-German author among the three who actually comes closest to (describing) the experiences of catharsis, wholeness, and coming home and full circle. The reason might be her close connection to African-Americans, especially to Audre Lorde, who taught her how to speak up and how to write about her African-Germanness. Even though Usleber's and Hügel-Marshall's works naturally leave open how their lives will proceed, by accepting themselves in the end their books do provide them with an incidental textual wholeness, a monument of their lives' paths. Massaquoi's autobiography takes on a special role, for he was already an older person when he wrote and published his life. Moreover, by filling in the gaps as a black boy in Nazi Germany, he transliterates an important chapter in German history and comes finally into being as the African-German he was born. Thus, he comes full circle and states, at the very end: "*Ende gut, alles gut*" (443). For him, it seems to be almost the unachievable wholeness of character and of his life. Through the autobiographical act he arrives at a textual wholeness of his cathartic journey as an African of the diaspora.

African-Americans and African-Germans go on a journey, mentally and geographically, to reconcile their hybrid souls. They travel to the countries of their ancestors and direct kin. The very fact of facing the truth and the past to retrace one's roots helps many African diaspora individuals to find an inner

---

[120] Massaquoi's case is a bit different: he first goes to Liberia, where his father is, and then he decides that his happiness lies in the USA.

peace, whether one is accepted by one's relatives or ancestors or not; it is the journey, the willingness of engaging oneself with oneself that intrinsically gives birth to one's catharsis, one's healing. Only when taking the journey does *home* transform from a geographical place into an inner point of reference that Africans in the diaspora can reach when searching for their roots and meeting with and affirming their pasts; then they are able to make peace with their identity quarrels. A difference is that African-Germans can often claim direct ties to America,[121] whereas African-Americans' long-ago ties to Africa were ruptured and Africans do not see them as kin anymore. When concentrating on the relationship between Africans in the diaspora and Africa, African-Germans have a higher degree of mediation between them and Africa, namely most often via their relations in the USA. The connection to Africa of African-Americans lies in the past, and thus they have to accept that they cannot relive the past or change it, and only then can they move on. "Autobiography is not a simple repetition of the past as it was, for recollection brings us not the past itself but only the presence in spirit of a world forever gone" (Gusdorf 38). Therefore, a reiteration of past events helps to heal and thus to find some form of being at peace with oneself. The product is a textual wholeness that supports the progression of one's life.

---

[121] In the cases of Hügel-Marshall and Usleber, their families embrace both authors. Hügel-Marshall even became a US citizen. Massaquoi takes fate into his own hands and in 1950 also became a US citizen.

Chapter Six: Concluding Thoughts

The preceding analysis supports Welsch's transculturality, which is a given in today's world; people of mixed genealogies oftentimes still struggle to combine culturally different identities inherent in them and/or to come to terms with a difficult past. Thus, identity issues stemming from a diasporic, hyphenated concept of the self remain; minority/ethnic writers usually deal with such issues through literary engagement. For them, the autobiographical act becomes a form of self-therapy. For mainstream society (or even the world, for that matter) it becomes an account which is capable of presenting an alternative view to dominant historical and scientific discourses. The involvement with these identity issues is one of the most prominent similarities that the analysis and comparison of African-American and African-German life writings brought to light in this research. African-Americans and African-Germans lost their kin in some way or another, and only when a strong community stands behind these hyphenated individuals are they able to deal with their genealogies and thus identity problems, most often brought about by racism. Searching and making peace with one's roots—be those roots African-American, as is often the case for African-Germans, or be they African, as is often the case for African-Americans—seems to be an existential question of accepting oneself as a hybrid self. Writing about one's trials and tribulations is an important step on the way to healing for the African-American and African-German writers at hand. The autobiographical act provides them with an ersatz wholeness, which is a textual instead of a real-life character wholeness, the latter of which is impossible to attain during a lifetime.

While African-Germans oftentimes have more direct links to the USA instead of to Africa, and because of their everyday battle against still existing racism in Germany, their main interest lies in the amelioration of present situations and circumstances and in their (re)connection to relatives in the USA. African-Americans have become a sort of guardian or idol for African-Germans due to their long history of battling for their rights, their traditions, and their achievements. An example of this idolization in literature includes the influence of Audre Lorde on female African-German student writers and on Hügel-Marshall, as well as Usleber's idolization of African-American culture and literature in general. However, although African-Germans look up to African-Americans and their literary achievements, and although they sometimes use African-American literary techniques like intertextuality, African-Germans also take on their own style of writing, as can be seen by Hügel-Marshall's dialectic racist discussion, for example. In addition, ethnic German life writing is still in its infancy. While African-Germans are in the phase of writing themselves into being, African-Americans have long ago done so through the process that was initiated by slave narratives. African-Americans, in turn, although also still partly facing deprivation, are on the one hand criticizing their own shortcomings while on the other hand digging deeper into the past and into their long-lost relations to Africa. Many African-Americans are still romanticizing about Africa. African-Americans thus do not write themselves into mere being any longer but are trying to get to the core of their history and identity issues. Whichever way Africans in the diaspora turn, this analysis shows that there are new tendencies of breaking the silence and breaking old habits in order to overcome wrong notions of the past as well as continuing racism and discrimination.

Through the battles and quests of Africans in the diaspora, and through their even differing backgrounds, the Black Atlantic takes on a new dimension. While searching for a *Heimat* and an identity that one can live with, Africans in the diaspora, in order to progress and not despair, must, and partly already unconsciously do, recognize that their consent and descent culture is not necessarily attached to a piece of land. All authors at hand experience that a place of their dreams, America or Africa, cannot cure their wounds. Rather, their point of reference and the aspect that connects them to each other is the Black Atlantic, which has given birth to this new folk—Africans of the diaspora—dispersed throughout the world. The texture of the Black Atlantic is diffuse and ever in motion, especially like the identities of Africans in the diaspora. Once they stop searching for this one, unified and fixed self, and once they acknowledge the diversity and elusiveness of identities in general, will they perhaps find peace with(in) themselves. The authors in this survey all portray this tendency towards accepting who they are and how they came to be that way, an accomplishment also of the autobiographical act itself, which then opens up new possibilities for further personal development in the future. Detaching oneself from notions of a fixed self or a self that can be cured by Africa (or America) can be compared to the meaning of Esu, an African divine trickster figure, who stands for infinite possibilities of interpretation, i.e., the "metaphor for the uncertainties of explication, for the open-endedness," in this case the open-endedness of identity development (Gates, *Signifying* 21). Paradoxically, just when the authors overcome their wish for a direct connection to African (or African-American) culture in order to cope, does an African trickster explain the fluidity of things and thus establish a connection—at least as a hypothetical thought—to Africa.

Obama's slogan, "Yes, We Can!" and his election as the first black President of the United States of America emphasize the achievements of African-Americans within American society. His appointment is a historical milestone, which also sent a message of equality and diversity throughout the world. African-Americans have become an integral and existential part of American culture, and some would argue that with the era of Obama the African diaspora has ended for African-Americans, who have finally been able to claim what is rightfully theirs as well. These recent developments in America have certainly boosted the self-esteem of many Africans, and not only the ones from the diaspora. On the one hand, Obama's achievement is a success for all people of color in a world which is mostly controlled by white people. On the other hand, this development in the USA underlines the already existing gap between the achievements and acceptance of African-Americans and other Africans in the diaspora, especially African-Germans, which have been analyzed in this doctoral dissertation. The future will show whether Africans in the diaspora move closer together and whether or not Obama's America can set the standards of a more equal and diversified African diaspora and world in general. It remains to be investigated how Obama's victory and his politics influences contemporary Africans in the diaspora, specifically African-Germans. Further research should occupy itself with the development of African-German publicity and culture, especially with the offspring of "pioneer" generations of African-Germans, who were the *Besatzungskinder*, or others like Massaquoi. In this new era, African-Germans also benefit from the cyber-age and can thus meet virtually, which makes community-building and mutual support easier. The question whether these new technologies and an ever-growing diversified Germany will support a German society, in which everyone accepts non-white faces as equal German citizens must be observed and surveyed in the future. More and more, African-German and other ethnic German literature occupies not only the bookshelves, but virtual blogs and other Internet sources, all of which will need further scholarly attention.

Apart from places, people, or other factors which are used to define and categorize people, let me end this study by referring to Usleber, who rightfully pointed out that it is not the color of your skin that determines who you are but

"[d]ie Farben *unter* [d]einer Haut" (141; emphasis added).

Appendix

German Abstract

Im Zuge der Globalisierung hat sich die Amerikanistik (*American Studies*) ebenfalls neu positioniert und somit hat sich auch ein umfassenderes Feld der Forschung aufgetan. Hier inbegriffen sind zum Beispiel Forschungsgebiete transnationaler und transatlantischer Studien. Die vorliegende Doktorarbeit lässt sich diesem erweiterten Begriff der *American Studies* zuordnen und beschäftigt sich mit zeitgenössischen *African-American* und *African-German* Autobiographien.

Ethnische Minderheiten suchen vermehrt literarische Wege, um aus ihrer Minoritätenrolle heraus von der Gesellschaft, in der sie leben, gehört und akzeptiert zu werden. In diesem Kontext können afroamerikanische Autoren auf eine lange literarische Tradition zurückgreifen, deren Wurzeln in der Sklavenliteratur verankert sind, welche sich wiederum afrikanischer Methoden wie der Griot Geschichtenerzählung (*griot storytelling*) bedienten. Vor diesem Hintergrund hat sich ein spezieller afroamerikanischer Stil herausgebildet, der sich zum Beispiel durch Intertextualität (*intertextuality*) und einem „sprechenden Text" (*speakerly text*) ausdrückt. Im Gegenzug können afrodeutsche Autoren nicht auf einer ähnlichen Tradition aufbauen, da sie keine gewachsene Gemeinschaft sind wie die *African-American community*. Deshalb untersucht diese Arbeit inwiefern afrodeutsche Autoren afroamerikanische Literatur und Errungenschaften als Vorbild verstehen und inwiefern sie eine eigene, eine afrodeutsche Tradition und Gemeinschaft mit den dazugehörigen Eigentümlichkeiten entwickeln. Ferner werden die Intentionen afrodeutscher vis-à-vis afroamerikanischer Autobiographen und deren Identitätsfindung als Individuen der afrikanischen Diaspora analysiert.

Zunächst erfolgt eine interdisziplinäre Synopsis der vorherrschenden Theorien (Autobiographietheorie, *African-American Criticism*, kontemporäre Gedächtnisforschung etc.), wobei eigene grundlegende theoretische Konzepte (*key concepts*) erarbeitet und erste Thesen aufgestellt werden. Im Anschluss werden die ausgewählten Werke im Hinblick auf bestimmte *motifs* wie zum Beispiel Schweigen (*silence*) analysiert und danach wird jeweils ein afroamerikanisches mit einem afrodeutschen Werk verglichen. Es zeigt sich, dass Werke innerhalb der afrikanischen Diaspora trotz Unterschiede im Hinblick auf ihre Tradition und gewisser literarischer Methoden (beispielsweise *signifying*) auf einen gemeinsamen Nenner gebracht werden können bzw. eine entscheidende Gemeinsamkeit haben: Ihre Autoren suchen nach ihren Wurzeln — sei es in Afrika oder in Amerika — und sie alle stellen mehr oder minder fest, dass allein der Weg zu den Wurzeln, *the routes to the roots*, und die Erkenntnis, dass man Verwandtschaft (*kinship*) nicht erzwingen kann, das Ziel und gleichzeitig die Lösung ist. Es ist die Diaspora und sinnbildlich dafür der *Black Atlantic*, welche die Verbundenheit mit anderen *Diaspora Africans* herstellen; und diese Verbundenheit drückt sich in den unterschiedlichsten Lebensgeschichten und Leiden aus. Der Akt des autobiographischen Schreibens hilft den Autoren zusätzlich auf ihrem Weg zu den Wurzeln und zurück zu sich, auf ihrem Weg zur Akzeptanz des eigenen Ichs. Das Schreiben an sich wirkt also als eine Art Wiederholung der Lebensschritte in Richtung einer „Heilung" von etwaigen Identitätsproblemen.

Works Cited and Consulted

Primary Sources

Golden, Marita. *Migrations of the Heart: An Autobiography*. 1983. New York: Anchor, 2005. Print.

Hartman, Saidiya. *Lose Your Mother: A Journey Along the Atlantic Slave Route*. New York: Farrar, 2007. Print.

Hügel-Marshall, Ika. *Daheim unterwegs: Ein deutsches Leben*. Berlin: Orlanda, 1998. Print.

Massaquoi, Hans J. *Destined to Witness: Growing Up Black in Nazi Germany*. New York: Perennial, 2001. Print.

---. *Hänschen klein, ging allein . . . Mein Weg in die Neue Welt*. Trans. Ulrike Wasel and Klaus Timmermann. Frankfurt am Main: Scherz, 2004. Print.

Obama, Barack. *Dreams from My Father: A Story of Race and Inheritance*. 1995. New York: Three Rivers, 2004. Print.

---. *The Audacity of Hope: Thoughts on Reclaiming the American Dream*. New York: Crown, 2006. Print.

Usleber, Thomas. *Die Farben unter meiner Haut: Autobiographische Aufzeichnungen*. Frankfurt am Main: Brandes, 2002. Print.

Secondary Sources

Adams, Timothy Dow. *Telling Lies in Modern American Autobiography*. Chapel Hill: U of North Carolina P, 1990. Print.

Anderson, Linda. *Autobiography*. New York: Routledge, 2006. Print.

Aristotle. *Poetics*. Trans. Malcolm Heath. London: Penguin, 1996. Print.

---. *Politics*. Trans. Benjamin Jowett. Mineola, NY: Dover, 2000. Print.

Asante, Molefi Kete. "African Germans and the Problems of Cultural Location." *The African-German Experience: Critical Essays*. Ed. Carol Aisha Blackshire-Belay. Westport, CT: Praeger, 1996. 1-13. Print.

Ashcroft, Bill, Gareth Griffiths, and Helen Tiffen, eds. *The Empire Writes Back: Theory and Practice in Post-Colonial Literatures*. London: Routledge, 1989. Print.

---. *The Post-Colonial Studies Reader*. London: Routledge, 1995. Print.

Ashley, Kathleen, Leigh Gilmore, and Gerald Peters, eds. *Autobiography and Postmodernism*. Amherst: U of Massachusetts P, 1994. Print.

Assmann, Jan. *Religion and Cultural Memory: Ten Studies*. Trans. Rodney Livingstone. Stanford: Stanford UP, 2006. Print.

Augustine. *Confessions*. Trans. Henry Chadwick. Oxford: Oxford UP, 1998. Print.

Bakhtin, Mikhail M. *The Dialogic Imagination: Four Essays*. Ed. Michael Holquist. Trans. Caryl Emerson and Michael Holquist. Austin: U of Texas P, 1981. Print.

Baldick, Chris. *The Concise Oxford Dictionary of Literary Terms*. Oxford: Oxford UP, 2008. Print.

Bergland, Betty. "Postmodernism and the Autobiographical Subject: Reconstructing the 'Other'." Ashley, Gilmore, and Peters 130-66.

Bhabha, Homi K. *The Location of Culture*. London: Routledge, 1994. Print.

Blackshire-Belay, Carol, ed. *The African-German Experience: Critical Essays*. Wesport, CT: Praeger, 1996. Print.

Boelhower, William. "The Making of Ethnic Autobiography in the United States." Eakin, *American Autobiography* 123-141.

Bressler, Charles E. Literary Criticism: An Introduction to Theory and Practice. 2nd ed. Upper Saddle River, NJ: Prentice, 1999. Print.

Brockmeier, Jens and Donal A. Carbaugh, eds. Introduction. *Narrative and Identity: Studies in Autobiography, Self and Culture*. Amsterdam: John Benjamins, 2001. Print.

Brockmeier, Jens. "Identity." Jolly. Vol. 1.

Brown, Timothy J. "Reaffirming African American Cultural Values: Tupac Shakur's Greatest Hits as a Musical Autobiography." *The Western Journal of Black Studies* 29.1 (2005): 558-73. Print.

Bruss, Elizabeth W. *Autobiographical Acts: The Changing Situation of a Literary Genre*. Baltimore: Johns Hopkins UP, 1976. Print.

---. "Eye for I: Autobiography in Film." Olney, *Autobiography* 296-320.

Butler, Judith. *Bodies That Matter: On the Discursive Limits of Sex.* New York: Routledge, 1993. Print.

---. *Excitable Speech: A Politics of the Performative.* New York: Routledge, 1997. Print.

---. *Gender Trouble: Feminism and the Subversion of Identity.* New York: Routledge, 1999. Print.

Chandler, Marilyn R. "A Healing Art: Therapeutic Dimensions of Autobiography." *a/b: Auto/Biography Studies* 5.1 (1989): 4-14. Print.

Chinosole. *The African Diaspora and Autobiographics: Skeins of Self and Skin.* San Francisco State University Series in Philosophy. Vol. 11. New York: Lang, 2001. Print.

Couser, G. Thomas. *Altered Egos: Authority in American Autobiography.* New York: Oxford UP, 1989. Print.

---. "Authenticity." Jolly. Vol. 1.

---. "Authority." Jolly. Vol. 1.

---. "Authority in Autobiography." *a/b: Auto/Biography Studies* 10.1 (1995): 34-49. Print.

Cross, William E., Jr. "The Psychology of Nigrescence: Revising the Cross Model." *Handbook of Multicultural Counseling.* Ed. Joseph G. Ponterotto et al. Thousand Oaks, CA: Sage, 1995. 93-123. Print.

David, Marian. "The Correspondence Theory of Truth." *The Stanford Encyclopedia of Philosophy.* Ed. Edward N. Zalta. Stanford University, 2009. Web. 22 Jan. 2010.

de Man, Paul. "Autobiography as De-Facement." *Modern Language Notes* 94.5 (1979): 919-30. Print.

Diedrich, Maria. "Afro-amerikanische Literatur." Zapf 415-40.

Douglass, Frederick. *Narrative of the Life of Frederick Douglass: An American Slave.* 1845. New York: Penguin Classics, 1986. Print.

Du Bois, W.E. Burghardt. *The Souls of Black Folk: Essays and Sketches.* 1903. Greenwich: Fawcett Premier, 1961. Print.

Dudley, David L. "African American Life Writing." Jolly Vol. 1.

Eakin, Paul John, ed. *American Autobiography: Retrospect and Prospect*. Madison: U of Wisconsin P, 1991. Print.

---. *Fictions in Autobiography: Studies in the Art of Self-Invention*. Princeton: Princeton UP, 1985. Print.

---. Forward. Lejeune viii-xxviii.

---. *How Our Lives Become Stories: Making Selves*. Ithaca, NY: Cornell UP, 1999. Print.

---. *Living Autobiographically: How We Create Identity in Narrative*. Ithaca, NY: Cornell UP, 2008. Print.

---. *Touching the World: Reference in Autobiography*. Princeton: Princeton UP, 1992. Print.

Echterhoff, Gerald. "False Memory." *Gedächtnis und Erinnerung: Ein interdisziplinäres Lexikon*. Ed. Nicolas Pethes and Jens Ruchatz. Reinbek, Ger.: Rowohlt, 2001. Print.

Emde, Helga. "An 'Occupation Baby' in Postwar Germany." Opitz, Oguntoye, and Schultz 101-12. Print.

Equiano, Olaudah. *The Interesting Narrative of the Life and Other Writings*. Ed. Vincent Caretta. New York: Penguin, 1995. Print.

Fischer, Michael M.J. "Ethnicity and the Post-Modern Arts of Memory." *Writing Culture: The Poetics and Politics of Ethnography*. Ed. James Clifford and George E. Marcus. Berkley: U of California P, 1986. 194-233. Print.

Fisher Fishkin, Shelley. "Crossroads of Cultures: The Transatlantic Turn in American Studies—Presidential Address to the American Studies Association, November 12, 2004." *American Quaterly* 57 (2005): 17-57. Print.

Fried, Johannes: *Der Schleier der Erinnerung: Grundzüge einer historischen Memorik*. Munich: C.H. Beck, 2004. Print.

Garvey, Marcus. *The Philosophy & Opinions of Marcus Garvey. Or, Africa for the Africans*. Vol. 1. Dover, MA: Majority, 1986. Print.

Gates, Henry Louis, Jr. *Figures in Black: Words, Signs, and the "Racial" Self*. New York: Oxford UP, 1989. Print.

---. *Loose Canons: Notes on the Culture Wars.* New York: Oxford UP, 1992. Print.

---. "Preface to Blackness: Text and Pretext." *Within the Circle: An Anthology of African American Literary Criticism from the Harlem Renaissance to the Present.* Ed. Angelyn Mitchell. Durham: Duke UP, 1994. 235-55. Print.

---. *The Signifying Monkey: A Theory of African-American Literary Criticism.* New York: Oxford UP: 1989. Print.

Georgi-Findlay, Brigitte, Maria Diedrich, and Heiner Bus. "Multikulturalität." Zapf 387-487.

Gerunde, Harald. *Eine von uns: Als Schwarze in Deutschland geboren.* Wuppertal, Ger.: Hammer, 2000. Print.

Gilmore, Leigh. Introduction. Ashley, Gilmore, and Peters 3-18.

Gilroy, Paul. *The Black Atlantic: Modernity and Double Consciousness.* Cambridge, MA: Harvard UP, 1993. Print.

Gunzenhauser, Bonnie J. "Autobiography: General Survey." Jolly. Vol. 1.

Gruesser, John Cullen. *Confluences: Postcolonialism, African American Literary Studies and the Black Atlantic.* Athens, GA: U of Georgia P, 2005. Print.

Gunn, Janet Varner. *Autobiography: Towards a Poetics of Experience.* Philadelphia: U of Pennsylvania P, 1982. Print.

Gusdorf, Georges. "Conditions and Limits of Autobiography." Trans. Olney, *Autobiography* 28-48.

Halbwachs, Maurice. *On Collective Memory.* 1950. Ed. and trans. Lewis A. Coser. Chicago: U of Chicago P, 1992. Print.

Haley, Alex. *Roots: The Saga of an American Family.* 1974. New York: Vanguard Press, 2007. Print.

Hall, Stuart. "Cultural Identity and Diaspora." Williams und Chrisman 392-403.

Hoffmann, Heinrich. "Die Geschichte von den schwarzen Buben." *Der Struwwelpeter.* 1844. 55th ed. Munich: Bertelsmann, 2001. N. pag. Print.

Holm-Hadulla, Rainer. "The Creative Aspect of Dynamic Psychotherapy: Parallels Between the Construction of Experienced Reality in the Literary and the Psychotherapeutic Process." *American Journal of Psychotherapy* 50.3 (1996): 360-69. Print.

Hopkins, Gerard Manley. *The Sermons and Devotional Writings of Gerard Manley Hopkins*. Ed. C. Devlin. London: Oxford UP, 1959. Print.

Hornung, Alfred. "Autobiography." *International Postmodernism: Theory and Literary Practice*. Ed. Hans Bertens and Douwe Fokkema. Amsterdam: John Benjamins, 1997. 221-33. Print.

---. "Postmoderne bis zur Gegenwart." Zapf 306-86.

Huddart, David. "Criticism and Theory since the 1950s: Postcolonialism." Jolly. Vol. 1.

Hurston, Zora Neale. *Their Eyes Were Watching God*. London: Virago, 1986. Print.

Janson, Deborah. "The Subject in Black and White: Afro-German Identity Formation in Ika Hügel-Marshall's Autobiography *Daheim unterwegs: Ein deutsches Leben*." *Women in German Yearbook* 21 (2005): 62-84. Print.

Jensen, Geeta Sharma. "Descendant of Slaves Traces Her Quest for Roots, Identity." *JSOnline*. 4 Feb. 2007. Web. 22 Jan. 2010.

Jolly, Margaretta, ed. *Encyclopedia of Life Writing: Autobiographical and Biographical Forms*. 2 vols. London: Fitzroy, 2001. Print.

Kaminer, Debra. "Healing Processes in Trauma Narratives: A Review." *South African Journal of Psychology* 36.3 (2006): 481-99. Print.

Keating, AnnLouise. "Audre Lorde." *Contemporary African American Novelists: A Bio-Bibliographical Critical Sourcebook*. Ed. Emmanual S. Nelson. Westport, CT: Greenwood, 1999. 284-288. Print.

Larsen, Nella. *Quicksand* and *Passing*. New Brunswick, NJ: Rutgers UP, 1998. Print.

Leitch, Vincent B., et al., eds. "Introduction to Theory and Criticism." *The Norton Anthology of Theory and Criticism*. New York: Norton, 2001. 1-28. Print.

Lejeune, Philippe. *On Autobiography*. Ed. Paul John Eakin. Trans. Katherine Leary. Minneapolis: U of Minnesota P, 1989. Print.

Lemke, Sieglinde. *Primitive Modernism: Black Culture and the Origins of Transatlantic Modernism*. Oxford: Oxford UP, 1998. Print.

Lusane, Clarence. *Hitler's Black Victims: The Historical Experiences of Afro-Germans, European Blacks, Africans, and African Americans in the Nazi Era*. New York: Routledge, 2003. Print.

"A Man of His Words." *Financial Times Weekend*. 17-18 Jan. 2009. Life & Arts 1-2. Print.

Marcus, Laura. *Auto/biographical Discourses: Theory, Criticism, Practice*. Manchester: Manchester UP, 1994. Print.

Massaquoi, Hans J. "Growing Up in Nazi Germany: An Afro-German and Former Editor-in-Chief of *Ebony* Tells His Story." *The African Courier* Dec. 1999-Jan. 2000: 27. Print.

---. Letter to the author 1. 12 Feb. 2005. TS.

---. Letter to the author 2. 27 June 2005. TS.

Meer, Sarah. "Slave Narratives." Jolly. Vol. 2.

Mercer, Kobena. "Identity and Diversity in Postmodern Politics." *Theories of Race and Racism: A Reader*. Ed. Les Back and John Solomos. London: Routledge, 2000. 503-20. Print.

Meyer, Michael. *English and American Literatures*. 2nd ed. Tübingen, Ger.: Francke, 2005. Print.

Misch, Georg. *A History of Autobiography in Antiquity*. Trans. E. W. Dickes. 2 vols. 1907. London: Routledge, 1950. Print.

N., Corinna. "Old Europe Meets Up with Itself in a Different Place." Opitz, Oguntoye, and Schultz 178-190. Print.

Nejar, Marie. *Mach nicht so traurige Augen weil du ein Negerlein bist: Meine Jugend im Dritten Reich*. Reinbek bei Hamburg, Ger.: Rowohlt, 2007. Print.

Nietzsche, Friedrich. *Beyond Good and Evil: Prelude to a Philosophy of the Future*. Trans. Walter Kaufmann. New York: Vintage, 1989. Print.

Ohlsen, Barry N. "Self." Jolly. Vol. 2.

Olney, James. "Autobiography and the Cultural Moment." Olney, *Autobiography* 3-7.

---, ed. *Autobiography: Essays Theoretical and Critical*. Princeton: Princeton UP, 1980. Print.

---. *Memory and Narrative: The Weave of Life Writing*. Chicago: U of Chicago P, 1972. Print.

---. *Metaphors of Self: The Meaning of Autobiography*. Princeton: Princeton UP, 1972. Print.

Opitz, May, Katharina Oguntoye, and Dagmar Schultz, eds. *Showing Our Colors: Afro-German Women Speak Out*. Trans. Anne V. Adams. Amherst: U of Massachusetts P, 1992. Print.

Opitz, May. "Racism Here and Now." Opitz, Oguntoye, and Schultz 125-227.

Owomoyela, Oyekan. "From Folklore to Literature: The Route from Roots in the African World." *The African Diaspora: African Origins and New World Identities*. Ed. Isidore Okpewho, Carole Boyce Davies, and Ali A. Mazrui. Bloomington: Indiana UP, 2001. 275-89. Print.

Pandey, Gyanendra. "The Prose of Otherness." *Subalterm Studies VIII*. New Delhi: Oxford UP, 1994. 189-221. Print.

Pascal, Roy. *Design and Truth in Autobiography*. Cambridge, MA: Harvard UP, 1960. Print.

"Performance." *An International Dictionary of Theatre Language*. Ed. Joel Trapido. Westport, CT: Greenwood, 1985. Print.

Philipson, Robert. *The Identity in Question: Blacks and Jews in Europe and America*. Jackson: UP of Mississippi, 2000. Print.

Popoola, Olumide, and Beldan Sezen. *Talking Home. Heimat aus unserer eigenen Feder: Frauen of Color in Deutschland*. Amsterdam: blue moon, 1999. Print.

Reimer, Maike: "Autobiografisches Erinnern und retrospektive Längsschnittdatenerhebung." *BIOS: Zeitschrift für Biographieforschung und Oral History* 17.1 (2004): 27-45. Print.

Rubin, David C. "Beginnings of a Theory of Autobiographical Remembering." *Autobiographical Memory: Theoretical and Applied Perspectives.* Ed. Charles P. Thompson et al. Mahwah, NJ: Lawrence Erlbaum, 1998. 47-68. Print.

Saloy, Mona Lisa. "African American Oral Traditions in Louisiana." *Louisiana's Living Traditions: Articles and Essays.* Louisiana Division of the Arts, May 1998. Web. 23 October 2009.

de Saussure, Ferdinand. *Course in General Linguistics.* 1965. Trans. and ed. Roy Harris. La Salle, IL: Open Court, 1986. Print.

Schacter, Daniel L. *The Seven Sins of Memory: How the Mind Forgets and Remembers.* Boston: Houghton, 2001. Print.

Schmidt, Siegfried J. "Gedächtnis – Erzählen – Identität." *Mnemosyne: Formen und Funktionen der kulturellen Erinnerung.* Ed. Aleida Assmann and Dietrich Harth. Frankfurt am Main, Ger.: Fischer, 1991. 378-97. Print.

Shapiro, Stephen A. "The Dark Continent of Literature: Autobiography." *Comparative Literature Studies* 5 (1968): 421-54. Print.

Sheringham, Michael. "Memory." Jolly. Vol. 2.

Smith, Sidonie. *A Poetics of Women's Autobiography: Marginality and the Fictions of Self-Representation.* Bloomington: Indiana UP, 1987. Print.

---. "Performativity, Autobiographical Practice, Resistance." *a/b: Auto/Biography Studies* 10.1 (1995): 17-33. Print.

Smith, Sidonie and Julia Watson. "Criticism and Theory since the 1950s: Feminisim." Jolly. Vol. 1.

---. *Reading Autobiography: A Guide for Interpreting Life Narratives.* Minneapolis: U of Minnesota P, 2001. Print.

Smith, Thomas R. "Agency." Jolly. Vol. 1.

Sollors, Werner. *Beyond Ethnicity: Consent and Descent in American Culture.* Oxford: Oxford UP, 1986.

Starobinski, Jean. "The Style of Autobiography." Olney, *Autobiography* 73-83.

Stone, Albert E. "Modern American Autobiography: Texts and Transactions." Eakin, *American Autobiography* 95-122.

Sturrock, John. "The New Model Autobiographer." *New Literary History* 9.1 (1977): 51-63. Print.

Welsch, Wolfgang. "Transculturality: The Puzzling Form of Cultures Today." *Spaces of Culture: City, Nation, World*. Ed. Mike Featherstone and Scott Lash. London: Sage, 1999. 194-213. Print.

Williams, Patrick and Laura Chrisman, eds. *Colonial Discourse and Postcolonial Theory: A Reader*. New York: Columbia UP, 1994. Print.

---. Introduction. Williams and Chrisman 23-26.

Wright, Michelle M. *Becoming Black: Creating Identity in the African Diaspora*. Durham: Duke UP, 2004. Print.

---. "Others-from-Within-from-Without: Afro-German Subject Formation and the Challenge of a Counter-Discourse." *Callaloo* 26.2 (2003): 296-305. Print.

Zapf, Hubert, ed. *Amerikanische Literaturgeschichte*. 2nd ed. Stuttgart, Ger.: J.B. Metzler, 2004. Print.

Zöllner, Abini. *Schokolandenkind: Meine Familie und andere Wunder*. Reinbeck bei Hamburg, Ger.: Rowohlt, 2004. Print.